WORDS OF PRAISE

It is a brilliant idea to publish an English translation of *Philosopher à l'infini*, one of Marcel Conche's most remarkable and daring books! Through a dialogue with the greatest philosophers of the past, Conche defines himself in comparison with them in a debate amongst equals. This initiative is doubly important because Marcel Conche is not only one of our most eminent historians of philosophy (Conche is the author of unrivaled works on the pre-Socratic and Hellenistic philosophers, and on Montaigne), but first and foremost, he is one of the very greatest French philosophers of our time. Though Conche has always kept his distance from fame, the latest trends and the media's glare, he is read and admired by connoisseurs and increasingly by a wider, appreciative, and cultivated audience. His thinking, nourished by an immense yet original and profound culture, is inspired by skepticism and naturalism. He finds the foundation of a universal morality, that of human rights, within the notion of infinite nature. Moreover, Marcel Conche is, in my view, one of the very rare contemporary philosophers who manage to avoid nihilism. His oeuvre is abundant and diversified but always remarkable and of a standard of excellence, forms part of the philosophical pinnacles of our era.

—**André Comte-Sponville**, author of *A Short Treatise on the Great Virtues* and *The Book of Atheist Spirituality*

Marcel Conche possesses three qualities which are rare among philosophers today: he conceives philosophy as an activity rather than as merely writing; since his early childhood, he has had a profound intuition of Nature as the Whole of reality; and he continuously rereads, with respect but no taboo, the philosophers whom he has studied all his life. He is a model and an example. To philosophize ad infinitum is both to think about the infinite but also to think infinitcly.

—**Christian Godin,** Université Blaise-Pascal de Clermont-Ferrand, France, author of *La Nature* and *La Totalité*

Marcel Conche is not only a great academic philosopher and the writer of great philosophical books, he is a philosopher who never ceases to develop and hone his thinking. He is also a man who has dedicated his life to teaching philosophy without being influenced by fads or ideologies. His philosophy is driven by the search for truth and the willingness to deal with what is essential, always starting with what is in front of us, which has always been and always will be accessible to everybody. His prose is clear and jargon-free. He is a model for all those who strive to help us to think freely.

—**Gérard Schmitt,** Redactor in Chief of *L'Enseignement philosophique*

Marcel Conche is probably the greatest metaphysician of our era. His thinking on the infinity of nature, which leads him along the paths of freedom and creation, combines itself with a moral philosophy and a reflection on the meaning of being in which humanity's fragile greatness is fully revealed.

—**Syliane Malinowski-Charles**, Université du Québec à Trois-Rivières, Canada

Marcel Conche provides the reader with deep, insightful, and sometimes controversial ideas on a number of philosophers: from Plato to Epicurus, and from Montaigne to Lao Tzu. He is engaged in a lively dialogue with each of them about the fascinating topic of the infinite. This is a revealing book about the meaning and the practice of philosophy in today's world.

—**Catherine Collobert**, University of Ottawa, Canada

Infinite Philosophy: this book paints a perfect picture of the life of Marcel Conche, a natural-born philosopher. His aptitude to question absolutely everything drove him to the pre-Socratics, even at an early age, in his relentless quest for the truth. With Montaigne, the thinker to whom he feels most akin, Marcel Conche stands tall as an exceptional figure in contemporary French philosophy, renewing and enriching a great philosophical tradition.

—**Françoise Dastur**, University of Nice Sophia-Antipolis, France

PHILOSOPHIZING AD INFINITUM

SUNY series in Environmental Philosophy and Ethics

J. Baird Callicott and John van Buren, editors

PHILOSOPHIZING AD INFINITUM

Infinite Nature, Infinite Philosophy

MARCEL CONCHE

Translated by
Laurent Ledoux and Herman G. Bonne

Foreword by
J. Baird Callicott

SUNY PRESS

Originally published in French as *Philosopher à l'infini* by Marcel Conche © 2005 Presses Universitaires de France 6, avenue Reille 75685 Paris

Published by State University of New York Press, Albany

Printed in the United States of America

For information, contact State University of New York Press, Albany, NY
www.sunypress.edu

Production by Jenn Bennett
Marketing by Fran Keneston

Library of Congress Cataloging-in-Publication Data

Conche, Marcel.
[Philosopher à l'infini. English]
Philosophizing ad infinitum : infinite nature, infinite philosophy / Marcel Conche ; translated by Laurent Ledoux and Herman G. Bonne ; foreword by J. Baird Callicott.
pages cm. — (SUNY series in environmental philosophy and ethics)
Includes bibliographical references and index.
ISBN 978-1-4384-5189-3 (hardcover : alk. paper)
ISBN 978-1-4384-5188-6 (pbk. : alk. paper)
1. Conche, Marcel. 2. Philosophy, French. I. Title.

B1802.C6513 2014
194—dc23 2013027105

10 9 8 7 6 5 4 3 2 1

It would be a lovely dream, and it is not an impossible one, that the post-Bergsonians concur with the pre-Socratics.

—Jean Wahl

Metaphysics does nothing more than transfer to within ourselves this dominant notion of the infinite.

—Louis Pasteur

I am permanently conscious of being immersed in an enveloping, infinite and incomprehensible nature.

—Jean Leyssenne

CONTENTS

FOREWORD

J. Baird Callicott

Marcel Conche is a philosopher after my own heart. He is, first and foremost, a student of the history of Western philosophy (and to some extent of Eastern philosophy as well), going back to the pre-Socratics. Especially to the pre-Socratics. Most twentieth-century Western philosophers on both sides of the Atlantic have narrowed the temporal scope of philosophy to a tiny and ultimately insignificant moment in the 2,500-year sweep of Western philosophy—to their own twentieth century.

Indeed, many Anglo-American philosophers actually think that all "philosophy" that preceded the professionalization of philosophy in the twentieth century was but a prelude to the real thing done by them. From lisping amateurs like Plato, Aristotle, Descartes, and Kant professional philosophers have inherited a suite of suggestive puzzles, which may now be definitively solved only by those properly "trained" in the methods of contemporary logical analysis. (Dogs, soldiers, and factory workers are "trained"; philosophers, I would prefer to think, are educated—very often, mainly self-educated over a lifetime.) The historical precursors of true philosophy are also a repository of incipient arguments that may be expressed in formal notation and examined, usually out of context, for validity. And, in extreme cases, "philosophers" who are, like Conche and me, intellectually engaged with the "philosophy" done prior to the twentieth century on its own terms have been banished from some American philosophy departments altogether and regarded as mere historians of ideas, not as philosophers proper.

While the professionalization and isolation of philosophy in its own disciplinary silo on the Continent has not been so extreme, the Continental tradition—that stemming from phenomenology, anyway—has been equally arcane, method-constrained, and dissociated from the thought of such ancestral figures as Descartes, Spinoza, Leibniz, and Rousseau, to say nothing of the Greeks.

Conche is a refreshing exception and contrast; he is not only a student of the entire, grand two-and-a-half-millennium-long sweep of Western philosophy, he positions himself as a peer among the giants of the past, upon whose shoulders he proudly stands. Hubristic? No! His is the only way to think boldly and creatively. One must imagine oneself as pressing that heritage forward in an ongoing historical dialectic of ideas in which oneself has a part. And in that project I join him. Otherwise, one simply settles for taking one's seat in the academic equivalent of a corporate cubicle, minding ones knitting, and being satisfied to toil away on some narrow bit of arcana that engages the attention of perhaps a dozen other clever fellows arguing over the same trifles. Occasionally some bit of trivia will capture the imagination of the corporate hierarchy and the lucky fellow who thought it up will have his fifteen minutes of fame and perhaps land a plum chair in a top-tier research university, there to rest on his laurels. That is not for Marcel Conche, nor is it for me.

So what is this "infinite" that Conche presumes to illuminate? It should be noted, as does Conche himself, that the infinite, or something like it, prominently appears at the dawn of Western philosophy. The archē of Anaximander—the ur-stuff, that from which all things come and that into which they all return—is the apeiron. The word is formed from *peras*, meaning boundary or limit, and the alpha privative. The apeiron is the unbounded, the unlimited. In my opinion, though not in Conche's, "infinite" is a misleading translation of Anaximander's apeiron. Why? Because the conventional sense of the word *infinite* now bears the indelible stamp of Zeno, who came along a century after Anaximander. Two of Zeno's four famous paradoxes of motion—the Stadium and the Achilles—turn on the infinite divisibility of a spatial continuum and the inexhaustibility of the infinite series of points that infinite dichotomous or geometric division discloses. His paradoxes of plurality turn on the concept of the possibility of an infinite extension. Zeno's infinite is essentially mathematical and was itself an achievement of a historical intellectual dialectic. Zeno defended the philosophy of his mentor Parmenides (who was also his lover, if Plato's gossip in the *Parmenides* is on the mark) by showing, via reductio ad absurdum, that the hypotheses of motion and plurality lead to contradiction—contradiction essentially involving infinite regresses. My mentor, José Benardete, wrote a book titled *Infinity* and it was not anything like the book by Conche that you hold in your hands; rather, Benardete's *Infinity* is in the genre of the philosophy of mathematics. No, Anaximander's apeiron is best rendered, in my opinion, not as the "infinite," but as the "indefinite"—a qualityless, homogeneous stuff, that is internally unbounded or undifferentiated. The idea that the infinite (that is, the apeiron) is infinite (in the post-Zeno sense), if I may put it so, never occurred to Anaximander.

And we must remember—though, strangely, Conche himself does not—that another signal appearance of the apeiron is also found among the earliest expressions of Western philosophy: the Pythagorean Table of Opposites, in which each column of opposites is headed by the Limit (peras) and the Unlimited (apeiron), thus:

Limit	Unlimited
Odd	Even
One	Many
Square	Oblong
Right	Left
Male	Female
Light	Darkness
Good	Evil

As Conche's peer, I must honor him with my best critical engagement, not patronize him with obsequious flattery. So this is just where I think that Conche goes wrong: he conflates two distinct senses of the infinite, the Anaxamanderian-Pythagorean sense, on the one hand, and the Zenoic sense, on the other. In Conche's defense, I might say that he is in good company because Plato does as well, if we may trust Aristotle's account of Plato's philosophy in the first book of the *Metaphysics*—as does Conche and so do I. According to Aristotle, opposed to the Numbers (forms), Plato posited the Infinite Dyad (the great and the small)—the quasi-spatial ideal continuum, first explored by Zeno, that is both infinite in extent (great) and infinitely divisible (small). But let us not come to this book by Conche with misleading expectations. The sense of the infinite that Conche wrestles with here is more the Anaxamanderian-Pythagorean sense and less the Zenoic. Although he wrestles with both, the former is not only primal but primary; the latter is secondary. And so I will concentrate on helping the reader of this English translation understand what Conche is up to in regard to the first and leave it to Benardete to help anyone wishing to pursue the matter further to understand the latter.

Nature, Conche posits, is infinite. We readers would be mistaken therefore to think this: Oh, contrary to contemporary scientific cosmology, Conche backwardly believes that nature is not a finite but expanding four-dimensional space-time continuum characterized by a Riemannian geometry; instead, he backwardly thinks that if one could drink from a fountain of youth and enjoy an infinite lifespan and inhabit a spaceship powered by an infinite fuel source, one could set out in Euclidean space and travel forever on a straight-line course and never reach the edge of the cosmos—because it is a Zenoically great infinite. No, Conche posits that one aspect of Nature is infinite (unlimited) in exactly the way in which Plato in the *Timaeus* and before him the Pythagorean cosmologists thought that it was. Yes, it may be Zenoically infinite, but more to the point, Conche's infinite is that which ever eludes and defies the power of the Limit to exhaustively render it pinned down, submitted to Reason, captured by Nous, answerable to the Logos. It is the chora, the matrix, apprehensible, Plato tells us in the *Timaeus*, only by a kind of "bastard reasoning." Why a bastard reasoning? Because the chora, the Receptacle, is the very opposite of the knowable, the definable, the namable; it is the nurse and mother of all becoming, informed—but only partially and incompletely informed—by the Limit and the Number-forms that the Limit proliferates.

In the Greek mythopoeic tradition, the kosmos is not created: it is procreated. From out of an original amorphous unity (later rationalized by Anaximander as the apeiron), the male Ouranos and the female Gaia were spontaneously and causelessly separated by Chaos and the first born was Eros—necessary, of course, to reunite Heaven and Earth sexually, so as to procreate the rest of the divine world order. So too, for the Pythagoreans and Plato, the Limit inseminates the ideal Unlimited and the Limit reproduces itself in the continuum of the Unlimited in the manner of biological cell division to become the Odd, the One, and then the definite Numbers—the forms, as Conche, wisely following Aristotle, understands Plato's forms to be. The Limit—no matter how virile and prolix and no matter how many and multifarious forms it gins up—can never ever exhaust the Unlimited, the Infinite, the apeiron—which, in its material manifestation, always remains un-formed, un-numbered, un-named, un-known, resistant, defiant, un-ruly, un-tamed, un-incarcerated, wild.

For the patriarchal and governance-obsessed Pythagoreans and Plato in the column of the Limit is the Good and the Male; in the column of the Unlimited is the Bad and Female, in need of discipline and control. But Conche is a man and a philosopher of his times—a contemporary, more or less, of Sartre and Foucault. The Pythagorean-Platonic valuation then of the Limit and the Unlimited, the Finite and the Infinite, are thus turned, by Conche, upside down and inside out. What is ever fascinating, ever self-renewing, and ever fresh is Infinite Nature in her wild, un-incarcerated, un-tamed, defiant, resistant, un-fully-knowable, un-named, un-numbered, un-formed, un-limited female essence.

So you see, I join Conche as a Neo-pre-Socratic philosopher, and he joins me as an environmental philosopher. Before I read his book, I did not know that; and unless and until he reads my foreword here, neither will he. We two lived and worked mostly in the twentieth century, utterly independently, but we are not of it. Both of us have survived and continue to work into the twenty-first century and Conche's philosophy is a harbinger of things to come—a new, scientifically informed metaphysics and ontology. I reach for that goal as well and only hope that I succeed as well as Marcel Conche. History will be our judge. And, hopefully, future philosophers will engage his work and mine over the distance of decades, perhaps even centuries.

TRANSLATORS' INTRODUCTION

Herman Bonne and Laurent Ledoux

> He wandered through the fields, a young boy of 16; he looked up and saw a trail of white herons flying through the sky, at a great altitude: and nothing else, nothing more than the whiteness of these white creatures rowing on a blue sky, nothing more than these two colors superposing each other, this ineffable feeling of eternity penetrated his soul at that very moment and untied what was tied, tied what was untied, so much so that he fell on the ground, as if overtaken by sudden death.
>
> —Hugo von Hofmannsthal

Why We Translated Marcel Conche's "Philosopher à l'infini"

"Enough talk *about* Marcel Conche. Why don't you pay him a visit to talk *with* him?" said Bob Starc to Laurent in June 2006 during one of their walks in the forest. For several years, Laurent had shared with Bob his pleasure and interest in reading Conche's books. Without a degree in philosophy but an interest in it since childhood, Laurent had previously followed the good advice of another friend, Jean Jadin, to study philosophy by choosing one single given philosopher. His friend suggested Conche. After reading his works, Laurent had some apprehensions about contacting Conche. What would a nonspecialist have to say to the great wise man, who had become a well-known writer in France? Nevertheless, Laurent decided to contact him and request to meet whenever possible. To his great surprise, he received a prompt but positive reply: "Come whenever you want!" This proved to be typical of Conche's openness and eagerness to spark earnest dialogues.

Marcel and Laurent spent a wonderful weekend together, discussing philosophy and the Infiniteness of Nature, while walking, eating, or sitting on a bench in front of a magnificent landscape. During that weekend, Laurent decided to translate one of Conche's books into English, in order to make his ideas known to a wider audience. When he asked Marcel which book he should translate, the answer was quick and without hesitation: "*Philosopher à l'infini*."

Laurent began translating the book during the summer of 2006 and despite his demanding position as manager of a commercial department at a large international bank, Laurent worked diligently each evening as well as weekends. In 2009, Herman Bonne, another enthusiastic reader of Marcel Conche's work and the owner and manager of a medium-sized company, was prompted by Conche to contact Laurent to help him finalize the translation. It took them another three years to do so, with the assistance of three native English speakers: Dan Tudor, manager of a company in the United States, Ian Swan, an Irish communications consultant living in Paris, and James Donahue, an American College teacher. Finally, J. Baird Callicott, a well-known environmental ethicist from the United States and a friend of Laurent's, introduced them to Andrew Kenyon of the State University of New York Press.

Why did two business managers, untrained in philosophy, decide to embark on such a long journey to translate a philosophical book by a French academic? The answer is simple: we both firmly believe that the notion of infinity is at the core of the crisis humanity is facing today. Every day, scientific advances offer us more insights about the infinitely small or the infinitely great. For the last two hundred years our economies have been running full speed, fueled by the implicit belief that natural resources are infinite. Today however, we finally understand that they are not and that we need to radically rethink the foundations of our economic system. Paradoxically, we believe that a solid philosophical reflection on the Whole of reality, on Nature as "the infinite" can help us properly address this unprecedented environmental crisis; Nature is indeed a perpetual challenge for the mind. Reflecting upon its infinity also helps to put man in his place, to evaluate our surroundings and ourselves according to their true proportion.

We hereby do not claim that metaphysics should be instrumentalized to help society resolve its problems. We want to acknowledge how reading Marcel Conche's works on infinite Nature has not only helped us grow and mature as human beings but also has helped us to take initiatives in our respective organizations and to change our managerial practices, leading to more harmonious, respectful, and sustainable long-term development where the progress and personal development of all team members is considered critical for the ultimate sustainable success and growth of the enterprise. It is in this spirit that Laurent leads the association Philosophy & Management (www.philoma.org) which organizes philosophy seminars for managers.

Since we have both significantly benefited from his insights, our goal is to render Marcel Conche's writings widely accessible. We have tried therefore to make this English version of "*Philosopher à l'infini*" as readable as possible:

Each chapter is preceded by a short summary entitled "Milestones" (as a reference to the milestones along the path Marcel invites us to take with the philosophers who influenced him). We have also added key word titles between some paragraphs of the various chapters in order to highlight the main ideas covered. Although the prose of Marcel Conche is straightforward, he sometimes jumps from one idea to another, making it less easy for nonacademics to follow. Hopefully, these summaries and additional titles will make it easier for the reader to follow his logic;

Book references of quotes and Greek or Latin versions of specific words have been converted into endnotes in order to lighten the text;

A glossary briefly introducing all thinkers, philosophers or "–isms" mentioned in the text has been added.

A Brief Introduction to Marcel Conche's Life and Work

Marcel Conche occupies an important place in today's French philosophical landscape. He is recognized by academics for his groundbreaking and authoritative works on Greek thinkers such as Pyrrho, Epicurus, Parmenides, and Heraclitus, as well as on Montaigne. He is also appreciated by the wider public for his more personal works.

Born in 1922 and emeritus professor at the Sorbonne, Marcel Conche has been made laureate of the French Academy and a corresponding member of the Academy of Athens for his life work. André Comte-Sponville, a best-selling French philosopher, considers Conche's philosophy as "one of the rare philosophies of our time" and has dedicated a book from an interview with him. To date Marcel Conche has written more than thirty-five books, most of them published by the *Presses Universitaires de France (PUF)*. Many of his books have been reedited several times. While he has long been known in academic circles, over the last decade his books have drawn a growing interest from the wider public. For instance, "Confessions of a Philosopher" has met with great success in French bookshops. A specialist in Greek philosophy and probably one of the world's best academics on Montaigne, his work combines erudite references to the history of philosophy with a highly personal and substantial search for "truth," all expressed in crystal-clear prose. This is illustrated by one of Conche's early works, "*Pyrrhon ou l'apparence*" (Pyrrho or Appearance), an audacious and successful essay that clearly distinguishes Pyrrho's philosophy from Sextus Empiricus's traditional skepticism.

Today, at ninety-two years of age and living in a small village in southern France, Conche remains as active and original as ever. Among his latest projects, he has recently translated as well as provided personal commentary on the *Tao Te Ching* despite his not speaking a word of Mandarin. He translated word by word, using dictionaries. In this book he draws an interesting parallel between the near contemporaries Lao Tzu and Heraclitus: the river of the Greeks is compared to the Dao of the Chinese.

With and Without Marcel Conche—
A Short Introduction to the Book

For Marcel Conche, Nature is infinite, both in time and space, and constitutes the Whole of reality. In this book, he introduces us to his view of infinite Nature, confronting it with that of other thinkers. Conche notes that, while the idea of infinity is present in many philosophical systems, time is often disregarded. Platonic thinking is focalized on an ideal and unchanging totality which does not allow for a temporal essence. Equally, for Aristotle, time is ruled from within by fixed forms which in a way annihilate its importance. Conche, therefore, finds his inspiration rather in Montaigne for whom "everything changes"; in Nietzsche, obsessed by time even when he writes about the "eternal return"; and in Bergson, who considers duration as the "background of reality."

For Conche, idealism—which has dominated philosophy since Plato—has corrupted our thinking on infinity. Infinity has been thought essentially to have a spiritual nature, perfect and achieved. It has been conceived as a well-ordered totality, meaningful and closed upon itself. Christianity has transformed reality into a "world" already completed and finite since God, who created it, can encompass it. Conche takes a radically opposite view: what comes first is nature as the Greeks have conceived it through the notion of "Physis" (or Phusis). Phusis is an infinite reality, that is, a reality that has always been there and always will be, unending, constantly creating and exploring new paths "like a poet," that is to say, without following a well-designed plan. Mankind is part of the Phusis and cannot extract itself from it. Mankind is, therefore, destined to death but also contributes to the creative process, to Phusis through its actions. Nature or Phusis, as "All of reality," must be distinguished from the worlds or universes that it encompasses. Science helps mankind to better understand these worlds but will never be able to do more than to scratch the surface of Phusis. For Conche, infinity is not only outside mankind. It is also inside mankind. Conche finds his inspiration here in Pascal. Mankind can indefinitely make an inventory of reality though science, though this action is a futile endeavor to understand or experience infinite nature. Mankind can, however, experience infinity through love. To love is by definition to love infinitely and to reveal the other's infinity. Here, Conche's naturalism (only Nature "is" and all transcendence is imaginary) does not lead to radical nihilism: the infinite character of Nature does not serve to undermine mankind, accentuating its irreducible finite character. Rather, mankind actively participates in the creation of this infinity through its own experiences, through its own life. This may help give some meaning to the human adventure. It may also let us think that mankind is free after all for it cannot be made prisoner of a religious, metaphysical or cultural definition of itself. Mankind's relation with Nature is precisely what makes mankind its own creator.

At the end of the book, an interesting insight into Marcel Conche's view on infinite Nature is gleaned through the correspondence between him and Gilbert Kirscher, an emeritus professor of philosophy. After having detailed why Marcel Conche journeys with and without various philosophers, the book culminates with a fruitful exchange that could have been subtitled: "With and without Marcel Conche." This earnest dialogue highlights the reasons why one might part with Conche regarding his views on Nature. The openness with which Conche shares this with us is, as previously mentioned, typical of him. He relishes engaging dialogues and is always ready to have his ideas challenged and to reconsider his positions. In one of his books on Montaigne ("*Montaigne ou la conscience heureuse*"—Montaigne or the Happy Consciousness), he openly yearns for a "good verbal duel" with him. For Conche, dialogue is the foundation of morality, as he argued in an eponymous book ("*La fondement de la morale*"). This also explains why, like Montaigne, Conche has never attempted to turn his ideas into a "system." He is well aware that his ideas cannot be put to the test and, as such, cannot be set against those who believe in a personal God, for example. The rather abrupt sentence in the appendix ("Between philosophers and believers—as such—dialogue has no meaning") should not be interpreted, therefore, as a refusal to dialogue with people who believe in God. His dialogues with Christians such as Montaigne, Pascal, or Bergson show otherwise (one with Meister Eckhart would have also been interesting, as he also seems to have made references to Nature as being infinite). Rather, Conche's sentence in the appendix highlights the need for both parties to always be ready to reconsider their beliefs in the face of new information or solid arguments, in order to philosophize and have a fruitful dialogue. Such a frame of mind seems, more than ever, critical in our global society. This is why we hope this book may spark a renewed dialogue on Nature and the infinite between men and women of different philosophies and beliefs.

Finally, let us remark that throughout his work and in this book, Conche develops inspiring ideas on the timeless and stimulating, but, in his opinion, inevitably limited dialogue between philosophy and science. Nevertheless, one may regret that in this book Conche does not present any scientific discoveries that could lend support to his thoughts, such as a mathematical treatment of infinity or contemporary cosmology. This should not be surprising, however, as for Conche no thought of Nature as the Whole of reality could be substantiated through scientific evidence. Philosophy is therefore condemned to remain an interpretation of Nature, which science can neither confirm nor invalidate. Here again we find infinity, in the unlimited number of metaphysical speculations and of philosophies about Nature. In Conche's own words: "Nature is infinite. This infinity reduces me to a point in space, a moment in time. But, I equal myself to it through thinking, not because I could have an "idea" of infinity, as Descartes said we could have an idea of God, but because my thought is like a door to infinity, which is nothing else than Nature offering herself to the consciousness and the reason of mankind."

To Julian, Miguel, and Alban, in the hope that Marcel Conche's book, whether in French or in English, will help them experience the infinity of Nature and dare to become the poets of their lives.

Laurent Ledoux
ledoux.laurent@gmail.com
www.philoma.org

Herman G. Bonne
hermanbonne@hotmail.com

PREFACE TO THE ENGLISH TRANSLATION

Marcel Conche

The main objective of this book is to define my philosophical position by differentiating it from the positions of the philosophers who have been most important to my own development. I have not defined my position from the perspective of the categories of Eric Weil. This was done by Gilbert Kirscher in a letter that is included in the Appendix. This letter does not just serve to understand my philosophical position; it provides a material example of the type of analysis that can be made according to the *Logic of Philosophy* by Weil while helping to elucidate Weil's own philosophy.

Why did I suggest to Laurent Ledoux that he translate this book rather than another one at the time of his request?

My works on the history of philosophy (Montaigne, Lucretius, Pyrrho, Epicurus, the Ante-Socratics) put aside, the works wherein I expose my own position were delineated, ensuing a process of elimination:

In *Orientation philosophique* (Philosophical Orientation), an ongoing work of investigation, I undertake a "deconstruction" of classical metaphysics, but I hesitate to commit myself to a new metaphysics;

Temps et destin (Time and Fate) takes the question of time as an isolated object and is not connected to the philosophy of nature;

Le fondement de la morale (The Foundation of Morality) confronts the notion of the "foundation" of morality, but does so without being subject to metaphysics (however, above all, I'm a metaphysician);

Présence de la nature (Nature's Presence) presents nature as I see it today: unending, everlasting, untotalizable, all-embracing, all-engendering. However, part of the book concerning Greek thought with the Greek language makes it rather difficult to read.

Finally, my choice centered on *Philosopher à l'infini*. It seemed to be a good idea to confront my own thoughts with those of the great philosophers known by everyone so that my thinking could be approached and understood in relation to them.

However, a synthesis of my agreements and divergences from those thinkers still has to be made, which is why after *Philosopher à l'infini*, one would benefit from reading *Métaphysique* (Metaphysics).

I

FLASHBACK

When I was a young man I used to work in the fields, vineyards, and meadows of my father's farm. This intense agricultural labor would consume practically all my energy, leaving little or no time for reflection. Indeed, my mind was so task-oriented that there was room for nothing else. Had I been able to "let go" I would have been naturally receptive to the concept of the infinity that surrounded me; my mind would have yielded to its natural propensity to wander and wonder, as it should do when one is so young and in the midst of this pure and transforming nature. But back then I had no notion of what infinity meant, virtually no knowledge of its existence at all.

Only today do I realize how alienated my mind had been; rather than surrendering to its natural disposition and absorbing itself in meditation on the infinite, it was stubbornly and exclusively preoccupied with what is contingent and finite.

As a schoolboy and, later, a college student, my mind would have been naturally receptive to conceive of infinity, but instead it was continuously limited by objectives of little scope, obliged to restrict itself to these narrowminded pursuits. I had to write essays and reviews, prepare this or that homework, and eventually, as an older student, submit my thesis. These scholastic efforts were presented for my headmaster's or professor's consideration, who in due time would then pronounce their final judgment. All this belonged to the contingent order of things. All that belongs to a human being that necessarily defines him or her as a philosopher was forgotten, brushed aside, or simply never stimulated or encouraged.

Human beings spend their lives accomplishing tasks, carrying out functions, performing roles that they have chosen or responsibilities that others have chosen for them. These tasks, functions, and roles might have been entirely different as a consequence of some other particular need, tradition, influence, or coincidence. How difficult it is to truly and deeply ascertain the universal human being beyond peoples' individual characteristics!

Having been spiritually educated in the Catholic faith, my teachers taught me that "God" had created the sky and the earth out of nothing; then he created light, the firmament, the planets, and the animated beings of the sea and air. I was told that he had created man in his own image; that a man called Adam had disobeyed him nevertheless; that Adam and his earliest of all sins had wrought evil, suffering, and death upon the world. But I was also told that, in his demise, man would take with him the promise of a savior who would return as Jesus Christ during the reign of Emperor Augustus.

From all this I could have concluded that God, World, and Man are all there is. Hence, I might have come up with the concept of the Whole: the Whole of reality, and therefore of the infinite, since there can be nothing else beyond the Whole of reality.

But that is not what I came up with.

God, World and Man tallied up without forming a whole; it did not cross my mind to consider them as going *together* at that time. Above all "God" meant a serious threat for "sinners" as well as a promise of eternal life in paradise for the "souls of the deceased," at least for the "just and good" souls amongst us.

Throughout my childhood and part of my youth, I attended an annual seven o'clock morning Mass, which was offered to God in order for my mother's soul to "rest in peace." I cannot at all remember having felt something resembling a love for God. Actually, I often felt a superstitious fear of this Supreme Being known to many as the "Almighty." Even back then, my mind never truly accepted what I had been told about Christ, the "God made man, second person of the Trinity, mediator, savior, dead and resurrected."

The Foundation and Spontaneity of My Rejection of the Monotheist Creed

The Judeo-Christian myth did not prepare me to reflect upon the ideas of the Whole and Infinity. God was of course "infinitely perfect," but this prerequisite did not really inspire one to think about the infinite. The Christian dogma never quite held a firm grip on my mind. So when I came to explicitly reject it, all I had done was to throw away a burden of imposed beliefs that did nothing but uselessly weigh me down. The so-called kindness of God did not appear to correlate with the utter magnitude of suffering here on Earth.

I had yet to develop the decisive argument needed to reject this religious dogma outright until the time I became aware of the sufferings of tortured children through reading Dostoyevsky and the "Diary of Mary Berg," among other texts. I considered their abject woe as having de jure no justification whatsoever. However, it was not the suffering of children that motivated my rejection of the monotheist creed: I had already rejected it. Rather, this suffering "became" the foundation for my rejection, and it was all I required to justify an anti-theist position, which had become mine spontaneously. Indeed, it had already been mine for quite some time.

Bergson, whose thoughts shall be discussed in chapter IX, writes that by taking into account only arguments, analysis, and rational motives, "we risk failing to see what is fundamentally spontaneous in a philosophical position."[1] My philosophical intuition freely induced me to reject the monotheist path. I had a premonition that my reason, my feeling of what is just, simple, and clear would be uselessly troubled by something that only made sense thanks to a dubious "Revelation." To my mind, this was as a cumbersome, hazardous, and complex construction.

"Impossible." This is what intuition "whispers in the philosopher's ear," says Bergson. And he adds: "What a strange force this intuitive power of negation! How is it that historians of philosophy have not been more greatly struck by it? Is it not obvious that the first step the philosopher takes is to reject certain things definitively, when his thought is still faltering and there is nothing definitive in his doctrine? Later he will be able to make changes in what he affirms; he will vary only slightly what he denies."[2]

As a matter of fact, I never once thought of turning back on my position on the monotheist creed. On the contrary, my negation became even more radical over time, up to the point of annihilating itself, having completely dissolved its object.

At first, the notion of God seemed to me most worthy of examination. At that time, part of my role as a university professor was to be able to explain the great theological philosophies of the world. Out of probity, I made an effort to align myself with the spirit that underlies and drives these theologies and to reconstruct their inner logic. However, this was quite an alienating experience as I had the patent feeling that doing so meant working against my true self.

Progressively, the meaning of the word *God* lost its meaning and eventually I tired of using it. In the monotheist system, notions of "God," "World" and "Man" are correlated. Once the notion of "God" is rejected, the notion of "World" cannot remain the same; a "World" is a whole with a defined, unifying structure. Do all finite beings, including "Man," form a "World?" For this proposition to be true, you need to postulate the existence of "God" for structure and unity. All finite beings become then a "world," a single one, unique and ordered, but also rational, reasonable, and harmonious. This is exactly how Plato, the Stoics, and Leibniz, among others, wanted the "World" to be, as will be shown in the coming chapters.

In contrast, once the notion of "God" is rejected, finite beings no longer need be thought of as forming a unique "World," though this does not mean that the notion of "World" becomes useless. Firstly, it remains useful as a phenomenological concept expressing the experience we have of all that we can see around us. Secondly, if all the finite beings no longer need to be brought together in *one* unique World, then we can consider there are multiple *worlds*. We can do so because we accept pluralist cosmologies, as Anaximander first did in the sixth century BC, or because we consider each species or even each individual as inhabiting "its own world," and finally, because we consider artists as "creating worlds."

The notion of "Man" fares no better than the notion of "World" against the disappearance of the notion of "God." Indeed, in the monotheist creed, the essence of man, the definition of what Man must be, and how he should live in order to qualify for salvation are all correlated to the notion of God. With God, eternal life, or immortality, is promised to Man; without God, his is a mortal destiny. In the monotheist creed, his "finitude" on earth means he must experience death, though that death would not be his life's end. The Loving God's promise gives sense to his life for, without God, his "finitude" becomes truly finite; his life ends with earthly death, as though he were an animal or a tree.

But what of his *being* then? "For why," asks Montaigne, "do we claim title to existence, on account of that instant that is only a flash in the infinite course of an eternal night, and so brief an interruption of our perpetual and natural condition?"[3] Montaigne speaks here as if he were an atheist. It is possible he was an atheist, albeit an intermittent one, as we will see in chapter VI.

Being and Appearances

To live during such a short period of time between the infinite past (when we were not yet) and the infinite future (when we will no longer be): can we really refer to that as "being"? Neither Plato nor Aristotle thought so, even though they needed the "forms" to be eternal so that they could be said to "be," as we will see in the next two chapters. Indeed, the lasting being is more real than the passing one. If Man only lasts one day, he is "the shadow of a shadow," states Pindar, the Greek lyric poet who lived during the fifth century BC.

Of course, in my daily life if I observe a table in front of me I might be moved to say: "The table *is*," or "This *is*." That is because I only see things in their present and current form or shape, forgetting the two infinities—the past and the future. I do not perceive what surrounds me as integrated into the infinity of time. Hence, I accept it as a firm reality.

But, if I could see all things within the infinity of time, they would appear to me as fleeting, incapable of taking the forms of firm *beings*. They would resemble "shadows and phantoms,"[4] states Philo, from the first century AD. He adds: "In a procession the first ranks get out of sight as they move further. In a torrent the waves stream faster than our capacity to perceive them. Similarly in life, things pass by, move away and although they seem firm, not one of them remains fixed for a single moment. All flee continuously."

As we limit time to a present flanked by a short-term past and future, we are thus able to say: "This *is*," "I *am*," etc. This occurs because we only succeed in living and acting in a "narrow" notion of time; the timeframe of the short lives and of the world we inhabit. However, let us now try to exempt ourselves from the need to act and consider our lives as brief moments in an infinite time. The time frame of the Whole of reality—Nature, as I call it—can be thought to be infinite in both space and time. Are we then still able to define ourselves with the words we use in the atomic time of our daily life? What are we then? Neither beings, nor nothingness: just appearances which do not refer to a being and which simply glide and flee, destined for oblivion.

Neither appearance-*of* (a being), nor appearance-*for* (for a being—a subject): such is the Pyrrhonian notion of Appearance. This concept is named after Pyrrho, the ironic philosopher considered by some as one of the fathers of Skepticism. In the monotheist creed, Man is the only being not destined to die. However, if Man has no destiny, then he merely appears for an instant until death extends its inevitable reach over all living things. All finite beings are then subsumed into the notion of Appearance. This whole of finite beings, the Whole of reality, is infinite since there is nothing else but this infinity, multiple and without unity. As will be shown in chapter V, this can hark back to the boundless universe of the Epicureans except that, in Nature, as I see it, there would be no substantial entities such as atoms, the infinite void, and gods. As long as our thinking limits itself to what appears to or before our eyes, we consider such entities as fictions.

Duties toward Shadows

But if human beings are only shadows, and if independently of what they do they quickly vanish, what becomes of our duties? Do we have duties toward shadows? There was a time when I thought that the reality of a being was implied by the unconditional character of the moral imperative that could be applied to that being. By "real," we can understand as we have just seen, either "that has the semi-reality of shadows" or "that has the full reality of what will surely last."

Since we do have unconditional duties toward particular beings, at least in particular situations, I concluded that these beings were fully real. I now understand they might have only a semi-reality. But that does not change our duties toward them in any way. We can therefore claim to have duties toward "shadows." Indeed, ontology should not interfere with morality; they play a different game. Ontological nihilism such as the Pyrrhonian philosophy only leads to a depreciation of beings, not of the duties we have toward them, or of the values we hold.

Where Pyrrho, Heraclitus, and Parmenides Meet

Was it possible for me to stick to the Pyrrhonian philosophy of Appearance, to such ontological nihilism? In order to answer this question, I should first state that my method is neither reflexive (examining myself), nor deductive (concluding from ideas to things), nor dialectic (limiting itself to the ideas game), nor eclectic (supposing a minimal agreement between different philosophies), nor intuitive (leading to the heart of things). My method is experimental, or rather "experiential." So I continuously confront *all there is, the Whole of reality* with *all that is offered to my experience.* Here we should distinguish between two forms of experience: on one hand, the narrow forms of experience such as those of the worker, the artist, or the scientist, and on the other hand, the global philosophical experience. The latter does not omit anything but rather takes all the aspects presented to us into account.

This leaves us with the following question: Can the notion "the Whole of reality" facilitate the experience one has of that reality or are there pockets of resistance? I think that it can, and that there is not one single pocket of resistance.

It is not by chance that I have tried to pull Pyrrhonism toward Heraclitus's philosophy and thereby bring together Heraclitus and Parmenides. Indeed, to defend as I do with Pyrrho the argument that there is nothing more than vanishing appearances is equal to defending the eternity of this statement. What there is now is not what there was yesterday, but whatever there is, to claim that "*there is*" remains always true. "*There is*" is the way I translate the "esti" of Parmenides, the Ante-Socratic philosopher who holds that the reality of the world as "One Being," an unchanging, un-generated, indestructible whole.

Parmenides's slightly younger contemporary, Heraclitus, claims what could be seen as just the opposite. For Heraclitus, everything is "in flux," as exemplified in his famous aphorism "*panta rhei*" which means "everything flows, nothing stands still."

With "*there is*," Parmenides and Heraclitus join forces to give eternity its rights. Indeed, when I say "*there is*," no notion of time is involved: "*there is*" demands no specification.

To test it, let us introduce the notion of time. Let us ask ourselves if, one day, one may have said or may say in the future: "*There is nothing.*" This would be contradictory. " '*There is nothing*' cannot be said or thought"[5] says Parmenides. "*There is*," on the other hand, can be equated to "neither there was, nor will there be, *because* it is now"[6]: the idea of "now" or "*nun*,"[7] used here, excludes the succession of moments in time and refers to an "eternal present": a present in no way bordered by a past and a future.

We can therefore say that everything happens in the world within an eternal present. Heraclitus's *panta rhei*, "Everything flows," implies an eternal present, just as Parmenides's *nun*.

Getting to See the "Real Force"

What diversity there is within this infinite constant! What diversity in this "*There is!*" We have only to open our eyes: a multiplicity of beings and appearances reveals itself to us. We will call them "beings" if we look at them in narrow time and "appearances" if we choose to do so in infinite time as seen above. However, this diversity, this multiplicity cannot be called disparate. What we see is an arrangement, a "world" (*cosmos*) in the phenomenological sense.

It would of course be pointless to ask why "*There is*" rather than "There is not": it has always been and always will be so. A more natural and rational question is to ask "Why is it 'so' rather than differently?" Aristotle observes: "For all men begin, as we said, by wondering that things are as they are."[8]

When we do wonder about it, we quickly note that no finite being can exist without an external source. Rain presupposes the cloud. The day presupposes the sun. The plant presupposes the seed. The animal has parents. All these beings cannot bring themselves alone into existence, or organize themselves in a world (a structured unity). Not even this world can justify itself. Should we then say this world conforms to an eternal model? We would thereby only shift the problem to another level.

So which creative force engendered this world? Observation and analyses of this world can give us a clue—on the condition that we are not blinded by some obsessive myth. The monotheist faith can prevent us from seeing what we have before our very eyes. We are told an Almighty being has created the world from nothing, and we must believe it, as absurd as it may seem. We are so blinded by this myth that we still would not understand it, even if we were to have real evidence reproducing all aspects of the world right before our own eyes. In order to truly see the real force, we first need to reject as imaginary the unsatisfactory "explanation": the absurd myth of "creation out of nothing."

When we finally succeed in rejecting this myth, then the real force naturally reveals itself to us. To sing the real force, to sing the renewal of nature in spring, the poet Lucretius uses the words *power, force,*[9] or even *love* (*Venus*). The Ante-Socratics called this real force "*Phusis*," which translates to Nature, always denoted with a capital N.

As the "real force," Nature can be said to animate the world. But it does this discreetly "in the background," as it were. Heraclitus says "Nature (*Phusis*) is wont to hide itself."[10] Heraclitus uses the word *phileo*,[11] meaning "to love," but also "to be in the habit of, to be wont to."[12] We can observe this over time as Nature shows or hides itself according to the seasons: it is a habit, the altering of the seasons being undefined. This power of life, Nature, hides itself and becomes invisible during the "dead" season. But after death, life; after life, death and so on. Each of these two opposites is needed. Nature keeps them together as they take turns to appear. A law of harmony governs the course of things but, as Heraclitus notes, "the hidden harmony wins over the visible harmony"[13]: the invisible governs the visible and holds its key.

Nature as Phusis, Nature as the Whole of Reality

The myth claims "God created the world," thereby implicitly acknowledging that the world is not everything. What is there beyond the world then? If we consider "God" as a cultural notion incompatible with our ingenuous experience of reality, could we then consider Nature as all that is "beyond" the world, as what encompasses the world we know and the multiplicity of other worlds and universes? If we do so, could we extend "*Phusis*," the "real force," "*Nature as what underlies the world*" to an all-encompassing Nature? Could Nature then be considered to be "*the Whole of reality*," "the only being that truly *is*" which does not flow away while all finite beings are no more than its fleeting manifestations?

We can only answer this question by plowing through with an ingenuous experience of reality and by contemplating it with renewed attention. This is precisely the purpose of this book. In the following chapters, I will attempt to define my philosophical position by differentiating it from those of the philosophers who are dearest to me. Hopefully, a certain idea of Nature will emerge from these chapters: Nature as infinite in time and space, as infinitely creative and in which Man, if he does not get bogged down with rigid concepts or blinded by contrived and deceptive myths and creeds can also be creative.

II

PRESENCE OF THE INFINITE

Plato and Science in Opposition to the Infinite

Milestones

In this chapter, Conche attempts to demonstrate how science, which is heavily influenced by Plato's philosophy, in reality blinds us to the presence of the infinite, from thinking of Nature as it is.

He first illustrates that despite the claims of positivism, infinity is the most important of the Positive notions. But thinking about the infinite, thinking about what the Whole of reality truly is, requires a certain freedom, a clean detachment from daily concerns, which most men—including scientists—often lack.

This leads us to reflect on the search for truth, which is, or should be, a philosopher's overriding passion. He argues that this search for truth should lead us to reject philosophical systems such as Hegelianism as they cannot assist us in the contemplation of the infinite. In order to erect their coherent and structured view of the world, such systems arbitrarily reject the notion of the infinite, be it in time and/or space.

The reflections on the limits of philosophical systems allow distinguishing two fundamental ways to philosophize: one in narrow time and one in eternal time. In narrow time things appear to be substantial whereas, in the infinite, eternal time, they would merely pass by.

Following the example of Socrates who was more puzzled by men with whom he lived than by Nature, Plato developed a philosophy searching for truth through dialogue. But the dialectical method is more suitable for a philosophy anchored in the narrow time. It inevitably leads to a truth-authenticity (built on "true," coherent opinions) rather than a truth-reality (the knowledge of what things truly are).

Plato therefore turned to "ideas" which he conceived as realities but as separate from the sensitive world. Together with mathematics, "ideas" allowed Plato to give opinions an absolute foundation and to turn them by so doing into a truth-reality. Furthermore, important Ideas such as Harmony or Good, which he called "Principles," again combined with mathematics, allowed Plato to explain other Ideas, which are themselves the causes of all things occupying the sensitive world. By doing so, he endeavored to show the link between the World of Ideas and the Sensitive World. This led to a philosophy where the "essence of things" (what things truly are) resides in Ideas that are numerical ratios. Plato finally thought that, in the World of Ideas, the dialectic or the art that governs the mix of Ideas goes from one Idea to another to end up in another Idea, just as music is the art that rules the union of sounds. Ideas are thereby composed in a system, so that the sensible world itself is a structured entity, an organism.

Such a philosophy and the science it inspires are incompatible with the hypothesis of a multiplicity of cosmos. It does, however, allow men to enter into dialogue with Nature. Unfortunately, through such an indeterminate dialogue, Nature will never entirely reveal itself. Paradoxically, science blinds us to the intimate nature of things, the "naked" Nature.

Infinity as the Most Important of Positivism's Notions

True positivism consists of taking into account everything which is present. Then, from the pen, springs that word *Infinite*. Littré himself writes: "We need to stare at the immensity and imagine the earth, a frail craft navigating the infinite spaces under the guidance of the sun, himself running an infinite course," while denouncing "the sterility of vague and contradictory notions suggested by theological beings."[1]

One could say Littré's wording is hyperbolic; he knows that the sun is not "running an *infinite* course." All the same, Pasteur, praising Littré, whom he will later succeed at the French *Académie*, objects that historical positivism "does not take into account the most important of the *positive* notions: Infinity."

Pasteur ingenuously poses the question that has preoccupied man for quite some time: "Beyond this starlit arch, what is there? Other starlit skies . . . ? And beyond those . . . ?" Mankind will never cease to ask: What lies beyond? Could he stop to look for it, in time or space? Whatever point he eventually reaches, it is still a finite grandeur even if it is greater than its precursors. The moment he begins to realize this, the implacable question starts to haunt him once again, and he is, as ever, powerless to silence curiosity's demands. It is of no use for us to respond with words such as "Beyond are spaces, times, or grandeurs without limits." Nobody understands these words. The notion of infinity has this dual quality; "It imposes itself upon us and yet it remains incomprehensible." Pasteur declares further: "This positive and primordial notion is gratuitously discarded by positivism." Positivism hereby discards metaphysics which "only translates within us the dominant notion of infinity."[2]

Pasteur's wording is not hyperbolic: The infinite is rigorously thought through as opposed to the finite. We could state that Positivism discards a "positive" notion; even the most positive of notions because all men, everywhere on earth, can watch the starlit sky, while many "facts" can only be observed in particular places. Men from across the millennia have been able to witness the starlit sky, while many "positive facts" that could be seen then, cannot be seen today. Whereas others never thought about are witnessed today. Polar bears in their habitat may only be observed in the Arctic; giraffes in Africa; and so on. In the fifteenth century, one never doubted there were knights in armor engaged in battle, but then nobody could have envisaged that soldiers would one day employ sophisticated tanks in warfare.

The starlit sky is far more positive than any of these facts because it remains unchanged regardless of cultures, peoples, or races. This grand and positive fact is of little interest to most men, who focus their attention on their own businesses and affairs.

On the contrary, it is safe to say that most men expect or hope that the starlit sky and its myriad constellations will pay attention to their affairs; indeed, many of them even believe they see signs of that. But in this way they encompass the starlit sky in the world of their daily concerns; hence, they do not permit their natural curiosity to wonder without purpose, to voyage to what lies beyond.

Freedom from Daily Concerns Is a Necessity in Order to Contemplate the Infinite

Thinking about the infinite presupposes a freedom from the world of daily concerns from which people have disentangled themselves. When I was a youth, my days would be crammed with diverse tasks related to life and work on the farm or at school. Nevertheless, I can recall a particular experience while my parents were working in a field close to the Route National 140. Free from my daily chores, I found myself in a state of mind that was "on vacation" gazing out at the wider world and asking questions like, Does this highway go till the end of the world? I deduced it did not go much farther than beyond the next turn and beyond that was a big void. But I needed to verify this, and so off I went, at the slow steady pace of a six-year-old boy. My father noticed my departure and came after me, putting an untimely end to the whole fascinating experience. I thought it useless to try to explain to him what I was trying to do.

The world is naturally thought of as not being infinite and not all-encompassing. Certainly for the Stoics this was the case. Thought is usually buttoned up and constrained within the cycle of daily concerns, much like a bird trapped in a cage.

This, of course, does not prevent Bergson from writing: "Even admitting that changes in the qualities turn around without exception in a finite circle, and that we are unable to find, outside fixed boundaries, anything perceptible to the sense, our mind however pushes us to go beyond, and refuses to be caught up in a space, however large, without desiring immediately to escape."[3]

The *Dasein* is *in-der-Welt-sein*, "open to the world," says Heidegger. This does not say enough. Beyond the world, the *Dasein* is at its very core open to the infinite, but the concept of "world" limits thinking to the pragmatic sphere, as it communicates a certain mental restraint. The world is a manner of being, a "character of being" (*Seinscharakter*) of the *Dasein*. So, what does that mean? The notion of "opening" excludes anything subjective. After the opening, however, comes the closing. In the eyes of the farmer, the field, the meadow, and the herd reveal themselves as they are; but the farmer does not allow them to simply be; no, he catches them without delay in the net of his projects. His thinking, initially open to the infinite, comes to a halt just as it was expanding in order to serve the pursuit of earthly and mundane goals. To keep the eyes open on the infinite, isn't this to forget that we are human beings "in situation," with our specific goals?

Positivists, as we have seen, reject the transcendental infinite. They are nevertheless no more amenable to the infinity that surrounds us. Should the reason for this be sought in the *Dasein* structure itself—of their *Dasein*?

Let us take the example of Auguste Comte. Comte's ambition was to develop a philosophy congruent with industrial societies and a political organization appropriate to their structure and capabilities. But this mattered only to man: This is a privileged moment in history and the problems of the time are ephemeral and vanish in the infinity of time.

Truth, the Philosopher's Passion

Without doubt, all of us are vaguely conscious of "a bottomless place in which we are plunged and that overtakes us from all sides."[4] We nevertheless repress this obscure consciousness, as do all men absorbed by a particular occupation: to plough a field, paint a portrait, win a battle, observe a chemical reaction, etc. This is the case with almost everyone, what interests them is not the *Truth*. They are only concerned with bringing to fruition what they have undertaken.

If they are not constrained by necessity, by an alimentary and vain labor, men are generally dominated by the passions related to the roles they perform in society—social passions. Accolades, money, fame, power, are the prizes that motivate them to act, often at the expense of their longevity.

The philosopher's passion is, on the other hand, so strong that all others succumb to it or become negligible: his is the passion for truth.

Some might find cause to doubt this as they witness around them career-driven philosophers continuously pursuing honors and even celebrity. If these thinkers don't search, above everything else, for truth, then they don't really qualify as genuine philosophers, instead they are merely "philosophers" in inverted commas.

So, Bergson believes his praise for William James can't be any higher when he writes of him: "No one loved truth with a more ardent love. No one sought it with greater passion."[5] Of himself, Bergson said that, while writing, he never bothered not to injure this or that belief, "he only cared for truth."[6]

Descartes preferred truth over human love. When he was thinking about marriage, he had nevertheless "actively courted," as Adrien Baillet mentions, Mme de Rosai. He even fought off a rival with a sword in hand for her attentions. But afterward "this lady wittingly revealed that philosophy had more charms than herself in the eyes of M. Descartes; and that, although he thought her rather beautiful, he had told her, trying to be gallant, he could not find any beauty comparable to truth."[7]

"The thirst, the search for truth, was the central and dominant passion of Simone Weil; if she had had to choose between divine love and truth she would have chosen truth. Weil opposed Dostoyevsky who said that, if Christ was not the truth, he would choose Christ's love against truth. She sustained that, under this hypothesis, she would choose truth against Christ, against love."[8]

The Rejection of Systems such as Hegelianism and the Search for Truth

What then must we understand by "truth?"

"What is true is the Whole" (*Das Wahre ist das Ganze*) says Hegel.[9] Bergson for his part writes that a philosophy is "a unique and global vision of the whole."[10] He hereby means: it is the work of one philosopher pretending to build an all-encompassing philosophy. He conceives philosophy to be as "necessarily collective and gradual." His own philosophy is unachieved.

Bergson's philosophy is by now already a philosophy of Nature, a Nature that would be itself an unachieved, continuously self-creating totality. Hence, Bergson's declaration to I. Benrubi: "Hegelianism is in my eyes totally wrong."[11] A philosophy of Nature can only reject a system in which thinking closes in upon itself. Indeed, Hegel believes that the Absolute is spirit: subjective, objective, absolute. But then what is this human, "subjective" spirit? What is this "objective" spirit embodied by customs, laws, families, and cities? What is the "absolute" spirit embodied by art, religion, philosophy, and human creations?

We should not forget either that the Hegelian philosophy, so-called "of nature," concerns the sciences elaborated by man. But then, what are all human productions if not remarkable accidents amid the abundance of things?

Not only Schopenhauer or Bergson, but any philosopher, conscious of the poverty of human knowledge when faced with the infinite and the enigma, rises to repulse the Hegelian system—even when one holds it in esteem as a remarkable analysis of the structures and articulation of culture. Philosophy is not sociology. Philosophy is of a higher order and in its background a certain unrest and anxiety always lingers.

The Two Ways to Philosophize: In the Narrow or in the Eternal Time

There are two ways to philosophize. We either anchor philosophy in the narrow time or in the eternal time.

In the first case things appear substantial, consequently the philosopher is a man of his time and develops a moral philosophy, or a philosophy of law, art, religion, or of the ethical possibilities that would be acceptable in the world he inhabits.

The principal moral predicament today is the justification and the extent of the "rights of man."

The difficulty with law pertains to international law and international jurisdictions.

The quandary with "contemporary art" is about its definition.

The problem with religion concerns its future.

Let us compare Hegel and Sartre, both of whom have philosophized in the narrow time, that is, as men of their time: The differences of the eras in which they have thought and worked are reflected in their different methods and concepts. Of course, we can define the boundaries of history so that Hegel and Sartre would not belong to different periods but rather to the same time, which began with the Declaration of Human Rights in 1789. Hegel and Sartre are sons of the French Revolution: For the former, the ideal of the Revolution is realized; for the latter, the ideal of 1789, completed by the ideal of 1793, is still to be concretely realized. On the one hand, a happy consciousness that accomplishes itself in the world and in the justification of Knowledge; on the other hand, a forlorn consciousness that holds out for the future.

Philosophies that have placed themselves at the mercy of the narrow, historical time are, after a few decades or centuries, no more than historical curiosities. Sartre, Hegel, expressions and embodiments of their times, have shaped their philosophies upon the ephemeral, *their times themselves*. Time erodes everything. All loses its importance. Refutation itself becomes useless.

One may also philosophize in the eternal time: unlike Hegel, Sartre, or Confucius, but akin to Heraclitus, Epicurus, or Lao Tzu.

Han-Yu blames Lao Tzu for not seeing the world that surrounds him, as though he were sitting at the bottom of a well. By thinking in this way, Han-Yu is himself a disciple of Confucius. Though sitting at the bottom of a well we are able to make an abstraction of the human world, we only see the starlit sky continuously changing the face of eternal Nature. In *Theaetetus*, Plato describes a philosopher who "knows not the road leading to the Agora,"[12] who has "no suspicion" of what is going on in the city—just as if we would be sitting at the bottom of a well. The philosopher described by Plato is the exact opposite to Socrates, the eminently sociable Athenian who was utterly at ease in the Agora. The philosopher Socrates, who meditates in symbiosis with his contemporaries and his time, is, in

Plato's eyes, the exact opposite of a philosopher of Nature, such as Thales, who observes the planets.[13]

The Limits of the Dialogical Method: Leading to a Truth-Authenticity, not a Truth-Reality

To philosophize in the historical time or in the eternal time implies that one goes toward truth via different methods.

The method of dialogue fits perfectly with the former but not with the latter. Socrates's method is the dialogical. Limited to itself, dialogue is not a means to know, since knowledge about *things* cannot result from an exchange of words. That is why Socrates renounced philosophizing about Nature; to speak truthfully about the nature of things, one has to deal with the things themselves.

Socrates is more puzzled by the people with whom he lives, by how his fellow citizens think about themselves with words, the meanings of which they don't fully understand.

It is likely they believe to have within their grasp a precise idea of temperance, courage, piety, etc., but their ideas do not resist closer inspection and their lack of coherence soon reduces them to silence.

So what is the point of dialogue for Socrates, then? "Let us make sure . . ." he says to Nicias, ". . . that you don't have a given definition of courage and that we have another one."[14] Socrates's dialogue aims at remedying judgments' disorders and to ensure that the citizens of a city agree on the same principles. Socrates's core goal in essence is to remedy the evil from which civil wars arise.

This is all well and good, but the problem remains: the truth we can reach through the challenge of dialogue is not a truth-reality but a truth-authenticity. The willingness to define virtue is the same as the willingness to define what a good man should be. Note that the definition of a good man obtained through such dialogue will not be absolute: It only gives the definition of the ideal man for the Greeks of the fifth century BC. For example, they agree on the value of courage in battles and it is evident that for them, this is a "very beautiful thing."[15] For Yeshayahu Leibowitz, on the contrary, the real value of a man has "never been measured according to his bravery," which does "not deserve our admiration."[16] Similarly, we might also evoke here the diverging judgment of Lao Tzu on military virtues.

The dialogical method can only help us to reach agreement but cannot help us know what things are. Plato's method arises indeed from the search for a definition through dialogue, but, as a dialectical method, it can only work for ideas. In order to be able to speak of truth and not simply of an agreement among minds, a contact with reality is necessary. Definitions, once agreed, make "true opinions" possible. We can say: "Laches is courageous." "Socrates is virtuous," etc., but these are only truth-authenticities. They are limited to the human sphere. "True opinions" can be compared to Dedalus's statues: Dedalus sculpted his statues to have a walking posture, so realistic that, it was said, they had to be chained up to stay in place. Similarly, "true opinions" escape the soul if they are not "chained up by causal reasoning."[17] Linked together by reasoning, true opinions take a "scientific" character. Science (*episteme*) provides the links, the enchainment of ideas.[18] But this only ensures the coherency of the ideas, not their truth. Their truth exists by itself, independently.

Ideas as Realities and Mathematics to the Rescue

Thus, we have to admit, for Plato, Ideas are realities, and are hence hereby separated from the sensitive world. So, Plato makes the hypothesis of the pre-empirical existence of souls in the region of truth, and of a transcendental experience in things themselves. Therefore "to know" becomes the same act as "to remember." Without "reminiscence" (*anamnesis*), we would remain stuck at the level of opinions; we would not reach the level of knowledge.

So, how can Plato therefore think he can transform the Socratic "definitions" or opinions into the realities he calls "Ideas"?[19]

To understand this, one has to remember that moral notions were inherent in Greek society; after Herodotus's lesson of relativism it was difficult to grant them, without solid foundations, universal acceptation. Nonetheless, there were other notions with an undeniable universal acceptation besides moral notions: mathematics. It is, however, possible to strip from mathematics everything that is related to sensitive observations and that is not demonstrable;

- Arithmetic then becomes only about numbers:
- Geometry is only about figures;
- Astronomy is only about combinations of movements that are not at all irregular such as those one can observe in reality and;

- The science of harmony is only about simple numerical ratios that ensure harmony.

These are sciences resting on hypotheses which spring from the mind and the mind alone. They attract the soul "of what is born to what is."[20] Plato hereby means that living beings that flit past are naturally more attracted to what remains and is eternal, than to what really is. Sciences help us therefore to accept the hypothesis of Ideas as realities, Idea-substances, and of their separation from the sensitive world.

Mathematical analysis must allow Plato to realize what Anaxagoras could not do. Plato quotes Anaxagoras as saying that "intelligence is the organizer and the cause of all things."[21] But in his detailed explanation of the phenomena, intelligence does not intervene and he resorts to the air, the ether, or the water to do so. Plato, on the contrary, explains things, including moral notions, from the first level, thanks to the hypothesis of the Ideas. So a beautiful thing is not beauty; it can be beautiful without being beauty by "participating" in beauty. "By beauty beautiful things become beautiful . . . by greatness only great things become great and greater, and by smallness the less become less."[22] Plato says thus that Beauty is the "cause" of beautiful things. Hereby, Plato strips judgments from their relativity and gives them an absolute foundation.

Principles and Mathematical Analysis Once Again to the Rescue

For which "things" will there be an idea then? If we have to give the "causes of all things," there must be an Idea for everything: Not only of "Justice, Beauty, Kindness and things of this sort, but also of Man, of Fire, of Water,"[23] of all living beings and, in general, of "each group of multiple objects that have in common the same name."[24]

But ideas themselves need to be explained: What constitutes Justice itself, or Beauty, etc.? Besides, there is a logical generation of Ideas,[25] which supposes to go back to a "Principle." Here, mathematical analysis comes in again. In order to demonstrate the existence of such "Principles," Plato first marks the primacy of arithmetic above geometry, of number above figure. Aristotle writes, "Plato and the Pythagoreans have established the Numbers as 'principles for beings'[26] because they believed the One (prime and un-composed number) a principle.

"Now, if the simplest being out of two has primacy by nature, then surfaces have primacy over bodies, lines over surfaces and points over lines; what mathematicians call 'points' or 'monads,' because points are absolutely not composed and have nothing that precedes them. Now, monads are numbers, therefore, Numbers are the prime beings."[27] Plato, however, "separated from the sensitive world the One, the Numbers, unlike the Pythagoreans."[28]

What now becomes of the relationship between Ideas and Numbers?

Ideas are the "causes" or "principles" for sensitive things.[29] Numbers are the "causes or principles[30] for the substance (*ousia*) of the other beings,"[31] including Ideas. Ideas are thus subordinated to Numbers. These Numbers, principles for the Ideas, are called "ideal" Numbers, as opposed to mathematical numbers. Together with geometrical figures, mathematical numbers are only intermediaries between Ideas and the sensible things.[32]

"Ideal" Numbers depend on two principles: the One and the undefined Dyad of the Great and the Small (a dyad, according to Pythagoreans, is the principle of "twoness" or "otherness").

"For from the Great and the Small, by participation in the One, come the Numbers."[33] So, Plato "relates sensitive things to Ideas, the Ideas to Numbers, raises Numbers to Principles (the One and the undefined Dyad), and lastly, details how they are at the origin of realities," writes Theophrastus.[34]

The equalization of the undefined Dyad[35] under the action of the One generates the number 2 that through duplication, generates the numbers 4 and 8. The application of the One to even numbers provides the uneven numbers 3, 5, 7 and 9, etc., thus the first ten numbers are generated. After the Numbers comes the generation of the Ideal Grandeurs, out of the One and the variations of the Great and the Small—long and short for lengths, large and narrow for surfaces, high and low for solids.

To claim afterward that Numbers are Principles for the Ideas implies that Ideas define themselves through numerical relationships. Since an Idea is a structure (structured by Ideal Numbers, structuring sensible things), these relationships are functions of *the measure* and *the proportion*—the prime goods, according to Plato's *Philebus*.

Aristotle also tells us that the Pythagorean Eurytos assigned a number to each thing. This number was determined by the number of stones needed to frame the shape of that thing. For example, 250 stones was the number for man.[36] According to Eurytos, there should be a particular number for each being of real phenomena: for each animal, for each stage in life, as well as for the movements of the sun or the moon. Following Aristotle, Hegel easily observes that such an abstract determination could fit too many different things. There is no reason to associate a particular number more to one thing than to another. "It is not due to the number 7 as such that there are seven vowels, seven cords in the musical scale or seven Pleiades. It is neither due to the number 7 if certain animals lose their teeth when they are seven, if the warlords numbered seven before Thebes," writes Aristotle.[37] But such a primitive symbolism has probably little to do with what should be kept as essential in Pythagoreanism.

Numerical Ratios, Dialectic, and the Essence of Things

"In other systems of physics," Nietzsche observes, "qualities were born out of combination or dissociation; Pythagoreans rather sustain qualities residing in the diversity of proportions."[38] Pythagoreanism, to which Plato is close in many ways, therefore implies that it is not simply about numbers but about numerical ratios.

So Heraclitus, similar to Pythagoras, tells us about the "conversions" (*tropai*)[39] of fire. It converts into sea, then into earth and into "burning blow" and then conversely.[40]

For Heraclitus, such conversions are made according to the same *logos*, which means according to constant proportions. Nietzsche tells us that, if Pythagoricians "had borrowed from Heraclitus the word *logos*, they would have hereby understood *the proportion*. *The proportion* fixes the proportions, just as *the limit* [41] fixes the limit."[42]

For example, music emerges in numerical ratios, amidst which we can define a proportion, called harmonious proportions. According to Nietzsche, this is why music is "the best example of what Pythagoricians meant."[43]

Plato follows the Pythagoreans' logic. "Pythagorean music allows him to see that the essence of things resides in numerical ratios, even more so than in numbers."[44] As a consequence, Ideas can define themselves as structured units, rather than as models referring to sensitive things. Also, the notion of "participation of Ideas among themselves" takes over the notion of "participation of the sensitive things to Ideas." Dialectic is then the art that governs the mutual participation or mix of Ideas, just as music is the art that rules the union of sounds.[45] So, "without using any perceptible data," dialectic "goes from one Idea to another to end up in another Idea."

Now, just as music cannot leave a sound isolated, because intervals also count, dialectic cannot leave an Idea isolated, because none can be thought of without links to others. Plato writes: "You destroy all discourse by separating everything from the rest; because it is through the mutual weaving of Forms that discourse is born."[46]

So, to the "Friends of Ideas" who want to keep them isolated and fixed, we need to oppose that, out of respect for Measure and under the "yoke of the Good," all is related to all in the "*totality of the being*."[47] By this notion we must understand here[48] the *cosmos* in its totality, encompassing not only the world of Ideas, but also the sensitive world. The world of Ideas is the truth of the sensitive world; both are inseparable within a one and unique world. Dialectic, as it does not leave any Idea outside its grasp, composes the Ideas in a system. There might not be a Platonic system but the World according to Plato is a system—a structured totality, an organism; Plato calls it a "Living."

Plato and Science against the Multiplicity of the Cosmos

For Plato, there can only be one World. If there was another one, "there should also be another, a third 'Living,' which would encompass the two former ones which would then be parts of the third one. In that case, we could rightly say that our sensitive world is the copy, not of the two former ones, but of the one that would encompass them."[49]

Science is Platonian. The scientist observes the sensitive world, or rather "questions" it armed with principles and hypotheses. He then submits his responses to a mathematical treatment and elaborates a model of the universe. There are thus numerous "systems of the world," from Plato to Einstein among others, through Laplace and his *Exposition of the System of the World* (1796).

Today, the word *universe*, rather than *world* is used to indicate "the whole of what exists in time and space."[50] Today, "we know, or believe to know," writes A. Koyré in 1954, "that our Universe is not infinite—although it has no boundaries, as opposed to what Aristotle believed—and beyond this Universe there is absolutely nothing, precisely because there is no "outside" and all of the space is "within."[51]

The philosophy that generates such an Einsteinian universe is Plato's "mathematical realism." "The philosophical attitude that proves right in the long run," adds Koyré, "is not Bacon's or Comte's, but the one of Descartes,

Galileo and Plato."[52] For Koyré, the modern cosmologists' models of the universe are as all-encompassing as the Platonian Model: The only difference is that Plato's universe is eternal while the modern cosmologists' universe is unfolding.

Beyond "Big Bang's universe," says Koyré, there is "nothing." This remains to be seen. There is indeed nothing for the cosmologist, but what about the philosopher?

For the cosmologist, the World (*cosmos*) is unique. Plato asks: "Would it have been more correct to say that there is a plurality of skies or even an infinite number of them?"[53] The hypothesis is rejected but is not judged as absurd. "The philosopher is the one who has the power to consider both all the hypotheses and their consequences," observes Monique Dixsaut.[54] This is precisely what Plato does in his *Parmenides*. The World's representation that he gives in *Timeaus* is presented as "probable," not as a truth. Dixsaut pursues: "The Democritean option [namely, that there might be infinity of worlds] remains possible": "It is possible that the world is the product of the chance and the necessity. However, if we consider that possibility, we will be undertaking a train of thought not apt to Plato."[55] The philosopher is thus free to see in the "Big Bang's universe" a *cosmos* in the sense of Democritus and Epicurus, outside of which there is not "nothing" but infinity of *cosmoi*.

Some "isolated" cosmologists do claim, in unison with the philosopher, "There are a myriad of continuously self-creating Universes, a vertiginous infinity of Universes with the most varied properties."[56]

However, the scientist, *in his role as a scientist*, cannot speak such words: if there were two universes, they would be resolved into one, as Plato shows. Because, if they are to remain two, there must be, in one of them—ours—enough to constrain us to admit the other one, so that they are to be two in one.

But the cosmologist who speaks as a philosopher—the metaphysician—may use such speculative language; after all, being beyond the reach of any experimental control, the metaphysician may formulate the hypothesis of the existence of infinity, of "Big Bang's universes," knowing that such a hypothesis is avowed to remain forever a hypothesis.

The Scientists' Unending Dialogue with Nature

Let us establish that there is a hiatus between the Nature that can only be known by the scientist if it is reduced to a world, and the infinite Nature that is thought up in the eternal time. Because the scientist, as the dialogical Socrates, thinks in the historical time, his work depends on a temporary and provisional developmental phase of science.

The dialogical method is also the method of the scientist. This is what Heisenberg writes from the outset in his book *Der Teil und das Ganze*: "Science rests on experiments; its results are attained through talks among those who work in it and who consult one another about their interpretation of these experiments. Such talks form the main content of this book. Through them the author hopes to demonstrate that science is rooted in conversations."[57]

As time passes, such discussions have—or seem to have—only historical interest. To prove it, let us remember the discussions between Einstein and Max Born on the interpretation of quantum mechanics. They did not agree. Einstein was obstinate in his conviction that "physics opens for us the gates to objective knowledge of the world" and that it is possible to describe the world in a nonequivocal way. Einstein's convictions were the results of philosophical postulates from another age, according to Heisenberg. For him, "It does not seem likely that science will ever find its way back to Einstein's postulates."[58] Heisenberg writes: "It does not seem . . ." Does this reflect a thought that Nature has yet to utter its last word?

There is, as we can see from the above, a great and essential difference between the Socratic dialogue and the discussion among scientists. The latter exchange ideas about the interpretation of observed facts, that is, about the interpretation of what Nature *says*, thus resulting in endless dialogue. Heisenberg writes: "The defenders of atomism had to recognize that their science was but a link in the infinite chain of the dialogue between man and nature and that their science may not continue to speak simply about a nature as such."[59] It is as if two speakers would ask themselves what a third speaker thinks. But as Galileo noted, this third speaker, Nature, expresses itself only in mathematical language.

In Greek, "Word" was expressed by *logos*; "conversation" by a short sentence[60] meaning "to converse with somebody in a common language to the speakers," that is, with the words of the tribe, in this case the Greek language.

Antonina Vallentin was present during a discussion between Einstein and his assistant, Professor Mayer. Formulas, series of numbers, words that made no sense to her were exchanged, she writes: "The two men might as well have conversed in Chinese."[61] The language Einstein and Mayer used is *logos*, the logos of science that Nature understands since through it, we obtain answers. But does that mean that, through this *logos*, we understand

Nature? The dialogue is "infinite" says Heisenberg. If the dialogue is infinite, there will thus always be a chasm, which the Greeks called *Chôrismos*, between the scientific logos and Nature itself.

So, once again we find in the Platonian *Chôrismos*, the chasm between the World of Ideas and the sensitive world, which Plato tried so hard to overcome. This *Chôrismos* is due to the infinite character of Nature, which cannot, by definition, be expressed in logos, in a language that would be understandable by finite beings, specifically by Man.

Nature offers itself to the scientific logos in the form of a world, that is to say, an ordered and structured world. Einstein acceded to the theory of relativity because he was—as was Plato—convinced of the "harmony of the world," as he himself said. The theory of the "unified field" expressed his search for a synthesis embracing the totality of the world—gravitational attraction was hereby reduced to an electromagnetic phenomenon.

It should be noted that, in the "dialogue between Man and Nature," both parties bring something to the table. Heisenberg writes: "What we discover and take to be the order and harmony of the world is merely the working of eternal laws or of the ordering power of our mind."[62] Let us write "and" rather than "or." The ordering force of mathematics is what we men bring to the table but the "eternal laws" are not ours.

Science Blinds us from "Naked" Nature

As we have just seen, Nature reveals and exposes itself in this scientific *logos*, which it depicts as a structured world. But *what exactly of Nature* is revealed? In my eyes, through the scientific *logos* Nature only reveals itself in as far as it can be measured, verified, and quantified. Nature itself remains illusive in retreat. Roland Omnès writes that science cannot reach "the intimate nature of things but rather the permanency of their mutual relations."[63]

None of the above therefore denies that the scientific *logos* has a grip on reality. It is able to do so because the order of the world has a logical and mathematical nature.

So, the scientific *logos* is able to catch something out of the system of rules in which the reality of our world is entangled. There is no doubt that science will always continue to increase its understanding of this system of rules; in fact, it will do so "indefinitely" as the dialogue between science and Nature is, as we have seen, infinite.

Nature itself will always dwell out of reach. The scientific *logos* cannot catch what in Nature cannot be turned into logic or mathematics. Nature is like a living body covered with a coat—the scientific *logos* might one day catch each of the coat's fibers that form a beautiful and harmonious whole, and find each fiber interwoven with all the others, but nevertheless, the coat is not the body of the person.

The paradox of all this, of science's unrelenting, progressing, but also infinite journey towards "understanding" Nature is this: Nature is constantly revealing itself to us "naked," without a coat. It does so in the guise of the sensitive, richly diverse world that all men, of all times and places, can witness. It is as if modern science, heavily influenced by Plato, would in fact blind us in its frantic pursuit from the presence of the infinite Nature.

III

WITH AND WITHOUT ARISTOTLE

Milestones

As Conche shows in this chapter, Aristotle, contrary to Plato, returns to a more immediate approach to Nature. Nevertheless, based on qualities (rather than on Numbers), his rationalism and determinism lead him to overdetermine Nature. In Aristotle, Phusis is "under control," doing nothing without reason; she is a force for organic growth leading to a perfect world or cosmos. This is, of course, compatible with his vision of the fixity and eternity of the species. Hereby, Aristotle negates Nature's capacity to "create," to be a "force of love," as Lucretius called her, guiding without a preconceived finality. Similarly, Lucretius's (and others') thesis of the infinite plurality of worlds contradicts Aristotle's intuition of one harmonious Whole and of the Goodness of the world.

Additionally, Aristotle's vision of the "infinity" of the cosmos is that it is "unlimited" because there is nothing beyond it. This is not the same as saying that the cosmos is actually infinite. To understand this, Conche distinguishes the "potentially" from the "actually" infinite, one of the key ideas of Aristotle's philosophy.

The distinction between potentiality and actuality leads him to distinguish the movement as such from the movement as a gesture, and the events that delimit the present from those that do not.

These distinctions are important to understand as considerations that Aristotle did not contemplate, but can be found at the core of the Stoic philosophy. Namely, beings exist as the succession of their parts, and nothing else is real except the present. Such reflections will prepare us to investigate the Stoic Chrysippus and his vision.

Aristotle's Return to a More Immediate Approach to Nature

Let us now leave aside the scientific, relativist and quantum *logos*, as Nature here is grasped only by her armature or her coat, the extremities shall we say, and not by "herself." Obviously this does not prevent us, as we mentioned earlier, from admitting that the practical effectiveness of knowledge and the capacity to use Nature for human goals does not require an absolute understanding of Nature. One could dare to make the following comparison in this regard: the perfect obedience of a woman, submitted to her "master" (her "husband") in cultures where this took place, did not imply that the latter understood her inner soul or feelings.

We need to go back to a more immediate approach to Nature, more precisely to the common experience each of us may have. That is exactly what Aristotle has done.

For him, Nature is offered to us: "to try demonstrating that Nature exists would be ridiculous."[1] Apart from artistic creations, most of the things that surround us, such as air or water, are only due to Nature. These things do not remain in place; change is an evident and universal fact.

Aristotle's "Qualitative" Rationalism and Determinism

Having said that, acknowledging what our senses tell us is not incompatible with being rational. Let us therefore briefly characterize Aristotle's rationalism.

First, Aristotle's rationalism minimizes the role of the Number, giving importance to the qualities alone. Beings are defined through their qualities. To say what a being "is" is to give its type and specific difference—that is, the quality which distinguishes that being from others of the same kind: the horse is a quadruped animal, a quality that distinguishes it from man—a biped.

Second, Aristotle's physical mathematics cannot be "*surpassed*" by the physical mathematics of Einstein; this is akin to saying that a swimmer's prowess could be "surpassed" by that of a champion climber.

In any case, Aristotle is as deterministic as Einstein. For him, chance does not contradict causality. Any effect is entirely determined by the sum of the causes from which it results, whether they are due to constant and regular phenomena or to random accidents and brute necessity.

But Aristotle's determinism is qualitative therefore of a different nature, and it does not allow for prediction. The future is, of course, to a large extent uncertain, yet the sky's rotation is perpetual. The seasons' cycle, the mutual generation of elements, the reproduction, generation after generation, of animals and plants are perpetual processes depending on the movement of the stars. There will always be winter and summer, therefore cold and the warmth, air and the winds, etc., and the same species of plants and animals; but what will be is *not* this water, this air, these individuals, etc. Future events, being singular, cannot be anticipated.

Aristotle's Apparent Contradiction Solved by His Overdetermination of Nature

This brief description of Aristotle's conception might give us a sense of its possible inner contradiction: a contradiction between the intuition of the *Phusis* and of her creative productivity (which comes from his return to a more immediate approach to Nature) and the concerns for cosmic order and structure that he inherited from Plato (this explains his qualitative determinism).

As we will argue, Aristotle has not kept himself close enough to the resolutely ingenuous experience of Nature's presence: he has overdetermined it, in the attempt to give it meaning.

That was unnecessary. In his philosophy, the meaning is already implicit: the world, which is the Whole of reality for Aristotle, is perfect. All that deserves to be, being truly real, already exists. So individuals only need to become what they are "in right" (de jure) to realize themselves according to the norms of their kind.

Therefore, the possible contradiction mentioned above cannot materialize. Nature's productivity is ruled, ordered, structured once and for all by cosmic dominance. At the same time, he neglects the original meaning of the word *Phusis*:[2] "birth, generation, and growth."

Aristotle's Methodical Finalism: Phusis as a "Fully under Control" Force for Organic Growth Leading to a Perfect Cosmos

More specifically, Aristotle starts by wondering to which of the following two meanings of nature he should give priority: to the nature-matter or to the nature-form? For him, natural beings are composed of matter and form. He finally concludes that, primarily, it is form that is nature:[3] "formal nature is thus more important than material nature."[4]

Without the earth, water, and their opposites air and fire, there would not be living beings, but it is the form[5] of the animal that makes them become food: not the form as such, in the simple universal idea, but the incarnated form in an animal, that is, a composite.[6] It is not the concept of "man" that generates man: it is a man.[7] Besides, forms have no reality beyond the beings in which they realize themselves.

But if these beings are generated by a composition of matter and form, these forms on the contrary are not generated by anything. Not being generated, they are eternal; being eternal they do not have the power of not to be. They are always actualized,[8] materialized, but they are actualized in individuals who are, from one generation to the other, forever new.

Now, where does it come from that beings generate other beings and then degenerate? For Aristotle, generation and degeneration are only due to the movement of the sun along the elliptic, alternative movement of the earth's approach and withdrawal.

From all of this arises the image of an achieved and stable cosmos where *Phusis* is fully "under control," and her power is reduced to almost nothing.

Of course, Aristotle often presents us Nature as a person, whose activity is governed akin to Leibniz's God by the principle of sufficient reason; but as such activity seems to be without deliberation or conscience, it is simply a way of expressing oneself at this point.

Nature, Aristotle tells us, "does not do anything by chance"[9]; she "does not do anything without reason,[10] neither in vain."[11] With her, nothing is "useless,"[12] "superfluous."[13] There is nothing that Nature does "without a goal."[14] She did not give eyelids to fishes: what would they need them for? Water,[15] just like air, does not contain a mass of corpses that would prevent seeing. The upright nature of man being to stand, Nature did not give him front legs. In contrast, as his intelligence makes him capable of using them, she gave him hands; he is not intelligent because he has hands, as Anaxagoras thinks, but the inverse. Nature acts as a "wise man" would.[16] She gives long legs to swamp birds and, as a corollary, a long neck: if it was too short, it would not allow them to hunt for food. The function "creates" the organ.

Finalism is, for Aristotle, a conviction. But before anything, it is a methodical finalism, which, as such, is still of value for the modern scientist in the study of living beings. Nature is a craft artist, an "organizer,"[17] writes Aristotle.

Aristotle's Nature is in this sense similar to the great physiologist Claude Bernard's "force of organic growth." Bernard's "guiding idea" has the same effectiveness as Aristotle's nature-form. Bernard writes: "In all living germ, there is a creative idea that develops and manifests itself through organization. While it lasts, the living being remains under the influence of this vital and creative force, and death arrives when the idea cannot achieve itself anymore. Here, and everywhere, everything arises from the idea, which alone creates and directs."[18] That's why, he adds, "in the organism of living beings, one must see a *harmonious* whole of phenomena." Unlike the physician and the chemist who "can trace back all ideas of final causes in the facts that they observe," the physiologist "is led to admit a harmonious and pre-established finality in the organized body, of which all parts are interdependent and generating each other."[19]

The same goes for Aristotle, with the difference that he would not speak of a "guiding" idea and that the object of his reflection, as a "physiologist" (in which there is the word *Phusis*), is the whole of the cosmos, which is for him a living being. Under the living and animated celestial bodies, "all things live truly, desire and love. All things tend towards the Good."[20] Nature, like Leibniz's God, "realizes, among all possibilities, the one that is best."[21] For Aristotle, the whole of the cosmos, Nature, is perfect.

Lucretius's Nature as a Force of Love Guiding without Preconceived Finality

Aristotle's conception of Nature could be well founded and true, but could also not be so, which is more likely, at least if one does not remain as the scientist with a method of postulates. In any case, Aristotle's vision goes much farther than what the immediate evidence tells us. So we must return to the evidence. Let us call upon Lucretius to help us.

When Lucretius sings the "power" of Nature in the spring he expresses what everybody feels, whether epicurean or not. This force called "love," each of us has lived this surging from within in moments of passion, a rapture taking us beyond ourselves, a leaving of the individual behind, only the species has, through generations of ephemeral individuals, a true and immutable reality.

What manifests itself is then is life itself and its meaning, which is forever to defeat death, whatever the extraneous individual goals might be.

There is a stunning imbalance between the force of love, which can rip lives, careers, and beings apart, and the cautious smallness of ordinary ambitions: on one hand, the meaning of life, with a horizon of undefined duration; on the other hand, the meager sense that the individual gives to his life, a derisory meaning since it has no influence on death (except for the capacity of works to delay oblivion just a little).

In order to define the gap between this and Aristotle's conception more precisely, let us discuss again the word that defines the power of Nature: "creation."

Aristotle does not use it. Animals, according to him, cannot be eternal as individuals but they participate *to* eternity, as each species imitates, through a perpetual succession of individuals, the eternity of the celestial movement. As species are immutable, Nature cannot be creative. Any animal presupposes, before it, an animal of the same species, hereby excluding "transformation" or evolution. Aristotle continues to think so, even though, already in his time, the idea of mutability of the species is more compatible with ancient Greek philosophies of the becoming (such as those of Anaximander and Heraclitus)[22] than their fixity.

Nature, counters Lucretius when echoing the teachings of Epicurus, "creates all things."[23] Lucretius opposes Nature, as he understands her to be against all that is divinity, providence, finality, design, plan, or the harmonious order of things. His Nature is a force that, without preconceived finality, "governs" or "guides"[24] all things. First of all, she brings all possibilities to existence. This, of course, has important consequences that are incompatible with Aristotle's vision of a perfect cosmos.

One Perfect Cosmos or a Multiplicity of Cosmoi?

For Lucretius, Nature brings all possibilities to existence. By this we should understand that, through her combination of powers, she brings to fruition:

1. All possible beings;
2. All possible worlds, without sorting for the "best";
3. All possible production modes.

For example, since the production of an eclipse is conceivable in many different ways, it is highly unlikely that eclipses occur in the same way throughout the universe's different worlds.

For Aristotle however, as for Leibniz, our world is the only one. It is the best out of all theoretically possible worlds, but Aristotle, like Plato, knows that he hereby does not refute Democritus as one refutes an error; he simply discards it on the basis of his own evidence. The thesis of the infinite plurality of worlds contradicts his intuition of a harmonious Whole, and of the Goodness of the world.

Such a thesis of the infinite plurality of worlds can only be sustained, according to Aristotle, through some sort of aberration. Yet this is precisely the thesis Epicurus and, before him, Democritus, sustain. Their thesis is based on a totally different intuition than Aristotle's, the intuition of the infinite.

In the previous chapter we quoted Pasteur. For him, the notion of infinite and grandeur, negated by Aristotle, is the most positive and pre-eminent of notions. How could we refuse to ponder what there could be beyond the skies? Still, for Aristotle, the answer is clear: there is nothing beyond the World, no fullness, no emptiness, and no location. The external surface of the stellar orbit is its limit, with nothing beyond it, because if all contact is something relative (being between two terms), the limit is not something relative.[25]

Aristotle's Nature: Potentially but not Actually Infinite

With his vision of a perfect cosmos and nothing beyond it, Aristotle would not have had any issue with the finite and spherical universe of Einstein.

But Einstein discards the Euclidian straight line because of the presence of matter, and replaces it with a ray of light assimilated to a Riemann line. Aristotle, however, limits the length of any real Euclidian straight line to the universe's diameter.

That goes as well for any length or grandeur: one cannot find grandeur greater than any grandeur of the same kind given in advance, because none can be greater than the world.

On the other hand, the Number, starting with the indivisible unity, is potentially infinite from the point of view of reason, because it is a being created by reason. If a line, or any other finite grandeur, cannot be infinitely increased, it is nevertheless infinitely divisible—in two parts, then three, etc.—since there is no end to the series of numbers. But no grandeur will be in practice divided in an infinite number of parts, and there is not an infinite number. The infinite exists "in a certain way," says Aristotle, since the series of movements is infinite, and even the series of Numbers and time, which is no more than the "Number of the movement" is without beginning or end.

But "how"[26] can the infinite exist? It only "potentially"[27] exists, that is, "in thoughts,"[28] not in reality or "actually."[29] When we say that a statue resides potentially in the bronze, we understand that the statue will perhaps one day be sculpted, that it will be actualized. On the contrary, when we speak about a potential infinite, we understand that it will never cease to have the potential to materialize one day. Formulated differently, it implies that we consider that only finite things are actualized.

However, the negation of the actually infinite contradicts the perception that we have of Nature as infinite, together with Anaximander, Democritus, Spinoza, or Pascal. Aristotle's definition of the infinite holds only, in our eyes, for the "unlimited."

Indeed, he defines *Apeiron*, the infinite, as follows: "The infinite is thus the opposite of what we usually call it: not that beyond which there is nothing, but that beyond which there is always something, this is the infinite." [30]

The Whole of what there is, in whatever way we understand it, is "that beyond which there is nothing." Since the Aristotelian cosmos is without exterior, he should have called it "infinite" if he had accepted that definition. That is where we see that calling the Whole "infinite" does not imply admitting the actually infinite, since Aristotle's World is finite.

My Vision of Nature: Actually Infinite

We have a different vision of Nature from Aristotle. Nature is, in our eyes, the whole of what there is (at least, that is our conviction) and she has not the character of a World, that is, an organic and structured Whole, which would imply that she is finite.

In which sense is she infinite? She is unlimited, but not only in thinking: really, actually. That means that if we apply the Number to the natural reality, letting in the series of entire numbers a new number correspond to a natural reality not yet enumerated, this bi-univocal and reciprocal correspondence will continue indefinitely, because there will be indefinite new natural realities yet to be discovered.

Since there is no end to the series of numbers and there is not one number that is infinite, Nature must be beyond any number, or any grandeur: We say she is actually infinite. The actually infinite is not simply "that [which] is actually greater than all given quantity of the same kind,"[31] but that for which all degrees of increase are given in advance, and which is hereby situated outside the concept of grandeur. There is no grandeur of Nature, even though all grandeurs are within her.

Aristotle's Vision of Beings: Reduced to a Finite Succession of Events

But for the moment, let us come back to the Aristotelian concept of the infinite and to what it can teach us. For him, there are only finite things. Of which kind is this finite, which is "potentially infinite," while it is "actually finite"? Aristotle clarifies it as follows: "We should not conceive the infinite as something determined[32] the way a man or a house can be. We should conceive it as being determined the way we speak of the present day or of a fight [occurring right before our eyes], of which the being does not exist as a permanent substance[33] but is always in a perpetual generation and a perpetual destruction[34] indeed finite, but always different."[35]

But what are the days or the combat we see at the Olympiads made of? The day is made of light and this light is made of rays that "do not cease to spring forward and vanish in turn, like wool we would throw away in fire";[36] while the combat is made of movements responding to other movements, calling for other movements.

But then what is man or a house made of? A man speaks, walks, writes, works, and looks for a place to sleep. Is he really that different from himself when he fights? The house has a red roof and green shutters; what are its colors? Only light? But one might argue color does not make this house. . . . All right then! But a house that appears to remain the same changes imperceptibly. For with all houses, one must account for the depreciation coefficient, in that they will always continue to age. So, beings are reduced to events and none can escape from being swept away in Heraclitus's universal flow.

Aristotle nevertheless informs us that man is a whole and as such is "achieved": "The thing with nothing beyond it is achieved and a whole because we define as a whole something to which nothing is missing; for example a man is a whole, just like a coffer is"[37]; at the opposite is the thing "to which is missing something that stays outside of it."[38]

But is man ever "achieved"?[39] This can be said of a body that possesses all its senses, limbs, functions, and faculties; but this body is not a man. A man to whom nothing is missing can only be conceived as a dead man. As for the coffer, it is only worth something thanks to the void it contains and is therefore nothing without the non-coffer. It can only be conceived through the event of being filled up.

As with the day or the combat, the potentially infinite only exists, says Aristotle, thanks to the succession of its parts. But all beings in the sensitive world can be reduced to a series of events; they are *in fieri*. They only exist, like the potentially infinite, through the succession of their parts.

Even so, they are not potentially infinite, because they are not "*always* different,"[40] that is, *indefinitely* different. There comes a time, the moment of death, when a man does not have *to be* anymore; he is nothing more than what he has been. From time to time we return to the idea that modern medicine could perhaps deliver man from old age and death. In this case, man would remain actually finite but would become potentially infinite, that is, *indefinitely* actually finite. Just as it goes for time itself, potentially infinite, only existing one part after the other, each part disappearing and being replaced by another, while in the case of spatial grandeurs, each part persists. Similarly, the life of a man only consists at any rate in a series of moments, the present and current one being the only *real* one.

Reality, Action, Movements, and Events

What should then be understood by "real?" For Aristotle, is "real" that which is "accomplishing itself," what is "actually?" It must be distinguished from what is possible or what is accomplished. All change can indeed be: (1) possible; (2) accomplishing itself; (3) accomplished. The expression "actually" is applicable to moment (2) as opposed to moment (1) (expressed by the words "potentially") and (3) (the "realized," actualized, and sustainable being resultant from this change). "Accomplishing itself" means therefore "opening itself to the accomplishment expressed by the moment (3).[41] Aristotle calls frequently (but not always) moment (2) ἐνέργεια (*energeia*) and moment (3) ἐντελεχείᾳ[42] (*entelechia*).

For Aristotle, action[43] is the foundation for the reality of time, inscribing it in the present. If there is no change, there is no time and there is no change if there is nothing that can change, that can act. The act delimits the present. The past is not anymore, the future is yet to be. But we can only speak of the present as having a "particular extent."[44] The act circumscribes the present, delimits it.

A hand passes me a bowl in which the evening soup is still steaming hot. The before is not anymore, the after is not yet; here is the now, which is totally different from the mathematician's infinitesimal instant, unreal fiction, which is not time, nor a part of time, of which we are therefore unable to determine the reality.

To the Stoics who split present, future, and past, Plutarch finds objection: "As we say, about the present moment, a part is the past and another is the future, so, about the action, one can say a part has been accomplished and another one will be."[45] In this case, what is left of the present? The present is nothing. And so, what is left then of the action? It is non-action, because the action is one and whole, and not the sum of countless mini-movements and stops in between.

It is true that we can hereby dissolve the action into what it is not, but since the movement of a hand giving me the soup plate is real, the view that analyzes and decomposes this movement leads only to a school exercise, without effect.

The Movement as Such or as "Gesture" and the Events

We talk about "act" or "action" in the case of a hand that gives a bowl of soup. This conforms to the common language. But when we use Aristotle's word *energeia*, we are led to discern two things in the movement: the movement as such and the movement as "gesture." Indeed, Aristotle opposes on the one hand the movement (*kinesis*) as "incomplete," "imperfect,"[46] and on the other hand the act, l' ἐνέργεια, the movement's end result.

The handing of the soup bowl implies a movement, of course, and therefore also, by now, the act that consists in the movement itself, "act of what is potential as such,"[47] "act" meaning here "realization," "passage." But to this we must add that the movement has the meaning of a gesture, which, while it leads to a result, also retains value in itself. This gesture, as such, fills in and delimits the present, which a simple movement cannot do. Because, although the gesture lasts, the before and the after give it meaning, so that together they constitute the present.

The movement of handing the soup plate is a movement, not potentially but actually. It is an act, if "the act[48] (ἐνέργεια) is the fact for a thing to exist actually, in reality[49] and not potentially[50] as we use to say."[51] Now, this act is an event.

Events that Delimit the Present and Those Which Do Not

This leads us to distinguish two types of events according to their capacity or not to delimit the present.

The being, as we said earlier, can be reduced to a series of events.[52] What there is *is* not "the" house, but *this* house, in front of my eyes, now, in the present. It does not seem to change but in reality it constantly changes; as Nietzsche says of a tree, it (this house) is "at every moment something new."[53] It represents countless mini-events but what delimits the present is not each of these events, but the event of the house. The event delimits the present only if it is complete, if it makes sense by itself, not if it is incomplete and unachieved. The clock strikes twelve times at noon. Neither the first strike, nor the second, and so until the eleventh, delimits the present. After the twelfth strike, the meaning of the eleven first strikes is given; the event is complete and delimits the present: it is noon. But if we say, "It's getting colder, winter is coming," the delimitation of the event is unclear, the one of the present cannot be clear either.

This leads us to declare what is real does not consist of events, some of which, making sense for us, would define what the present is. The event, however simple and short in duration (the pulse of a heartbeat, the tick of the second hand on a watch or the bell strike of a clock tower) or composed (simple events), if it is complete or achieved, delimits the present. And nothing is more real than the present, as the Stoic Emperor Marcus Aurelius wrote: "[When we'll die], we will only be deprived of the present, as this is the only thing we possess."[54]

Setting out from Aristotle's position, we have now arrived at the Chrysippian stance.

IV

WITH AND WITHOUT CHRYSIPPUS

Milestones

In the previous chapter, Conche argued that, despite his more immediate approach to Nature, Aristotle's vision of Nature's finitism and fixity negated her creativity and productivity. However, with Chrysippus, we move a step closer to grasping Nature's creativity in some ways. But Chrysippus does not bring his observations and reasoning to a conclusion and ends up with a peculiar mix of Aristotelian and Heraclitean finitism.

The sensitive Stoic Chrysippus observes that "beings" are in reality no more than a succession of events: beings coincide with doing; the reality is event. He hereby senses and thinks that there is no other time for the body than the present, delimited by action.

Yet Aristotle's mark on Chrysippus is still evident: for him, the individual form or individualizing quality (idiôs poion) of beings remains eternal and hereby he is not fully "Heraclitean." The eternity of these forms is secured by the doctrine of the "eternal return," so dear to Stoics. The world, according to this doctrine, "regularly" conflagrates and then recomposes itself across successive worlds; small changes, or external "accidents" occur so that the worlds are not exactly the same. These "accidents" however, do not affect the individual forms. The coherency and the perfection of the successive worlds remain, compatible with Zeus's will. This leads Chrysippus and the Stoics to consider that wise men are those who succeed in remaining unaffected by external "accidents"; they remain true to their individual form, their identity, their idiôs poion.

As a result, Chrysippus's belief in destiny does not allow him to consider individual creativity as a force that allows individuals to maintain a stable basis; even though, coinciding with their doings, they constantly change.

Reducing Beings to Events?

My preoccupation is to always return to the most immediate grasp of what surrounds us. This is what we have just done with Aristotle. Aristotle says that we should start with what is most within our reach. He also says this is why we cannot doubt nature's existence. I could not agree more, but, as we have just seen, we nevertheless had to leave Aristotle's vision because his perception of Nature as finite and fixed negates her creativity and productivity.

We are told that Stoics such as Chrysippus were "sensitivists" for whom all notions find their origin in the sensitive representation. This is also my starting point, however I intend to anchor thinking to a more ingenuous immediacy than the so-called sensorial immediacy.

The eye does not see by itself; indeed, the notion of "organ of the senses" is a learned notion. We have the feeling to see things themselves and not to see them "through" the organs of the senses. "All I have got till today that is truest and most assured, I have learned it from or through the senses": so writes Descartes at the beginning of his Metaphysical meditations. Such a start is not ingenuous; the author uses a notion that is already the result of reasoning.

I open my eyes and I see: a cloud passes by in front of the sun and makes a shadow. This is an event. The bird flies away; this too is an event. By writing this, am I not reducing beings to events; are the sun and bird not beings? What does Chrysippus tell us about it? Following some interpretations of his work, we might think he says such reduction is impossible. Is this really what he says? Let us investigate.

Stoics only accept singular propositions and in such propositions the subject is always individual. But the verb cannot be decomposed into a copula and an attribute, such as in "Socrates is virtuous." Rather, the verb in Greek has to be taken in its unity, expressing an event: "Socrates exercises his virtue." Similarly, in Greek, we will not say, "The tree is green," but "The tree turns green"; not "The body is warm," but "The body warms up," etc.

Unreal Events—Real Beings?

If the attributes are events, then the subjects are beings. Subjects are thus bodies, and subjects are therefore real. Events, on the contrary, are only the objects of the discourse (*lekta*), of what we say about the subjects. They are "incorporeal," unreal. Bréhier calls them "unreal because they are only the products and results of the bodies or of the reciprocal action of these bodies, the bodies being the sole real agents."[1] But, Bréhier also tells us that dialectic "deals with the existence or non-existence of an event which is not the object of current perception, *l'adilon*,[2] such as the existence of gods, or the survival of the soul."

This being said, we could not speak of an event as "existing" or "not existing" if it did not have already some reality. So, the event might not be a being or it might be a non-being, but it is nevertheless "something" (*ti*). Hence, it might be excessive to say that events are "unreal": what has no reality is nothing. Nevertheless, the distinction between beings and events cannot be easily dismissed. What should, however, be understood is this: by maintaining this distinction between beings and events, we might fail to see how radically Chrysippus renewed the notions he borrowed from Aristotle. Let us see why.

Aristotle's Notions Renewed: Bodies Are Events; Reality Itself Is Event

One can argue that the Aristotelian analysis of the substance in matter and form can be found again in Chrysippus. In Chrysippus's analysis, the form is the agent; it is the active matter, opposed to the passive matter and encompassing it. According to Aristotle, the body constituted by the matter and the form is nevertheless very different from the body or the being (*ousia*). The body for Chrysippus is the "only real agent," says Bréhier, and it is, above all, action. That is why there is no other time for the body than the present delimited by the action. "Man is what he does," we wrote in the former chapter. So, for Chrysippus, the being of the body merges with its doing. Bodies exhaust themselves in the present and the events they produce. "The tree turns green," rather than "The tree is green." But then, what is a tree and what is turning green or blossoming?

For Chrysippus, bodies define themselves through the events they cause. Therefore, God, the supreme cause, being only what he does, is not separated from what he acts upon: the world. Zeno, Chrysippus, and Poseidonios all declare that the "substance"[3] of God, what he consists of, "is the entire world and the sky."[4] God penetrates life[5] and all the things through and through; he extends through the ether, the air, the fire, the water, and the earth.[6] All the events are, in the end, effects of this cause and are divine. So, in the proposition "The tree turns green," the predicate "to turn green" is not to be distinguished from the tree, the being; it "is only distinct and un-corporeal in our thinking," writes Bréhier.[7]

Very well, but we say that "the tree turns green" because it *really* turns green. We can see that when we open our eyes. For the Stoics, "the being coincides with the doing," the reality itself "is event."[8]

The Eternity of Individual Forms Secured by Their "Eternal Return"

Despite this, Aristotle's mark on Chrysippus is still recognizable. For Aristotle, forms are not subject to becoming; from them, there is no generation and they are, in this sense, eternal. The same is true for Chrysippus, up to a point: for Chrysippus the form[9] is an individual form. The form is the proper and individualizing quality.[10] Being indivisible, it can only appear or disappear (at death) "at once, in one strike,"[11] having guaranteed, throughout the entire duration of life, the identity of the individual to himself. For Aristotle, on the contrary, individuals go by (they are born and perish) but the species remains. For Chrysippus, the individual, although being born and perishing, must remain.

This could not be possible if the world were unique. It is therefore necessary that the world be born again, identical to itself and this without end.[12] Chrysippus says: "It is obviously unavoidable that, after our death, after many time periods, we would be re-established in the same form that we currently possess."[13] Since the doctrine of the "eternal return" is essential to Stoicism, not only is this unavoidable according to him, it is also necessary.

Accidents in the Successive Worlds that Do not Alter the Identity of Individuals but Distinguish Worlds

However, the return of individuals in their identical forms does not imply that they would come back as perfectly identical due to "accidents." If some Stoics have maintained that, in each successive world, individuals do come back exactly identical, down to the slightest detail, it must be because they have not properly understood the doctrine's raison d'être. The same individuals do come back but with variances.

"There will be again a Socrates, a Plato,"[14] but with all the changes that there can be yet without them ceasing to be Socrates or Plato. Successive worlds are not repeating themselves identically in the slightest details—the world is an individual. It has its individualizing quality, its *idiôs poion,*[15] which ensures its permanency across time. "Following periods of time decided by destiny, the entire world goes up in flames, after which it puts itself once again in order."[16] During the conflagration (*ekpurôsis*), all reenters the divine substance, which is identical to fire; after which, this original fire, extinguishing itself spontaneously, produces the air and then the liquid element, which is the germ from which the world's order recomposes itself (*diakosmèsis*). But this recurrence does not mean that there will always be the same snowfall at the same place, at the same time, or the same fog in the same valleys, etc. Why cannot it be so?

This has to do with the nature of time, which has no reality other than through events. An instant in time distinguishes itself only through dissimilar events. Therefore, if the exact same events took place in a successive world, one period in time could not be distinguished from another; there would then be only one world, one period in time, and there could not be indefinitely a periodical return. The notion of "eternal return" only makes sense if there are some differences between the successive worlds, even if the individuals, the *idiôs poia,* within each world remain the same. This is surely what Chrysippus admitted.

What changes, then, if the individuals remain the same? Alexander of Aphrodisias explains with clarity: "For the beings with proper qualities or individuals (*idiôs poia*) that exist afterwards, the differences with anterior beings are only related to specific external accidents. They are similar to the changes affecting the philosopher Dion when he remains the same during the course of his life. These changes do not alter who he is, his *idiôs poion.* He does not become a different person if, for example, on his face he no longer bears the warts he had before. Stoics state that, for beings with proper qualities, there are similar differences in a world compared with another."[17]

For Stoics, "accidents"[18] were thus a very different affair than for Aristotle. For the former, accidents are far from being the principle of individuality, as they were for the latter. On the contrary, for the Stoics, accidents do not in any way alter the individual, he who is solely defined by his proper quality.[19]

It might be useful here to mention two distinct Stoic categories. One category is related to what is "corporeal" and real: the substrate[20] (the matter without qualities) and the quality that determines the material substrate. A second category is related to what is "incorporeal"; although they are not bodies, they are nevertheless "something"[21]; they are the "way of being"[22] and the "way of being in a relationship."[23]

What the individual makes or what happens to him, his successive ways of being and his varied relations with what surrounds him are "things that are told" (*lekta*). They belong to the second category and can be different in each successive world. Socrates will come back an infinite number of times; within the successive worlds he will have the same physical and moral qualities but his actions and ways of being will be as varied as possible, as long they remain compatible with the fact that he remains the same Socrates. If, on the contrary, he came back holding exactly the same speech, repeating the same actions, walking down the same streets of Athens on the same day, wearing the same clothes from the former period, and if this were the case for all individuals who make the world, the successive different worlds—as they would not differ in any way from each other—would merge into one world. There would be no infinity of time periods, with some periods before and others after ours.

Cicero quotes this "Stoic formula": "In all the reality there is not one hair, not one grain that is identical to another one."[24] There can't be two eggs or two twins that are *exactly* the same. Cicero takes the example of the Servilius twins: "People in the street could not tell them apart; but at home they were distinguished; strangers confounded them, but not their parents."[25] The Stoic named Nemesius, says for his part that, from one world to another, "everything will happen in the same way and without differences,[26] in the slightest details."[27] But this is impossible, and this testimony should not be considered, since it can be argued that for the Stoics, as for Leibniz, "in all reality," there are never two things that are exactly the same. In the innumerable worlds that preceded ours, there will be infinity of Socrateses, all different. Twins are dissimilar, clones are even more so. Socrates has had, and will have, innumerable clones that have kept and will preserve only the essential qualities that constitute the individualizing quality, l'*eidos*, l'*idiôs poion* of Socrates.

Different Events, All Compatible with Zeus's Will

Just as there cannot be two identical individuals, there cannot be two identical events. Everything is linked in the world; the world is an organic entity, a coherent whole in which everything resonates with everything. If each event is linked to the totality of the events, then two identical events will have, in their background, the same events and will therefore be only one and the same event. In other words, if just one event happens differently in a world, then all the events in this world happen differently and the resulting world is a different one from the others.

This particular difference can only be about the "ways of being" and the "ways of being in relationship," not about the substrates or the individualizing qualities. The successive worlds can thus be the same world in terms of their substance (*ousia*), with the same individuals.

Now, let us admit that (1) "nothing, neither in ways of being or in relationships, produces itself in contradiction to Zeus's will, which is identical to destiny (*eimarménè*)," [28] and (2) in the smallest events, there can be variations. Should we therefore understand that in the multiple worlds, there will be multiple Zeuses and multiple destinies? Of course not; Zeus and destiny always remain the same. The different events, which do not change the identity of the beings, remain all compatible, not "contradictory" with Zeus's will. For example, if I buy a piece of bread and if I have in my pocket a dozen one Euro coins, it is quite irrelevant whether I pay with one or the other.

Only the Wise Is Free, Unaffected by External Events

We can therefore understand why Stoics distinguish two kinds of events: those affecting the identity of beings and those "external accidents" as quoted in Alexander of Aphrodisias's passage mentioned above. Beings express themselves freely in the world or they deviate from themselves under external influences. For example, a domesticated animal is not free any more; this implies that the radical difference established by the Stoics between the wise man and the foolish one is far from arbitrary. The wise man always acts according to the spontaneity of his nature (the Taoist *ziran*). He does so whatever the antecedent cause that may have led him to act. He behaves in the way of a cylinder rolling down a slope, in a tumbling fashion, whatever the impulse that led it to glide.

"The wise man," says Cicero, is the "one who does not say anything, does not do anything, does not think anything that is not out of his own movement and out of his own will,[29] the one for whom all decisions and all acts find in himself their principle and goal, who does not allow anything to prevail on his will and judgment."[30] Only the wise man is free, since to be free is what we have just mentioned. The one without wisdom, the foolish one "raves"; he is always carried away, "outside of himself," having moved away from his own nature, which is always good. He is a slave, since slavery is "the submission of a broken and vile soul, without free will."[31] Cicero later enumerates those who are slaves to their properties, to their ill-gotten works of art in Greece, to their passions, to their responsibilities and honors, to their regrets and fears, and so on.

Aristotelian and Heraclitean Visions Combined: Perfect Worlds but Forever Somewhat Different, Due to Changes in Small Events

Chrysippus, we might suppose, combines the finitism resulting from Aristotelian cosmology with the finitism associated with Heraclitean fluidity.

According to Aristotle, the life of the world is a periodic life. Its period, the "great year," is the smallest common multiple of all the periodic celestial revolutions. The movements' periodicity of the celestial bodies leads to the periodicity of their impact on the corruptible world. Generations and corruptions occurring now already happened before, and will happen again an infinite number of times, as the revolution of the supreme sphere, the First Sky, is continuous and perpetual. "So, the first circular revolution is periodical and so is the sun's; the diverse seasons have therefore a circular generation and come back, and since they follow a circular course, the same happens, in their turn, to all the things that are dependent on them."[32] Together with the "great year," Aristotle also considered the "great winter," with torrential rain,[33] and the "great summer."

But for Aristotle, vicissitudes brought with the great year only concern the sublunary world. The skies and the stars, on the other hand, remain perpetual. Herein lay the difference with Chrysippus for whom the world transforms itself in fire, as if fire was its semen (*sperma*), and from this fire it reproduces itself again in a form similar to the one it had before.

Chrysippus nevertheless agrees with Aristotle in acknowledging the perfection of the world. For both of them, the organization of the world, the structure or shape of its parts cannot be improved upon, and the forms are once and for all what they should be. For Chrysippus, however, these "forms" are now individual, as we have seen earlier.[34] So, each individual has his irreducible originality that makes him irreplaceable and un-substitutable. Each individual feels at home in the world and is perfect in his singularity; within him he carries something of the goodness of the world. As a living unity, the world itself is nothing more than the sum total of its distinct individuals.

Chrysippus's cosmology, with its perpetual revolution of the celestial spheres, leads therefore to the conception of a complete world, to which nothing is to be added. It is a finitist and static thesis where the forms are stable and no evolution occurs. However, after the great summer, which precedes and announces the destruction of the world in fire, and after the destruction itself, a new world is born that is substantially similar in its core but not in its details. As new worlds will be born, there will be new details, because "we cannot enter twice the same river": that is the Heraclitean side of Chrysippus.

Chrysippus's Belief in Destiny: Obstacle to Consider Individual Creativity as a Force Allowing Individuals to Maintain a Stable Basis, Even Though They Constantly Change

According to Heraclitus (*panta rhei*), fluidity concerns everything, that is, all things *in themselves*. There are no such things as immutable things, nor is there, for each individual, an *idiôs poion*—the master quality which, through the flow of things, would assure its identity—if at least we understand by this an upright pole that would resist change.

Undoubtedly I am, at any moment in my life, the one whom I resemble most: any change, however, has its effect on the whole of me. As we have seen earlier, Chrysippus says the subject is inscribed in reality through the verb, that is, the event. "Socrates walks," and not "Socrates is walking," as Aristotle would want it.

I think Chrysippus is correct on this, but for me Socrates does not remain Socrates thanks to destiny but thanks to himself. He constantly becomes different, but with himself as a basis, and that's how he continues to be himself while changing.

If Chrysippus had envisaged things in this way he could have acknowledged individual creativity. He could not have conceived the world any longer as perfect and achieved, but, on the contrary, as uncertain and constantly in danger. He could have then taken into account a creative time. But he did not pursue his discovery regarding events to a conclusion, and therefore, Aristotle retained the advantage.

V

WITH AND WITHOUT EPICURUS

Milestones

Despite Epicurus's feeling for Nature's immensity which he shares, Conche parts with him because of his willingness to explain everything and his methods of doing so.

Epicurus wished to explain why the world is this way and not different. This leads him to reject the hypothesis of a creative God and to pretend finding in the atom and in chance the basis of his "explanation" of everything. This "explanation" is not convincing, however. First, he fails to tell us what an atom actually is. Second, he does not acknowledge that, even if a cause may produce an effect, the cause may be incapable of explaining the effect itself.

These considerations lead Conche to distinguish reductionist from emergentist materialisms. Conche could feel an affinity with emergentist materialism if only Epicurus had a clearer notion of matter. But he fails to provide it; he explains what has to be explained: the sensitive world that is offered to us, but it is explained through what is not explained—the atom, the space, and the movement.

Epicurus's failure should not surprise us; the Whole cannot be "explained." On the basis of what could it be possibly explained, since it is precisely the Whole? At least Epicurus's failure teaches us a worthy lesson: to try grasping infinite Totality, we should first stop trying to explain everything.

Epicurus's Imagination and Common Sense

"All these things, sky, earth and sea, are nothing compared with the totality of the great whole." So says Lucretius the Epicurean.[1] If there is one thing about which we are entirely certain, this would have to be it. Nevertheless, it is on this idea of the Whole that I will separate myself from Epicurus.

The Epicurean totality is a construct of our imagination. However, the way I see things, totality, the Whole of reality is the experience of the infinite Nature and this, before anything else, is given through an experience sui generis. Otherwise, the place where we are would have to be somehow limited. But what would there be beyond such limits? We would be unable to say.

Having said this, I believe Epicurus could have taken a different approach to his conception of the Whole. Without a certain feeling for this immensity from the start, he could not have imagined a Whole beyond all imagination in terms of immensity. He ignored, however, this feeling and initially tried to limit himself to what was presented directly to his eyes. This is why he favored the "sensation" or sensitive experience.

The path taken by Epicurus and his understanding of the sensitive experience comes very near to the "common sense" that we find with Thomas Reid, the "common sense" philosopher par excellence. Schopenhauer, on Reid's *Inquiry into the Human Mind* (1764), writes that it deserves "to be read ten times more than all the books published since Kant, put together."[2] Reid rejects the ideas or images brought forward by Descartes, observing that, for most mortals, "it is the external object that we immediately perceive."[3] "Nobody" he says, with an irresistible and immediate conviction, "believes in seeing images of the objects, but precisely the objects themselves." Reid speaks about "perception," understanding herewith "exclusively the sensitive perception."[4] Reid's "perception" corresponds to Epicurus's "sensation." What is offered to us through the "sensation" is the thing in itself, real and independently of us. What is offered to our senses is the sensitive world, which Epicurus limits to the stars, since our sight cannot see beyond them.

Epicurus's Starting Point: The World, not the Whole

The starting point of Epicurus's thinking is not the Whole as such but the world and for this there is only one reason: he wishes to explain everything. But the Whole cannot be "explained"; what could possibly explain it, since it is precisely the Whole?

We could of course renounce explanation; this is, after all, what Aristotle does. For him, the world is eternal in its matter (un-generated, indestructible) and in its organization; it exists indefinitely in time. Forms—types of biological organizations—realize themselves temporarily through individuals who give, across generations, an uninterrupted series, a perpetual succession.

So then, the world, the sky, the living species, man, nothing can really be explained according to Epicurus. The world and all that it contains represents a problem for him: *the* problem par excellence of philosophy. For Epicurus, we need to explain why the world is this way and not different; not only does he want to find an explanation for the world in general, but in addition, for all world beings and phenomena.

The hypothesis of a creative God would have seemed too easy for Epicurus, although a premise such as this could be invoked all the same, if the world was totally different. For him, on the contrary, we need to explain *this world* and none other. The explanation must be able to deal with the details of what is offered to our eyes and nothing else, because for him, to explain is to demonstrate how the things we see have become what they are. To do this we may rely on reasoning, on things we cannot see. We explain the visible through the invisible, acknowledging as true the hypothesis whose contradictions are weakened by experience.

So, for Epicurus the world presents itself as a whole of composed bodies arranged in a certain order. He explains the order of these sensitive bodies starting with the absence of order, and, according to the principles of chemical analysis, he analyzes composed bodies starting with simple bodies. This leads him to consider the composition and the organization of bodies as products of chance, repeated a great number of times.

He admits that "nothing can be born out of nothing," because, if the opposite were true, the world could not be what it is; anything could be born out of anything, etc. For the same reason, he admits that nothing can be annihilated; if the opposite were true, there could be sudden annihilations, etc.

The Basis of Epicurus's Explanation: The Atom

Epicurus therefore acknowledges the basic element of all things, to the simplest indivisible body, namely, the atom; the necessary properties in order to explain the properties of composed bodies, the formation and structure of the cosmos, and the apparition of life and man.

So then, the atom is absolutely full, surrounded by void, perfectly solid; its impenetrability is absolute and indestructible, it is henceforth eternal. Bodies are composed of atoms that cannot die. The Whole is made of bodies and of void. It is infinite, as are the void and the number of atoms; being a body, the atom therefore possesses form.

In order to explain the great diversity of qualities and sensitive forms, he must suppose that the number of the varieties of atomic forms is inconceivably great, but without inferring that it is infinite. Still, for Epicurus, the number of atoms in each form is "infinite": whatever the number of atoms, there will be atoms that cannot be accounted for. For example, if an atom has the form of a try square, it appears as being comprised of two inseparable parts; if it has the form of a triangle or a trident, it has three parts and so on.

So, the atom can be deemed to be composed of particles,[5] which are not infinitely tiny and whose movements are uninterrupted and eternal. Atoms always maintain the same speed, which is superior to light speed even in solids and bodies of greater density. For Epicurus, a ray of light is composed of colliding atoms whose friction diminishes their "flight," lessening the speed of light relative to the atoms themselves.

Gravity, collisions and "slope" (*clinamen*)[6] are the causes of atomic movement. "Conglomerates" are born from the chance collision between atoms whose forms take the shape of nebulous clouds, and in some cases, when organized they produce worlds. The number of worlds is infinite for Epicurus. All composed bodies emanate a multidirectional flow of atoms, which can emerge from the nucleus or the surface, depending on the body. Surface flows are called semblances,[7] which can be said to convey the shape of the bodies.

For Epicurus, the soul is a corporeal element of the body, and after death it is no longer contained by the body but dissipates in the air.[8]

Epicurus's Failure to Explain

We should observe at this stage that this so-called explanation of everything, on the basis of one element, the atom, is not an explanation at all: it fails to tell us *what exactly an atom really is.*

For Epicurus, an atom is an extended something, with an invariable form and an invariable grandeur. It is colorless, odorless, tasteless, tangible (*en droit*), ultimately durable, and impenetrably dense. It is heavy, surrounded by void, forever in motion, and deviates without clear reason from the linear path. These essential properties of the atom fail, however, to tell us *what it is made of.* We can say of a musical instrument that it is made of "wood" or "metal," but we cannot say what the atom is made of.

What is the world made of? According to Epicurus, it is bodies and nothing more than bodies. But then, what are these bodies made of? Atoms! Fine, so what are the atoms made of then . . . ?

Descartes would tell us that the atom is only an extended space because, "We have the same idea of matter than we have of space."[9] Epicurus cannot give such an answer because in this case, the difference between the atom and the void would disappear for him. There would be no void, for according to him, the atom is full. But of what is it full? Being? To merely say that *it is* does not help, because in order *to be*, it needs to be something; if not, it is nothing. If it is something, we need to say what it is!

In Epicureanism, as we have just seen, the atomistic explanation of the order of things is no more than a figment of the imagination; this does not however diminish the quality of Epicurus's initial view on Nature. He attempted to justify, with irresistible argument, what is revealed and evident before any reasoning: Nature is the absolute source of everything and invents herself by inventing everything; Nature does not create according to any pattern defined in advance. On the contrary, the meaning of words used to indicate specific beings in the sensible world can only be understood after these beings have "been." Beings cannot be simply explained away by "a God's creative power."

If this God created man, how could he have known what the word *man* meant before there were men?

Chance as the Origin of Everything

As with Epicurus and various Ante-Socratics, we rather think Nature created man blindly; she did not create him according to an image inscribed in her, but on the contrary, she did create him not "knowing" in advance what he would be. And so it goes for any living being, because no guiding idea could have presided over the formation of a living organism that did not yet exist. From this primitive intuition of Nature, Epicurus has the idea to put chance at the origin of everything and then attempts to clarify the way this chance and her role could be conceived.

For a start, he considers this: in the void, atoms of varied forms and grandeurs trace trajectories independent from each other so any encounter they may have is fortuitous. All the rest is derived from this initial fortuity. This seemed sufficient for Democritus. Epicurus adds nevertheless to this view with his famous *clinamen*. Through this *clinamen* the atom deviates arbitrarily from its trajectory by a negligible degree (just enough to ensure a deviation), though not an infinitely small one (Epicurus rejects the division ad infinitum). Let us note here that Lucretius defines this trajectory as a "straight line": "When the atoms are carried away by their own weight from top to bottom in a straight line[10] through the void, they might constantly deviate slightly from the vertical at undetermined moments and at undetermined points."[11]

Did Epicurus suspect then what we now know, namely, that there is no such thing as a straight line, in the Euclidian sense, in Nature? It's possible. He might have had the presentiment that geometry is modified if we cease to make abstraction of matter. Deviations occur then discontinuously and arise unexpectedly, in contrast to any anticipation or prediction. Should we therefore believe things occur as Democritus and Epicurus describe them? Montaigne suspects these two eminent philosophers do not quite believe it themselves. The model of the universe, born of their imagination and reasoning, finds its motivation and reason for being in the primitive intuition that Nature is the source and unique origin of all things, and that man, as a natural being, is destined to death.

Capacity or Incapacity of the Cause to Explain the Effect

Democritus and Epicurus want to show that it is possible to explain everything with only the intervention of causes without purpose, that is, not driven by a final goal. Now, to explain something is to show what causes it. The cause is the necessary and sufficient condition of a particular effect. The cause is such that, should it exist, its effect also exists. Let us suppose that we want to explain the cohesion of the solids. We want to explain why parts of a solid do not detach themselves, why they bind together, so that, unlike a liquid, a solid does not need a recipient to contain it. Lucretius explains that solids are essentially formed of "hooked atoms of which the ramifications form, between themselves, a very dense tissue."[12] Troubling each other with their hooks or branches, they mutually truss each other inside the body, with the atoms on the periphery the only ones being thrust outside to form semblances.

What is then the cause of solids? According to Lucretius, it is the fact that atoms move in the void at maximum speed (the speed at which a composed body can move itself is lower) in an extremely reduced space.

But this does not in any way resemble what is observed in the effect: the cohesion. One could argue well that the cause produces the effect, that is, it ensures that the effect occurs. Nevertheless, in this case, the effect is not fully contained in the cause—it is something new, unless this cause can also explain the sensitive qualities. Can it? Epicureans will say that atoms of different forms penetrate the sensory organs, the pores and conduits of these organs having different structures. Smooth and round atoms will give an impression of softness; sharp atoms will give an impression of spikiness. With the cause come forms and movements; with the effect come the qualities.

Do we want to explain changes in coloration, for example, of the sea under the effect of wind? We will then suppose a mix of atomic forms on the surface of the colored body and a stirring up of these different forms leading to a modification of their mix. A blind man may well understand the cause of the changes in coloration of such bodies, but he won't be able to see the color. He will know the cause of something that, as a sensitive quality, will remain forever unknown to him. This is an example of how the cause may explain that an effect takes place without explaining the effect itself. This incapacity of the cause to explain the effect is not acknowledged by Epicureanism or later forms of materialism.

Reductionist and Emergentist Materialisms

According to a definition attributed to Auguste Comte, materialism is the "doctrine that explains the superior through the inferior," for example, "moral nature through the physical one."[13] But we can't explain the superior through the inferior. Indeed we cannot hereby formulate a new concept. For example, with the concept of matter, we won't be able to forge the concept of "life" or the concept of "spirit."

"To be materialist," writes André Comte-Sponville, "is to sustain that everything is matter or produced by matter."[14] If "all" is matter, including life and spirit, we then have reductionist materialism: life and spirit are only "explained" by suppressing what they have as most irreducible. This explains why the "soul" is no more than a parcel of the body according to Epicurus. If "everything" is simply a "product" of the matter, we are left with emergentist materialism. All beings, including living and thinking beings, find their condition in materiality and "there is consequently no spiritual reality or autonomous idea."[15]

Material conditions are necessary for there to be life and spirit. When the necessarily sufficient material and corporeal conditions exist for life and spirit to emerge, the consequence is indeed "superior," and is produced by what is "inferior" as its cause. However, it cannot be thought of as being what it is due only to its cause. I have addressed this in another book: "The cause produces the effect; it does not explain it."[16] "It is the brain that thinks," modern materialists will say, which is, unfortunately, unthinkable—if the brain is body and the thinking is spirit.

But materialists have no need to accept the reductionist temptation, unless they are incapable, as was Epicurus, of conceiving a spiritual reality. But in this case . . .

I could feel an affinity with emergentist materialism if I only had a clearer notion of matter, a notion that would be authenticated through experience. But while I am able to deal with Nature simply by opening my eyes, I only deal with matter by reading books, be they by Aristotle or by today's physicians. Epicurus himself talks more about "bodies" than about "matter." The atom, the ultimate principle of his explanation, is only a solid reduced to its form. This could be conceived as a geometric being but instead, it is for him a physical being, and thus by all accounts he should describe what it is made of. For him, the atom is endowed with just enough essential properties to explain what there is to explain, and the retained hypotheses are established by the fact that their contradictions are weakened by experience; Epicurus's empiric-rational method has therefore perfect rigor.

Epicurus supposes that an infinite number of atoms in the infinite void have always been in perpetual motion. He explains what has to be explained: the sensitive world that is offered to us, but, it is explained through what is not explained, that is, the atom; the space and the movement are not explained in Epicureanism. Perhaps, then, we should take the time to question the Epicurean methods of explanation. If we try to grasp the infinite Totality and not just the sensitive world, it is precisely this notion of "explanation" that seems to be beside the question.

VI

WITH AND WITHOUT MONTAIGNE

Milestones

Conche appreciates that while Epicurus wished to explain everything, Montaigne's humbler approach does not pile up certainties.

Montaigne is, however, on the side of Epicurus and admits innumerable worlds. This is the foundation of his wisdom and also Conche's. Montaigne's meditation on the infinite helps him distinguish what endures from what is fleeting.

But his ingenuous vision of an infinite Nature in time and space is constantly contaminated by his Christian outlook: his notion of an all-seeing, all-controlling, purpose-giving God remains with him and cannot be detached from the rest. As Conche shows, God and Nature are continuously intermingled in Montaigne's essays. For him, Nature has a unity as such, assuring the unity of reality, and is guided and guiding through some kind of purpose, as if she were the servant of a sovereign God and at the same time could be confounded with Him. Besides, the notion of "Providence" also allows Montaigne to feel Stoic and to speak about deriving the future out of the present; this leads him to contradict his intuition of Nature's creativity.

Finally, Conche remarks that Montaigne shares with Taoists, such as Lao Tzu, the idea of a unity of Nature (while the notion of "world," implying the finite, is compatible with the idea that there would be an infinite number of worlds). They also see as evident the fundamental Goodness of reality, meaning that it is good to live. Yet, for the Taoists, this does not imply one's admission of a divine governance of the world. Their idea of the eternal return allows them to discard what Conche calls the "contamination" by the divinity. Without having to resort to chance or providence to associate the characteristics of unity and goodness with Nature, Nature's creativity is infinite and does not admit restrictions, which would have the effect of converting Nature into "world," an organic and finite totality.

Montaigne's Humble but Ambiguous Way to See Reality as a Whole

At this stage, I would like to make clear that I share Montaigne's humble approach in that he does not pile up his certainties. They survive the time of evidence and then delete themselves, even if they are to be subsequently reinstated. They are not like the stones upon which an edifice is built, but if we compose them, we will obtain a particular image of Montaigne and his philosophy. The skeptical idea dominates because the hesitation to assert always remains; nevertheless, there are some pieces of evidence that ring true more than others. Montaigne does not *conquer* them as Descartes did with his method of doubt; they come to him and, ultimately, he cannot rid them from his sight. What is un-doubtful is not what resists the doubts we try to have, but what previously discouraged these doubts. That "everything changes," "everything flows" (*panta rhei*), how can we contest such statements? And how can we dispute therefore that "we have no communication with being"[1] because "what suffers change does not remain one and the same, and if it is not one and the same, it also *is* not."[2]

Moreover, how can we contest this: the one who speaks like this, using the word *everything*—"*everything* changes"—is only a man, who, for his part is ignorant, the truth being "but rather elevated to an infinite height in the divine knowledge."[3] Evidence is a human thing, indeed much too human. On one side are reason and evidence, on the other is faith. Descartes justifies, by the proof of God, the human evidence and lays herewith the foundation for the human claim to knowledge. The proof of God is, however, only a human confirmation. According to Montaigne, we can't avoid to pray and say our *Pater*. In opposition to the insubstantiality and temporality of human affairs, God *is*, in the immutability of his eternal present.

The way Montaigne sees reality as a whole—his metaphysics—is essentially ambiguous, because his ingenuous vision of things is constantly contaminated by his Christian outlook. This ambiguity would only be apparent if one of the sides to his metaphysics were not as strong as the other, if his fideism were no more than a "deceptive mask," as the abbot Zbigniew Gierczynski considered it to be. Once the "mask" was removed, there would remain only a pure naturalism that could be similar to Spinoza's. Montaigne is, however, a genuine believer, I see the proof of this from what he writes in his *Diary*, in Italian, while he has no reason to believe it will ever be published (which by pure chance it finally was). In 1581, Montaigne was at the Bagni della Villa, close to Lucca in Tuscany. Suffering from *lithiasis*, or kidney stones as we say today (from *lithos*, stone), and having just passed a large stone he wrote: "There would be too much weakness and cowardice on my part if, finding myself every day in a position to die in this manner, and with every hour bringing death nearer, I did not make every effort toward being able to bear death lightly as soon as it surprises me. And in the meantime it would be wise to accept joyously the good that it pleases God to send us. There is no other medicine, no other rule of science, for avoiding the ills, whatever they may be and however great, that besiege men from all sides and at every hour, then to make up our minds to suffer them humanly, or to end them courageously and promptly."[4] So, in his solitude, with nobody to control what he thought or wrote Montaigne thought that divine will and not chance was at the origin of what ailed him (acknowledging suicide as acceptable if one suffers too much).

If he had not been sincere, he could not have written his essay "About Prayers," or this, for example: "There is nothing so easy, so sweet and so favourable, as the divine law: she calls and invites us to herself, sinful and detestable as we are; she stretches out her arms to us and takes us into her bosom, no matter how vile, filthy, and besmirched as we are now and are to be in the future. But still, in return, we must look on her in the right way. We must receive this pardon with thanksgiving, and, at least for that instant when we address ourselves to her, have a soul remorseful for its sins, and at enmity with the passions that had driven us to offend her."[5]

Merge God and Nature

We are, for Montaigne, under God's governance but equally under the governance of Nature. Montaigne switches from one to the other without apparent difficulty.

So, in this passage from the chapter titled "About Experience," God and Nature are continuously intermingled: "As for me, then, love life and cultivate it just as God has been pleased to grant it to us. . . . I accept with all my heart and with gratitude what nature has done for me, and I am pleased with myself and proud of myself that I do. We wrong that great and all-powerful Giver by refusing his gift, nullifying it, and disfiguring it. . . . Nature is a gentle guide, but no more gentle than wise and just. I seek her footprints everywhere. . . . There is no part unworthy of our care in this gift that God has given us; we are accountable for it even to a single hair. And it is not a perfunctory charge to man to guide man according to his nature; it is express, simple, and of prime importance, and the creator has given it to us seriously and sternly."[6] God and Nature are mingled in

Montaigne's mind. So he writes this about miracles: "[B]ut reason has taught me that to condemn a thing thus, dogmatically, as false and impossible, is to assume the advantage of knowing the bounds and limits of God's will and of the power of our mother Nature."[7] Sometimes the word *God* is struck out and replaced by the word *Nature*. For example, Montaigne had written: "And the things that are the greatest within our knowledge we judge to be the utmost that nature can do in that category. . . . We must judge with more reverence the infinite power of God, and with more consciousness of our ignorance and weakness."[8] In the manuscript, he substitutes "Nature" for "God," attributing thereby to Nature the infinity of the divine might.

The limitation of the world in the biblical myth of the Creation is rejected for the sake of the innumerable worlds of Epicurean and Lucretian materialism.

Montaigne's Chasm with Epicurus

It is clear that Montaigne admits the extensive infinity of Nature. Quoting an extract from Cicero in which the Epicurean Velleius speaks of the "boundless immensity of space," he adds *et temporum*, "and of time." This implies he admitted the infinity both of space and time. "An infinite of atoms" circulates in this infinity, says the Epicurean. Montaigne changes however *atomorum* into *formarum*. He writes that we discover "an innumerable number of forms"[9] in the infinity of Nature. This modification is truly a reversal of ideas. Indeed, atoms are the principles from which Epicurus explains everything, while the "forms" are not principles but the effects of Nature's productivity. Montaigne thus rejects the atoms and the materialist explanation but nevertheless keeps the Epicurean idea of Nature as a principle of multiplication, proliferation, fertility, and, it must be said, of diversity and variety. Indeed, "Nature has committed herself to make nothing separate that was not different."[10] There is, however, a chasm between the Greek Epicurus and the Christian Montaigne. For Epicurus, Nature is dissolved, disseminated in an infinity of natures, without a reality as such (denoting an infidelity to the notion of *Phusis*), and therefore more or less confused with the universe, that is, a quantitative totality.

Nature's Unity through God's Purpose

For Montaigne, on the other hand, Nature has a unity as such, assuring the unity of reality, and is guided and guiding through some kind of purpose, as if she were the servant of a sovereign God of goodness, and at the same time could be confounded with him.

"Himself all good, he has made all things good," we are able to deduce, from a written addition in the Bordeaux version of his Essays.[11] Is he referring to God, to Nature, or both of them?

Nature is, however, for Montaigne, the mutability itself, the becoming, and in her plays the Heraclitean opposition of contraries while God is the Being itself, "the only one that *is*."[12] God remains thus in his transcendence, does not mingle in any way with Nature, or cannot be confused with her because time, not even eternity, can be associated with Him. To place Montaigne on the side of Pantheism would be a major mistake. For him, there is what we can talk about—what is offered to us, Nature—and there is the One for whom there is no human word because he is not to be seen. He has "revealed" himself and there is only his Word. And, "it belongs to God himself to know and interpret his works."[13] Therefore, we should not try to conceive what the relationship between God and Nature can be, since at least one of the two is inconceivable for us. It is here, to some extent, where I feel very close to Montaigne. For me, who does not admit such a "Revelation," the word *God* (monotheist) has no meaning. For Montaigne, God eludes any human meaning. The only difference between us regards his Word. Montaigne believes God on his Word; I don't. When I still used the word *God*, I was dwelling on the question of evil: if God is "kind" and "just" and "almighty," "for which just motive are children condemned to suffer such evils?" asks Saint Augustine in his letter to Saint Jerome on the origin of the soul (415).[14] This question was decisive for my atheism. Montaigne observes, however, that this language is just human language using human notions, which can't be transposed as such into notions that would apply to God. The question of evil is not answered but it ceases to be one as soon as we understand the human presupposition of God's humanization it implies.

Montaigne's Meditation on the Infinite: Foundation of His Wisdom

I feel close to Montaigne on account of our common meditation on the infinite, which is the foundation of his wisdom and almost my own—at least on certain days it is! On one side there is what lasts, and on the other what is fleeting. We are far too preoccupied with what just passes by. What is it that makes newspaper headlines grab our attention so? What for? Tomorrow or the day after tomorrow something else will make the front page. Let us not be moved by these headlines; let them pass us by. Let us listen to Montaigne: "We are all huddled and concentrated in ourselves, and our vision is reduced to the length of our nose. Socrates was asked where he was from. He replied not *Athens*, but *The world*." Because "he embraced the universe as his city"—unlike us, who look only at what is underfoot. "When the vines freeze in my village, my priest infers that the wrath of God is upon the human race."[15] Today, wherever we may be, we know about what happens elsewhere in the world, but the events that are not directly related to us touch us very little. While I write these lines, in November 2003, we are currently discussing actively the new police speed radars, a holiday that will be cancelled, the precise meaning of a new hit song on the radio: could this be of interest to anyone reading these words today? Montaigne lived the greater part of his life in a province several times ravaged during periods of civil war. He is admirable when he puts even this into perspective: "Seeing our civil wars, who does not cry out that this mechanism is being turned topsy-turvy and that the judgment day has us by the throat, without reflecting that many worse things have happened, and that ten thousand parts of the world, to our one, are meanwhile having a gay time?" (ibid.). Back in June 1941 during World War II, a war that left few places in the world intact, I pondered such things differently, considering that it (the war) would be relatively short anyway—three to four more years. I tried to make an abstraction of it by imagining the peace that would ensue; I was even already preparing myself for my studies.

We need, however, to go beyond such reasoning. We need to consider the immense and eternal Nature and contrast her with the frailty of our lives, indeed, the sheer insignificance of our daily worries. Montaigne perfectly expresses what the proper philosophical attitude should be: "The consideration of nature is a food fit for our minds; it uplifts us and swells us, makes us disdain base and earthly things by comparison with loftier and heavenly things."[16] In these lines, the memory of the philosopher's description made by Plato in the *Theaetetus* shines through. Let us further read the lines that inspired Pascal. The reflection on infinite Nature contained in the following lines was further developed by Pascal under the title "Man's Disproportion"[17]: "But whoever considers as in a painting the great picture of our mother Nature in her full majesty; whoever reads such universal and constant variety in her face; whoever finds himself there, and not merely himself, but a whole kingdom, as a dot made with a very fine brush; that man alone estimates things according to their true proportions. This great world, which some multiply further as being only a species under one genus, is the mirror in which we must look at ourselves to recognize ourselves from the proper angle."[18] "Our world," Montaigne says elsewhere, "has just discovered another world." "This other world will," perhaps, "only be coming into the light when ours is leaving it."[19] Montaigne refers to "our world," the "new world," and maybe others, because we don't know if the "new world" is to be the "last of his brothers." Such is for him the "great world," in which "Cannibals" and other types of men and cultures lead us to put into perspective our absolutes, our cultures. Great as this world may be, as Epicurus thought, for Montaigne there is still a multiplicity of such a "great world" in the immense universe. Montaigne prefers however, as it is too much of a quantitative notion, the word *Nature* to the word *universe*. Understanding by "great world" the entire face that Nature takes for us, he considers that Nature as an infinity of faces, as many as the worlds she creates. Each animal lives in its own world, impenetrable to others, unknowable to us. Montaigne attributes to the hedgehog, the swallow, the elephant, the dog, the fox, etc., the analogues of what we call "judgment," "imagination," "foresight," and "reasoning": "When I play with my cat, who knows if I am not a pastime to her more than she is to me?"[20] The difference between Nature and the universe is that Nature hollows herself out in innumerable worlds, the universe does not.

Emptying Nature from the God-Person

I made clear in *Orientation Philosophique* what we should understand by "world," and I would like to reiterate it here: "We can propose the following *exclusion principle*: we can only "see" things in a certain way by *not* "seeing" them in another way. We can only see a house from one side by not seeing it from another side. We can only observe the stalk of a plant through a microscope by not looking at it with the naked eye. We can only recognize somebody's face by not reducing it to a sum of cells or organs. We can only think of the rainbow as a scientist by not appreciating it as a poet. We can only consider the flower as a bee does by not considering it as a man, as a dog, etc. Each time we put together everything that can be put together from a certain point of view, with the exclusion of what can't be put together from the same point of view, we have what I call a 'world.'

"Examples: the fly's world, the Neanderthal world, the art world, etc. (to take but a few disparate examples). Now, the exclusion principle holds the structure of reality, considering the way it (reality) is composed. The idea of a gaze that could observe from all sides at the same time (God's gaze) is therefore absurd. That's why the richness, the profusion, of reality is in principle not to be unified; a 'God' is always something far too simple when faced with the complexity of reality."[21] So I follow Montaigne in his view of Nature as infinite, realizing everywhere "infinite difference and variety,"[22] creating indefinitely in dissemblance.

However, due to the exclusion principle, I must here part with Montaigne, as I conceive that Nature hollows herself out in innumerable worlds. He indeed wants to maintain the idea that is incompatible with the structure itself of reality, that of the all-seeing God.

"God" is no more than a cultural icon that the philosopher uselessly throws in to show among his pieces of evidence. Besides, everybody knows that he is alone in the world and that there is, in his mind, no room for another look at things other than his own. "There is no one but yourself who knows whether you are cowardly and cruel, or loyal and devout."[23] "Only you [and] God?" Can I not be seen just as who I truly am by the one who loves me out of an absolute and clear-sighted love? Maybe I can then assume that God is the absolute *You* who loves me similarly? However if God is a *You*, we are then of the same species. There is communication between him and me, and so innumerable other beings remain outside this relationship. We could go on to suppose that there is, for example, a god for the flies, a god who can see the world as a fly does; and a god for the bee, and so on.

This would imply a multiplication of the gods and this fantasy that "God" is never more than a sort of accompaniment to man. Within Nature, there is nothing other than what man believes visible. Nature herself must be emptied of the characters of the God-Person, the God of prayer.

When Montaigne speaks about Nature as the "Mother," he means a benevolent unity. "Nature has universally embraced all her creatures; and there is none that she has not very amply furnished with all the powers necessary for the preservation of its being"[24]; "But there is nothing useless in nature, not even uselessness itself. Nothing has made its way into this universe that does not hold a proper place in it"[25]; "The laws of Nature teach us what we rightly need"[26]; "We have abandoned Nature and we want to teach her a lesson, she who used to guide us so happily and so surely."[27] These passages, and others of the same kind, point to a purpose in Nature, an immanent finality. Nature works toward what is good for her creatures. We thereby must understand: to ensure life in conformity to the nature of each of them. We could then ask ourselves: In order to find Nature as she truly is, could we not just strip her from the characteristics Montaigne gives her owing to his contamination by his Christian vision, characteristics such as unity, "all kindness," "infinite might," discrimination of the best, etc.? This contamination cannot however be negated since Montaigne, as we pointed out earlier, uses the two words, *God* and *Nature*, interchangeably.

The Stoical Side of Montaigne

As some of his work obliges us to do so, let us now take into account the Stoical side of Montaigne, such as this: "In all affairs, when they are past, however they have turned out, I have little regret. For this idea takes away the pain: that they were bound to happen thus, and now they are in the great stream of the universe and in the chain of Stoical causes. Your fancy, by wish or imagination, cannot change a single point without overturning the whole order of things, and the past and the future."[28] Here, Nature is similar to the one we can find in Cleanthes's *Hymn to Zeus*, caught in the embrace of the logos of destiny. Indeed, this "chain-maker of causes" is just another definition of destiny itself: destiny is a "chain of causes," as the Stoic Aetius wrote.[29] But destiny is also "reason" (*logos*), immanent reason to the cosmos and governing the production of events, or as Chrysippus says, "reason of the things governed in the world by providence (*pronoia*)."[30] This notion of "Providence" also allows the Christian Montaigne to feel Stoic, and this despite the ineluctable chain of causes so dear to the Stoics. Here is another Montaigne sentence that a Stoic might have easily made: "It is one and the same nature that rolls its course. Anyone who had formed a competent judgment of its present state could infer from this with certainty both all the future and all the past."[31] This text makes us think of the famous text of Laplace and contradicts absolutely the "divine word" of Plato: "Nature is nothing but an enigmatic poem."[32] Indeed, if Nature is a poet, the future is not yet comprised within the past.

Nature, under the reign of divinity, be it the transcendent God or the immanent Zeus, must have the characteristics of unity, providential kindness, and perfection.

It is therefore tempting to think that Nature owns them thanks to the contamination by the divinity and conversely that, without the idea of God, these characteristics of organic and orderly unity, of a harmonious lot in motion, would vanish leaving a Nature that indifferently and blindly creates in the manner of Epicurus's Nature. Why, then, should not we put the creative chance, rather than the straightening reason, down as the origin of things?

Lao Tzu and the Fundamental Goodness of Reality

If we have a look at Taoism however, specifically Lao Tzu and his *Tao Te Ching*, what do we find? The Tao, the "Way," could also be called *Phusis*, "Nature," as thought by the Ante-Socratics. In no way is it a divinity; it is not somebody, and we cannot invoke it as with the Absolute *You* of the Christians or Cleanthes's Zeus. Everything, however, proceeds from a preeminent unity, the Tao, the Nature. Indeed, there is *one* Nature, while the notion of "world," implying the finite, is compatible with the idea that there would be many worlds, even an infinite number of them. From this Unity, infinitely rich in resources, is born everything that lives and life is good. The virtue (*te*) of Tao is the force of kindness that gives life to all beings. This is a nonviolent force; harmony and balance are in accordance with the Tao and Nature, violence is not, nor is excess (*hubris*)—both are human in essence. Montaigne, the Stoics, and Lao Tzu see as evident the fundamental Goodness of reality, yet this "Goodness" should not be understood in a moral sense, only meaning that it is *good* to live. All living creatures harbor a sort of self-approbation of life, and it can be said that they necessarily abhor, or are repulsed by, death.

Now, to speak of an imminent Goodness in the course of things does not imply one's admission of a divine governance of the world. Faith in the divinity is not possible without faith in Providence. All creatures are consequently under the control of the universal reason; Time is entirely filled in by all that must be; the end of the world is ordained and nothing new will happen. Montaigne contradicts his intuition of Nature's creativity when he speaks about deriving the future out of the present. Indeed, the one who "has sufficiently judged the present state of things" and thereby derives all the future and all the past, exists: the God of monotheism.

In Taoism, on the contrary, future and past are derived easily from the present state of the world. Indeed, according to the eternal return, the future has already happened before, the past must happen again, and there is nothing new under the sun.

So, having discarded what I called the "contamination" by the divinity, the characteristics of unity and goodness can still be associated with Nature, as we see with Lao Tzu, without having to resort to chance in order to explain things. In monotheism and stoicism, the field of possible creatures is predetermined. God knows which creatures will be created, and for Stoics, there are no creatures other than the ones that exist during the whole life of the world. For Lao Tzu, on the contrary, Nature's fecundity is infinite. She does not admit this restriction, which has the effect of converting Nature into "world," an organic and finite totality. Here, Lao Tzu is on the side of Epicurus who admits, in the infinite universe, the birth and destruction of innumerable worlds.

Now, as we have seen in some Essay passages, Montaigne is also on the side of Epicurus and of the innumerable worlds. However, the thought of an all-seeing, all-controlling God remains with him, and Lucretius's influence is not enough to eradicate it.

As Malebranche said, the Greek *Phusis* is incompatible with Christianity. Montaigne looks with temptation toward the Greek *Phusis*, but hindered by his Christian anchorage, he can't resign himself to naturalism.

VII

A MOMENT WITH OMAR KHAYYAM

Milestones

Although Montaigne could have written some of Omar Khayyam's quatrains, he, like Conche, could not have remained stuck in Khayyam's nihilism, taste for wine or negative feelings. Like Khayyam, they recognize that eternal Time has the upper hand on all finite things; unlike him, they nevertheless share the will to ever increase the difference between what has value and what does not. This will is tragic, however, since everything is condemned to be annihilated.

Despite all this, Conche feels to some extent closer to Khayyam than to Montaigne, admiring his courage as a free thinker who dared in an eleventh-century Muslim country to not pay attention to contemplation in mosques and to doubt the Lord, in particular, to doubt the Lord's interest for Mankind. And, of course, Conche also appreciates Khayyam's presentiment of the infinite and final refuge in love.

Where Khayyam's and Montaigne's "Nihilisms" Meet and Part

Having left Montaigne, I meditate for a moment with Omar Khayyam whose quatrains (*robaîyat* in Persian language) with their nihilistic tone, could match the maxims of Montaigne's "library." Like Montaigne, I however cannot remain trapped in nihilism. So then, what about Omar Khayyam?

Let us begin with his self-portrait:

On this multi-coloured earth someone walks
Neither believer nor atheist, neither poor nor rich
He worships not Allah nor laws human
With no faith put in universal truth, nothing he confirms
Who is this courageous and sad person walking our multi-coloured earth? (108)[1]

Montaigne might have written something similar but for this: Montaigne revered God, he believed in truth, at least in "divine knowledge," and of course, he wasn't what you would call a sad human being.

The desperate tone of the Persian poet cannot be Montaigne's; even when Montaigne came close to nihilism in some of his "sentences," he remained happy. His was always a happy "nihilism."

Here are nevertheless a few examples of sentences from Khayyam that Montaigne could have painted on the exposed beams of his "library":

> Life is as short as a sigh (63)
>
> Our life is as short as a raging fire: flames the passer-by soon forgets,
> ashes the wind blows away. A man's life (90)
>
> Life passes by, fast caravan!
> Stop then your mount and try to be happy (68)
>
> Our days pass as fast as the water of the river or the desert wind (20)
>
> This evening or possibly tomorrow you may not be here anymore (117)
>
> Enjoy this fleeting moment we call life (43)
>
> I concluded that it is impossible to affirm or deny anything (150)
>
> Poor soul, you will never know anything (164)
>
> Scholars have nothing to really teach you (105)

At certain moments, notably when he was writing the *Apology of Raymond Sebond*, Montaigne has been indeed tempted by nihilism. He could have then agreed with Khayyam's following quatrain:

> Our great wide world—a piece of dust
> All human knowledge—words
> People, animals and flowers of the seven continents—shadows
> The result of our meditations—nothing (26)

Together with the poet, Montaigne could also have been tempted to write:

Listen to the melodies lovers play on their lute;
These are the real psalms of David
Don't concern yourself with the future or the past but savour
this moment
That's the secret of inner peace. (64)

Or:

Surrender your soul to the Now. (130)

However, Montaigne possessed a spirit that continuously propelled him forward, and being fully dedicated to the search for truth, it made him reject and surpass his desire for the present. He also had a confidence in life, in the being (that is, in "reality"), such that he could not have written either of Khayyam's following lines:

Stop talking, words are deceptive.
Quick, hand me my cup!
I have grown older again . . . (79)

Nor:

Convictions and doubts, folly and truth,
These are but words, as empty as an air bubble . . . (91)

Beyond his regularly shifting opinions Montaigne had his convictions; He loved the search for truth through dialogue, which he greatly valued, and he made firm judgments on what he considered unsustainable. Above all, his confidence and love for life would have urged him to reject the Theognisian (from Theognis of Megara, Greek gnomic poet, circa 540 BC) pessimism expressed in the following words:

Happy is the child who died on the day he was born!
Even happier is the child who never came to the world! (36)

Montaigne might have sometimes approved or remained impartial, and perhaps on occasion even disapproved when he read Omar Khayyam.

Here is a quatrain, the first part of which he might have approved, the second most definitely not:

> What do you prefer?
> To sit down in a wine house and there investigate yourself and your conscience,
> or to kneel down in a church or mosque without your soul participating?
> I don't even think about whether or not we have a Master
> And what he will do with us if he exists? (2)

It is indeed better to examine one's conscience in a tavern rather than kneel down in a church with an unrepentant soul. Nevertheless, Montaigne would have considered as unwelcome bravado and useless the claim to "have no interest" in knowing whether we have or not a Master, the Lord.

Montaigne would have acknowledged the justness but not the intention of this quatrain:

> Stringed instruments, perfumes, wine cups, lips, long hairs, eyes,
> Mere toys that are destroyed by time, toys!
> Frugality, loneliness, labour, meditation, prayer and renunciation,
> Mere ash that time will blow away! (170)

Of course, the eternal Time has the upper hand on all finite things. What has *value*—as much as what has no value—meditation, prayer, love, and effort are all condemned to be erased, annihilated. The difference in worth nevertheless exists, and the tragic wisdom resides in the will to ever increase this difference, despite the nothingness.

Khayyam's Taste for Wine and Negative Feelings

Omar Khayyam was a poet and a scientist. In his foreword to Khayyam's *Robaîyat* (translated by Franz Toussaint), Ali Nô-Rouze says of Khayyam, "he was the most famous scientist of his time." Khayyam was nevertheless ready to forsake all his knowledge and all the sciences for a glass of wine:

> I'll give all kingdoms for a good glass of wine!
> All books and science for the soft scent of wine!

All love songs for the song of wine flowing!
All of Freidun[2]'s glory for the play of colours in this glass!
(166)

Omar Khayyam would even barter the Koran itself, which he called the "supreme Book," in exchange for the "suave smell of wine" brought to his lips in a cup. That is quite an effort of values' "transvaluation"!

Omar did not negate the wisdom contained in the Koran; however, the wisdom provided by wine was more readily available to him. Such wisdom intoxicates:

Wine gives the Sages intoxication such as that of the Chosen.
It gives us back our feeling of youth, all that we have lost
and all that we still wish for.
It can burn us like a devastating sea of fire,
but it can also transform our sadness into refreshing water.
(127)

On certain days, Montaigne himself might not have had any difficulty in following Omar to exchange a "sacred Book"—the Koran, the Old Testament—for more earthly pleasures, which could have been not much more than a simple glass of Bordeaux. If Montaigne never dispraised wine, he nevertheless did not like to get drunk. The so-called benefits found in drunkenness by the poet were nothing more than illusions for Montaigne, his essay "Of Drunkenness" condemns this as a "gross and brutal" vice, which reverses the capacity to think and leads to loss of self-control.

All the same, Montaigne was not a very severe man. This was first out of indulgence toward the Ancient Greeks and Romans for their fondness of the grape—some Stoics went so far as to recommend occasional drunkenness. Second, because to him drinking was "less malicious and damaging" than other vices such as disloyalty or cruelty. And finally, isn't it "as it were the last pleasure the course of years deprives us of"?[3]

Having said that, Montaigne despised ugly or negative feelings such as bitterness far more than drunkenness, misanthropy, or pessimism, like those expressed in this text:

Be happy that you have few friends.
Don't feel obliged to show them endless sympathy.
Before you shake hands, before you consider someone a friend,
ask yourself whether you are not shaking a hand that may
one day beat you. (8)[4]

He would have equally loathed the pride expressed in this:

I look back at my life
and I again hear my mother say to me:
"Allah will forgive you."
But I refuse a forgiveness I never asked for. (71)

And the mistrust in this:

When you see ripe almonds along the road,
Don't eat them; they may be poisonous. (53)

Although I identify with Montaigne, including the repudiation of negative feelings, Montaigne, being of a more generous disposition, did not have a certain "disdain" I have, always mixed with some pity.

By "negative feelings," I don't mean, for example, a mother's cries of anguish for her child, because this pain and these tears express an immense love. I don't mean the torment of the scorned lover either, where it is love that once again cries out, or injustice's hatred that leads to conflict and sacrifice. No! I mean the bitterness of the one who feels "wronged," badly rewarded, or not held in regard to his "just" value, not arriving at the "place," or not reaping the accolades he thinks he deserves. I also mean, without getting into too many details, jealousy, envy, resentment, unjustified sadness, mistrust, vanity, presumption, arrogance, egocentrism, calculated self-interest—in short, everything that is mediocre. Sadness and despair are not negative feelings if they are normal human reactions to an event that is negative, such as the death of a loved one; on the contrary, sadness in the face of somebody else's success, or an unjustified sad mood, is a negative emotion. Montaigne condemns them in his essay *Of Sadness*.

Khayyam's Courage as a Free Thinker

Despite all this, I feel to some extent closer to Khayyam than to Montaigne. I admire him, who, in an eleventh-century Muslim country, dared to not pay attention to contemplation in mosques and to prayers, did not believe in Heaven or Hell, doubted the Lord, and, in particular, doubted the Lord's interest in Mankind.[5]

He no longer opened the Koran, devoting himself only to free thinking:

Close your Koran.
Think in freedom and look with open minds
at Heaven and Earth. (128)

He only went to mosques to sleep or rest:

In days past, when I used to visit the mosques,
I didn't go in to pray but I always returned home
filled with hope. I still often go to a mosque,
because the shadows there are so restful. (107)

Religious buildings were for him the artifacts of the fear for death:

In convents, synagogues, mosques, churches,
the weak, those who are afraid of Hell, take refuge. (24)

Omar despised the hypocrisy he saw in praying:

I despise the hypocrite mumbling his prayers. (92)

He took certain and doubtful pride in the fact he never prayed:

Everyone knows that I never mumbled prayers. (1)

Why pray? He asked, for "Heaven"? For "Hell"? These are but mere words.

To believe in eternal rest: folly (72)

And what of God? Is there a God?

People talk about the Creator. (76)

God is only a rumour. If there is a God, he must be a sublime chess player, indifferent to our vices and virtues:

Let us speak clearly and without parable:
We are pawns in that mysterious game played by Heaven.
We are played around with on that chess board of the being
And we are finally thrown back, one by one, into the box of nothingness. (103)[6]

This gives the hope of being freed from *everything*, if death is nothing.

This story of Tchouang-Tse expresses pessimism even more vividly: "During a trip, Lie-Tse was eating on the side of the road when he noticed an old skull amidst the tall grass. He brushed aside the grass, pointed his index finger to the skull and said: 'Just you and me, we know that you are neither dead nor alive. Are you really unhappy? Am I really happy?'" [7]

Lie-Tse seems to give to the dead a pseudo-life, similar to the lives of Homer's shadows. Whether the dead, in their uncertain state, are really unhappy is as unclear and difficult to answer as whether we the living are truly happy. Maybe there is no "real" death, nor "real" life. Maybe there is just some sort of a swamp. In which case, why would we bother to commit suicide then? After all, in the end we can never "get away" from this nebulous swamp!

Khayyam's Sad View of the Human Condition

Omar Khayyam is sad, and his sadness, due to his human condition, is fundamental; it is incurable, ontological, and therefore rather normal. Man indeed does not know who he is and what his life means, and even after his death, he still does not know it. Should he resolve all the other problems, including "the creation enigma," the question of Man's raison d'être and his meaning would still remain:

> Let's assume that you have finally solved the riddle of the creation—what's your fate?
> Let's assume that you found the deepest layers of truth—what will be your fate?
> Let's assume that you have lived a hundred happy years and will live another hundred—what will be your fate? (27)

In short, why is there mankind?

By the time Omar composes his *Robâïyat*, he is already more than seventy years old. He remembers the scientist he once was:

> When I was young I had eminent teachers.
> I was quite happy with my progress, with my triumphs.
> When I remember the sage I was, I compare that sage to water,
> That takes the form of the vase or with smoke that is blown away by the wind. (151)

He had written Astronomic Tables, a Method for the extraction of square and cubic roots, an Arabic treatise on algebra,[8] a Treatise on a few difficulties related to Euclid's definitions. He had not separated algebra from geometry, thereby paving the way for the modern analytical geometry. Above all, as director of the Merv Observatory, he had reformed the calendar.

As with the Julian, the Persian solar year traditionally counted 365 days and 6 hours, but when the Persians fell under Arab caliph domination, the vanquished were forced to accept both the religion and the lunar year of their new rulers.

But the end of the eleventh century saw Malik-Châh shake off the yoke of the caliphs and a new dynasty was established. Malik-Châh wanted to return to the Persian solar year and asked his astronomers what form it should take. However, advances made in astronomy in the intervening period rendered this return to the old way impossible; the solar year was now recognized to be short by about eleven minutes. Omar Khayyam had the idea of inserting one day every four years, seven times in a row, and upon the eighth time this was to be repeated only after every five years.

He thereby obtained an insertion, which, much later, was said to be to some extent far more precise than the addition obtained by Pope Gregory XIII's reform of the Julian calendar in 1582. Persians were so proud of this that they passed a law through which they reserved for themselves the right to study astronomy.

As a poet, Omar saw humans as images against the world's curtain:

> The dome-shaped sky under which we wander;
> I compare it with a magic lantern,
> whose light is the sun and whose screen is the world
> On which our images are moving. (115)

Khayyam's Presentiment of the Infinite

Omar Khayyam the astronomer had a presentiment of the infinite:

> The big wheel turns without following our human
> calculations.
> Abandon your vain efforts to count the stars. (34)

For how long have stars been going around in circle? Myriads of centuries:

Millions of centuries have seen dawn, have seen twilight.
Millions of centuries stars have passed through the sky. (48)

We are only a "twinkling," said Montaigne, "in the infinite course of an eternal night."
Omar wrote in the same vein:

Beyond the earth, beyond the farthest skies,
beyond the infinite,
I try to find Heaven and Hell. (15)

Should we find here a real intuition of the infinite? Why not? Didn't Ferdowsi write, only a century before this: "The world seems an infinite ocean, so deep that one cannot see its bottom."?[9]

Like Pascal, Omar Khayyam struggled with the silence of the universe, with the incomprehensible, with the enigma. But in the company of friends and some good wine—he was fearless:

What are your thoughts, my friend?
Are you thinking about your ancestors? They have returned to dust.
As to their merits? See how I smile.
Take the decanter and let us drink and listen, quietly, to the great silence of the universe. (83)

But his intellect suffered when confronted with the world's enigma:

How mysterious, all those stars,
moving around in space (66)

So much so that he resolved "not to contemplate the sky anymore."

Khayyam's Final Refuge in Love

Man is then left with this: to forget his sad condition, however, two things can help us deal with it: wine and love. We have discussed above his taste for wine. All that remains is love.

For Khayyam, outside love, "of bliss we know no more than its name" (61). But love itself is disappointing, except for the precious pleasure that is received and given:

We shall perish along the path of Love.
Fate will trample us.
Yeah, tempting young woman, get up and give me your lips
before I return to dust. (60)

By "love" we should herewith understand the infinite sweetness that comes from "the" woman:

Scholars really have nothing to teach you.

But from the soft touch of the eyelashes of a woman
You will know all there is to know about happiness. (105)

Sadness itself gives way to the look of the loved woman:

Each new morning my heart feels heavier again,
But your glance makes me forget my sorrows. (124)

Dissociated from love and from any loving friendship, wine leads to drunkenness and forgetfulness or to false lucidity. Only love can give meaning to life. Without love, we are unable to see the "world in all its splendour":

How wicked a heart that does not know how to love,
That does not know what it is to be drunk with love.
If you are not in love, how can you enjoy
the blinding light of the sun, the soft light of the moon? (10)

But what is the solution if the love of a woman is missing, if loved we are not? Then, it only remains for us to meditate on this sublime quatrain:

When you are so full of sorrow that you can't walk, can't cry
anymore,
and think about the green foliage that sparkles after the rain.
When the daylight exhausts you, when you hope a final night
will cover the world,
think about the awakening of a young child. (147)

VIII

CONCERNING NIETZSCHE

Milestones

While Conche was able in the previous chapters to share the truth-seeking road "with" Epicurus and Montaigne, only to differ to some extent from them, he is unable to do so "with" Nietzsche. With him, there is not one single road but many.

Conche asks, first, what Nietzsche's originality is and finds it in his emphasis of the word eternal in his doctrine of the eternal return. But to what does he refer? To the eternity of events' recurrence or "of the present"? The core idea developed in this chapter is that, according to Conche, Nietzsche rejects the cyclical recurrence of events.

To show this, Conche first presents the mythical usage by Nietzsche of his doctrine; it is meant to serve as the "foundation of an oligarchy above people and their interests." By believing in eternal recurrence and living accordingly, man becomes the "overman."

Secondly, Conche presents Nietzsche's perception of the world and of Nature and reveals its ambiguities, due precisely to the doctrine of eternal recurrence. Nietzsche has an intuition of Nature as infinite and denounces, therefore, in many texts the concept of the Whole of reality as an organism. Yet the eternal recurrence of all things and of events would imply the connection of each thing to each other. This in turn would imply, just as with the Stoics, that the Whole of reality is an organism, that is to say a "world," a cosmos. But, in the end, the idea that we need "to get rid of the all, of unity . . . some force or other, something unconditional" seems to dominate and leads Nietzsche, at least in some texts, to admit the infinite plurality of worlds and of an infinite Nature.

While still unsure of what Nietzsche really had in mind, these reflections allow Conche to interpret the notion of "eternal recurrence" as the eternal return of the moment, and not of the event. This means that there will always be a new instant, indefinitely: whatever we do, we can always do it for the first time.

So, while the eternal recurrence of events would signify nonliberty, the eternal recurrence of the moment signifies the immensity of our freedom. This helps Conche to interpret the overman as a free man, the only and ultimate decider of himself. And in that light the expression amor fati can be kept in the sense of amor casus: it is because the future has not already happened and depends on chance and randomness, that I can do what is new, that is to say, create.

Nietzsche's Originality: His Emphasis on Eternity?

Over the course of the following pages it is my intention to express and explain my own understanding and vision of infinity according to Nietzsche. I would also like to point out that my motivation is not to speak about myself per se, but rather write about what seems to me to be the truth. If I use the word *I* it is so that the reader may freely consider that this is merely *my* truth and none other. I have been able to share the truth-seeking road "with" Epicurus and "with" Montaigne, only to differ slightly or more than slightly with them. This I have been able to do by virtue of understanding them. I cannot however share the road "with" Nietzsche because simply put, with Nietzsche there are not *one* but many roads and so many ways of understanding him. Therefore, let it not be said that I have not "understood" Nietzsche; this is simply not what I have sought to do. I have, moreover, noticed that Nietzsche has very often "served" as a pretext.

For all his worthy insight, Nietzsche did not "see" much that had not already been seen. A few days after the Surlei vision, he wrote to Peter Gast that on several occasions he was unable to leave his room. Why was this? "Each time, I had cried too much the evening before while walking, and not sentimental tears, but tears of joy, to the accompaniment of which I sang and talked nonsense, filled with a new vision far superior to that of other men" (Letter of August 14, 1881). Nevertheless, he forgets that among the "other men" were the great sages—Epicurus, Pyrrhus, Buddha, and Lao Tzu, to name but a few—and that wisdom has always represented the triumph of a "new vision."

However, as far as the old Greek and Archaic idea of eternal recurrence is concerned, is it not true that at the beginning of August 1881, at Sils-Maria, he had a revelation that allowed him to see this recurrence differently than his forerunners before him had seen it, and then he himself had seen it before? If it is indeed the case that eternal recurrence occupies a "central place" in the philosophy of Nietzsche, and if it is the "star around which all the decisive ideas" of this philosophy orbit, as Philippe Granarolo[1] believes it to be, it is important to know what to expect regarding how he intends this notion to be understood. Well, it would be interesting to know it, but is it really that important? Probably not. Indeed, Granarolo makes the somewhat discouraging observation that "The simulacrum of the eternal recurrence concept often trapped him in its web, and we can even make the assertion that, from 1886 onwards, our thinker was to have difficulty in distinguishing the simulacra of this thought from its true formation. By systematically and constantly using the inversion argument to an almost nauseating degree, the philosopher, tired of recent writings, gets caught in the trap of simulacra denounced by Zarathustra."[2] In this case, let us not try to understand what Nietzsche wanted to say, and he undoubtedly varied, but what he was able to say that has a truthful meaning for us.

According to Daniel Halévy, the originality of Nietzsche is in emphasizing the word *eternal*; "'Everything returns,' said the ancients, who were not familiar with the notion of the eternal. Everything returns ceaselessly, writes Nietzsche, which is to say eternally. At the same time as there is a Return, there is an Eternal Return. Such is the expression he will always use, and in this expression the accent always falls on the Eternal." [3] The Stoics do not say otherwise, and, without speaking of Homer's gods "who are forever,"[4] Heraclitus's "ever living" fire,[5] Parmenides's being "without beginning or end,"[6] the word *eternal* had already been used by Anaximander, it would seem.

In any event, it is used in Mélissos,[7] in Hesiode's *Shield*,[8] in the *Homeric hymn at Hestia*, during the archaic period. Of course, it is to be found again in the classical period. The use of the word is therefore not "unknown to the Greeks," as Halévy rashly says.

Eternal Recurrence of Events or Eternity of the Present?

However, it is one thing to speak about the eternity of recurrence and another to speak about the eternity "*of the present*." Does not this consideration of the present as eternal constitute the originality of Nietzsche? Daniel Halévy explains: "Each instant that we live, which is destined to recur an infinite number of times, bears the mark of eternity and is itself an Eternal Thing. . . . The eternal is no longer to be found in the unfathomable beyond: it is particular to each instant, at each moment we are filled with it."[9]

For certain, the idea of considering each moment as eternal and not only lived eternally is not to be found in Greek thought; it cannot be found there, because to make the moment eternal would be to immobilize it, which is impossible. What recurs for an infinite time,[10] for the Stoics, is only the passing moment, which, however, for the wise can suffice for happiness. It is also certain that as pleasure is not of the order of movement and process, "it is possible to feel pleasure independently of time," as having occurred in an indivisible moment, this, according to Aristotle,[11] while such experiences can only last a "short time." On the other hand, the friends of Epicurus, particularly during ritual meals, feel that so rich, so complete is the present moment that they are devoid of future.

This is what Epicurus calls living "like gods," when the present seems neither to be held between the past and the future but to be outside of time. Nevertheless, the present moment is usually fleeting and an infinity of evanescent moments will not make a moment permanent. Certainly eternity is in a sense always there, because if what there is, is constantly changing, the fact that "there is" (the *esti* of Parmenides) is eternal. This is true whether or not there is an "eternal recurrence." On the other hand, it will always be true that what is happening now has happened in such a way that what escapes with the passing of days is memorized in the eternal memory, even if there is nobody to remember. Yet neither has that anything to do with the "eternal recurrence."

Nietzsche's Rejection of the Cyclical Recurrence of Events

Besides, in the second of the *Untimely Meditations* (1874), Nietzsche rejected the cyclical recurrence of events: "Fundamentally what was possible once could only be possible a second time if the Pythagoreans were right in believing that, with the same constellation of the heavenly bodies the same events had to be repeated on earth, down to each miniscule detail: so that whenever the stars have a certain relation to each other, a Stoic will join an Epicurean and murder Caesar, and ever again with a different configuration Columbus will again discover America."[12]

Yet, "the true historical Conexus of causes and effects, which once fully comprehended, would only prove that the dice game of the future could not give rise to a completely similar constellation."[13] A posthumous fragment specifies that "[i]f everything happened again—in the Pythagorean sense, it would then be necessary to know the past and the constellations in order to precisely identify their reappearance. But nothing happens again."[14]

Nietzsche does not believe in eternal recurrence as a physical theory. He criticizes, moreover, all the concepts that come into play in the formulation of the hypothesis: the concept of truth, the concept of knowledge, the epistemological categories such as causality, the metaphysical concepts such as the notions of "all" and "world," the scientific concepts such as force, the logical concepts including the notion of noncontradiction. All that remains is myth and its usage.

Nietzsche's Mythical Usage of the Eternal Recurrence

He dreams of the "foundation of an oligarchy above people and their interests."[15] For this he needs a "great selective thinking": "We need a doctrine that is strong enough to exert a selective action: strong enough to have the effect of breeding: strengthening the strong, paralyzing and the weak and world weary."[16]

He sees his philosophy as the "hammer" that will be the instrument of selection: "My philosophy brings the victorious thought of which all other modes of thinking will finally perish. It is the great cultivating thought; the races that cannot bear it are condemned; those that feel it as their greatest benefit are destined for rule."[17]

What is efficient for changing mankind is not the body but thought: "You say that food, location, air, society transform and condition you; well, your opinions do so even more since it is they that determine your choice of food, place, air and society. If you incorporate this thought within you, amongst your other thoughts, it will transform you. If for everything that you wish to do you begin by asking yourself: 'Am I certain I want to do this an infinite number of times?' this will become for you the heaviest weight."[18]

Nietzsche wrote "Eternal Recurrence: A Prophecy"[19] from this, and here we get to the core of his teaching: "My friends I am he who teaches eternal return. I teach that all things recur eternally, and you yourselves with them and that you have already existed infinite number of times before and all things with you. I teach that there is a great year of becoming, a colossus of a year; this year must turn itself over like an hour-glass, tirelessly, so that all these years resemble one another in the greatest things and the smallest. When dying I would say: 'You see, you die and in an instant you shall be nothingness; and there remains nothing of you as you, for souls are as mortal as bodies. The complex of causes which created you this time will return and it will create you again: you, yourself a speck of dust among dust, are part of these causes of the eternal recurrence. When you return, it will not be to a new life or a better life or a similar life but to this identical and self-same life, in the greatest things and in the smallest.' This teaching has not been given on earth, that is to say this time on earth and in this great year."[20]

One who has had, during and after the war, "a broken body" will have and will have had it an infinite number of times; the same goes for an AIDS sufferer, one who has Alzheimer's or anything else. One who has experienced unrequited love innumerable times, or rather an infinite number of times will always do so. Those people whose children die of hunger (one every seven seconds in 2004), will have dying children an infinite number of times. An Auschwitz, Sobibor, Dachau, Dresden, or Hiroshima will occur again and again.

The Thought of Eternal Recurrence Creating the Overman

Nietzsche then asks the question: "Is humanity ripe for such a thought?"[21] It is "the most grave"—the heaviest—thought and "its probable effect, if we do not guard against it beforehand," is that "it will shake everything to its foundations."[22] It will therefore be necessary to prepare for its probable consequences. The "way to bear it": the "revaluation of all values,"[23] that is to say, the reversal in the assessment of all values. This implies "living in a world stripped of morals":[24] "To endure the idea of the recurrence one needs freedom from morality," and correspondingly, the "greatest elevation of the consciousness of strength in man as he will create the overman."[25]

The "overman" is what man becomes when he is able to dominate the situation that is made for him by believing in eternal recurrence. The strong will extends "to a Dionysian affirmation of the world as it is, without subtraction, exception, or selection—it wants the eternal circulation; the same things, the same logic and illogic of entanglements. The highest state a philosopher can attain: to stand in a Dionysian relationship to existence—my formula for this is *amor fati*."[26]

The will to power cannot be accomplished via the conquest of economic, political, military, religious, and other supremacies because it involves going beyond man: "Man is something that must be overcome," said the Prologue to *Zarathustra*. Then there is this note from posthumous Fragments: "Abandon the inferior degrees of power in order to reach the higher degrees."[27]

He who reaches the higher degree of power "will dominate," but "dominate" does not signify "being master": "What I demand is to produce beings to dominate from their higher position the whole of the human race, to sacrifice themselves for this purpose, oneself and their 'kin.' One of the tendencies of evolution is, necessarily, the one which levels humanity and creates great anthills etc. The other tendency, my tendency, on the contrary tends to accentuate differences, widen distances, suppress equality, and create monsters of power. The former produces the 'last man'; my tendency produces the overman. The goal is absolutely not to conceive the latter as masters of the former; two types and species are to exist side by side, separated as far as possible, like the gods of Epicurus the one paying no heed to the other."[28]

So, what can we make of all this? We know that Nietzsche was guided by the idea of a "hierarchy." He dreamed of an "oligarchy which would rule over people." Yet, between the Epicureans gods, and therefore the "overmen" and the humans, there can be no question of "hierarchy": they are *other*. It can be admitted that becoming wise, or a true philosopher, is to *separate oneself* from the crowd; but this does not in any way imply any demeaning judgment nor contempt. The sage, like Nietzsche's Dionysian philosopher, says "yes" to everything that happens to him—because it happens to him and that is the way of things. This is what Montaigne, who has no belief in eternal recurrence, does. However, for the sage, saying "yes" to what happens to him is not to say "yes" to what happens *to others*, just as Montaigne condemned torture, witchhunts, and the cruelty of the New World colonizers.

Because injustice in this world is a fact and each man bears a responsibility toward other men, and today perhaps toward *all* men. Nietzsche opposes the "strong" and the "weak," unaware, at least in the way that Lao Tzu was, that there is a force in weakness, and then forgetting that the ultimate example of weakness is the child, in such a way that the future and salvation of humanity hinge upon what duty of care we have and should have for the child.

Nietzsche's Denunciation of the Concept of the Whole as an Organism: Nature as Infinite

Leaving aside the mythical usage of the doctrine of eternal recurrence, let us ask ourselves how Nietzsche really perceives the world and what elements of this are worth holding on to.

Having caused a certain dizziness and a great temptation, the image of an eternal recurrence of all things "functions" as a foil of sorts.

Nietzsche returns and reinvigorates his intuition of nature as infinite, which he had expressed in a note during the year 1872: "All knowledge reflects its object in forms that are clearly determined which don't exist a priori. Nature knows no form, no greatness: it is only for a subject knowing that things show themselves to have greatness or smallness. The infinite in nature: it has no limits anywhere. For us alone there is the finite."[29] "The *infinite* is the primordial fact," he adds.[30] Yet the eternal recurrence of all things implies the connection of each thing to each other, and so, just as we see in the Stoics, the concept of the Whole of reality, "Everything," as an organism, that is to say, as "world" (*cosmos*).

That "God" and "world" be corresponding notions,[31] this is what appears to Nietzsche. The cosmic God, immanent in the world as principal organizer, is essentially different from the God-will of the monotheists, who imposes himself on human will. Nevertheless, monotheism, whatever its form, is not compatible with a dehumanized vision of nature: monotheism unavoidably tends to view Nature, the Whole, as a living (human-like) organism. Nietzsche denounces the tendency of sages or modern philosophers of Nature to conceive the Whole of reality as an organism.

The same applies as much today as it did in the nineteenth century, and it cannot be otherwise, because science, by the structure of logico-mathematical logos as a unifying power, necessarily involves a unique universe which is a *cosmos* and which is the Whole of reality.[32] This necessity is reflected in the organic philosophy of Whitehead, in which he calls "Nature" a system of interdependencies, an organism where each part is in solidarity with everything.

But Nietzsche writes: "The modern scientific counterpart to belief in God is belief in the universe as an organism; this disgusts me. This is to make what is quite rare and extremely derivative, the organic, which we perceive only on the surface of the earth, into something essential, universal and eternal. This is still an anthropomorphising of nature! . . . If everything could become an organism it would already have become so. We must think it as a whole precisely as far as possible from the organic! . . . Let us believe in the absolute necessity of the whole and beware of maintaining, with respect to any law, that such a law is dominant in this whole and is an eternal property. All the chemical qualities have been able to become what they are and to disappear and return. Innumerable 'properties' have been able to develop, which are impossible for us to observe from our temporal and spatial recess. The change in a chemical quality is also happening now but at such a subtle level that it escapes even our finest calculations."[33]

". . . such a subtle level." Heraclitus's river is the real one, is the Essence: the permanent, the identical are only surface effects linked to the coarseness of our powers of perception.

So, let us take care not to ascribe absoluteness to qualities, properties, laws and structures: "We must always remain sceptical with regard to all our experiences, and say to ourselves that we cannot assert an eternal validity of any 'law of nature'; we cannot assert of any chemical quality its eternal permanence; we are not fine-tuned enough to see the absolute flow of events; anything permanent is there only by virtue of our crude organs. . . . The tree is something new at every moment: we assert the form because we are incapable of perceiving the most precise absolute movement. . . . The lines and the surfaces are introduced by us according to the principles of the intellect, and it is in this that the error consists: we admit identity and permanence because we can only see the permanent and only remember what is similar."[34]

In a general way—Nietzsche wrote this in 1872—"for us alone, there is the finite." An organism is a finite whole. So, "the whole is not an organism."[35] Nietzsche was to have great difficulty in freeing himself from the prejudice of the whole (of the whole organism). He would still write: "[A]sking that a thing be other than what it is, is to ask that everything be other."[36]

Nietzsche's Rejection of the All Unity

But the moment finally comes when he writes the following: "It seems important for me to get rid of the all, of unity . . . some force or other, something unconditional. One would not avoid regarding it as the highest court of appeal and baptising it 'God.' One must shatter the all and unlearn respect for the all. . . . The all would always bring the old problems with it: 'how is evil possible etc.?' Therefore: there is no all, the great Sensorium or Inventarium or repository of force is missing."[37]

Therefore, neither God nor one World, but a multiplicity of worlds is at the heart of an unquantifiable Nature. No longer *Deus sive natura*, but: "*Chaos sive natura: the dehumanisation of nature.*"[38]

If I am quoting these texts it is because they are texts I could almost write myself. Like Montaigne, I willingly borrow the words of another when they express my own thinking. But let us look again at a thought from Pascal.[39] By changing a word, I could say, "It is not in Nietzsche, but in my own self, that I find everything I see there"—at least everything I see as true.

And here, finally, is the passage that Nietzsche entitles: "My hypothesis opposed to the cyclical process": 'Would it not be possible to have the laws of the mechanical world derived as though they constituted exceptions and up to a certain point, chance happenings in the whole of the being? As one possibility between various innumerable possibilities? To consider that we are thrown by chance into this corner of the universe where mechanical order reigns? That every kind of chemical reaction in turn forms an exception and chance inside this mechanical order of things, and that the organism finally constitutes the exception and chance inside the chemical world? . . . [S]o that all our mechanical laws would not be eternal, but have become among countless different laws left over from them, or having prevailed in certain parts of the universe but not in others?' It seems that we need randomness, a real lawlessness, only an ability to become lawful, . . . Is not everything much too multiple to be born of the one? And the numerous chemical laws, and in their turn the species and organic structures, do they not remain inexplicable from the One? Or the Two?"[40]

What then of this "aptitude for lawfulness?" It is nothing other than the product of chance itself. On condition that there be no combinatory limit, therefore, under the condition of the infinite, order necessarily comes from disorder; this is only one particular case of this. In infinite Nature, limited by neither form nor size, it is easy at least by right, to explain that forms and structures are born. Order can be explained if we presuppose the existence of disorder, but from order how can we explain disorder? Especially with regard to God who is only Reason and Goodness, how can evil be explained?

The Epicureans, following Democritus, admit only the hypotheses that are necessary so that the world that offers itself to our senses may be explained. But from these very hypotheses also come the infinite plurality of worlds. He who wishes to explain that in space this organized and structured whole that is the world is formed in infinite space where an infinite number of atoms subject to chance and necessity are formed, is forced to admit that the worlds are infinite in number.[41]

Nietzsche's Admission of the Infinite Plurality of Worlds

Following his new hypothesis, which, going against the cyclical process, favors chance and places randomness at the heart of reality, Nietzsche can admit the infinite plurality of worlds in the sense of the Epicureans. Added to this is what he calls in *The Gay Science* "our new infinite." Because nature is not thought simply by extension, it encompasses the fact that innumerable worlds, which can be called "subjective," turn inward upon themselves and their interior.

However, Nietzsche hardly reflects on anything but the multiplicity of perspectives that it must be admitted is beyond our own perspective, "our corner": "I should think that today we are at least far from the ridiculous immodesty that would be involved in decreeing from our corner that perspectives are only permitted from this corner. Rather has the world become 'infinite' for us all over again: inasmuch as we cannot reject the possibility that it may include infinite interpretations? Once more we are seized by a great shudder; but who would feel inclined immediately to deify again after the old manner this monster of an unknown world?"[42]

Nietzsche writes "world," but it is Nature that is concerned.

Formerly, instead of "Nature," I used to say simply the "Whole,"[43] and I used to distinguish:

1. *The Whole (reality in its entirety)*: It includes everything, but is not a whole, has neither structure nor real unity. Not having unity, it has no meaning;
2. *Those beings having life and the vital worlds*: Each being lives in his world and not in all the real. This applies to man or flies;
3. *The global universe as the whole of material reality*: Together, as the Epicureans would wish, it is insurmountably broken up into parts that cannot, even by right, be reassembled: it is the un-combinable;
4. *The world of scientific knowledge (for example, the universe of the Big Bang)*: Science turns the Whole into worlds in function of the variable aspects of the Whole which it investigates;
5. *The other human worlds, real,* (the world of the aristocracy, that of the farmer, etc.) *or imaginary* (mythical, religious etc.).

I keep these distinctions; but today I say "Nature" rather than "Whole," because the Whole is simply *thought*, while Nature is *given*.

Eternal Recurrence of the Moment: Time Is Infinite

At this point in our analysis, let us return to the notion of "eternal recurrence." Let us try to interpret it in a sense other than that rejected above, bearing in mind not so much what came to Nietzsche's mind, as what seems just and acceptable. That there be an eternal recurrence *of events*, this simply cannot be, and besides, is incompatible with the thinking of

Heraclitus, to whom Nietzsche likes to think of himself as loyal: "[N]othing of what is, he says, has always been, nothing will always be: the future of Heraclitus."[44]

The moment must be dissociated from its content—from events; from what happens or has happened in the instant. What has happened now will never happen again (even if the truth that it has existed remains), but there will always be a new *instant* indefinitely. This means that the world, in a certain way, always begins from scratch, an eternal return to the "starting point."

So what is the result of this reflection? Saying that the world always starts from scratch is something totally different from saying that the world always begins with what has already happened. This is even the opposite. If I admit that whatever I do, I have already done, there is no longer future or past. But if chance is at the heart of reality, things happen here without connection to what happens elsewhere. If everything is linked to everything, the fabric of things is so tight that anything really new is impossible and any initiative is suffocated. The Stoics understood this very well. However, if the fabric of things is loose, lots of causal series independent from each other, new and unexpected, can insert themselves into a reality that is still happening. What I do, I can do *for the first time*. The moment has recovered its meaning, which is to close the past and open the future. At each moment, something is ending, something is beginning, and I am at the beginning. Yet, that applies to everything in the world.

Thus, we can say that the world is not born once and for all, but at each moment we are at the dawn of the world. If eternal recurrence is only the eternal return of the moment, and not the event, that means that there has always been time: time is infinite. Time is not under the control of eternity. For us, who are finite, eternal recurrence of the moment means that at each moment we are given another chance, which can be to completely reevaluate our lives, and to start again, to "recommence." As the eternal recurrence of events signifies non-liberty, the eternal recurrence of the moment, and therefore of creative time, signifies the immensity of freedom.

During the seminar on "Nietzsche" that took place at Royaumont in 1964, Jean Beaufret quoted the following text as signifying not the endless recommencement of what has been, but the return to the beginning, Nietzsche wrote: "I teach you to free yourselves from the eternal flux: the flux does not cease to flow into itself, and it is always anew that you enter this flux that is always the same, always equal to yourselves."[45]

Here is my understanding of this text. We think first of Okéanos, in Homer, whose waters flow back on themselves unceasingly without any source or beginning. The current has no origin. It is always the origin of itself. It has neither an end nor a purpose. It leads to nothing, flows without progressing, and thus remains the same as itself. Whether we enter the river earlier or later, it makes no difference. We always newly enter it as though we had never done so before. We are still so poor, so helpless, and so free, faced with life to be invented each day. "I teach you to free yourselves from the eternal flux." Put another way, the flux does not carry you away; it is you yourself who always newly enter the river, that is to say, who choose life. Each time, you have to overcome the same anguish, without there being at one time or another the slightest progress. If the "recurrence" means eternal recurrence of the same life, what is left for me to do? To sink into despair or assert myself in accordance with the strength I have.

We can imagine that "yes" to always having the same life is the cornerstone of my strength and my love of life. But if I can say "yes" at each moment to every life other than the one that has, in the moment, become only the past, when I alone determine my choice, then I am far from being dependent on the order of the world for what I do. It is the world that depends on what I do; it being understood that here the word *world* changes meaning: in one case, the "world" is the Whole of reality, "Everything"; in the other, the "world" is only one world among many in infinite Nature. Man in Nature is the result of chance. There could have been no mankind. In Epicurus, by the set of innumerable combinations of atoms in infinite time, an organism as complex as man can only be the result of chance, at one time or another. This reassuring consideration is absent in Nietzsche. Man is the result of an absolute chance, and so am I, the man that I am. If God, whose creature I am, exists, a certain definition of my life is fixed by the same principle. If the Whole of reality is a great organism where everything is linked to everything else, my place and my role are also fixed. But there is no Whole. The Real is only a river where erratic blocks that are unaware of each other creep in.

So, having support only from within myself, in my own energy, what am I if not a kind of god? Nietzsche says that the overman is similar to the god of Epicurus. But the overman who defines himself by "yes" to the world as it is, which eternally recurs, is only a fictional being, because the eternal recurrence of the same event is unthinkable, as it abolishes time. The overman which is a reality is the man who, having separated himself from everything that weighed on his freedom without originating from him, can be the only and ultimate decider of himself. He is solitude among other solitudes. Perhaps each one of Epicurus's gods was alone.

Is this really Nietzsche's way of thinking? In any event, that is how I see it—without being able to satisfy myself that it is, as we shall see in the final chapters. My approach is not that of a historian. If we are serious about radically freeing ourselves from God, from the Real as a whole organically linked to the Unity of the Real, we cannot stop at the *amor fati*. Indeed, if wanting *what is* means wanting what cannot not happen, which must happen anyway, where is then the difference between the Christian and Muslim unconditional submission to the divine will? "*Fiat voluntas tua*?" (Will Thy be done?). "Supposing that we say 'yes' at a given moment, at the same time we have said "yes" not only to ourselves but to all of existence."[46]

These words of Nietzsche are only acceptable in the following way: if I say "yes" to the event that is happening to me in this instant. It does not follow that I say "yes" to all events, because the present event is linked to certain events, not to all, but I say "yes" to this event without which there would be no event: existence itself. Each "yes" at each moment of my life is a *yes to life*. However, the expression *amor fati* can be kept in the sense *amor casus* because says Nietzsche, "extreme fatalism is identical to chance and creative activity."[47] It is by the fact of chance that my destiny is always decided, and it is because the future has not already happened and depends on chance and randomness, that I can do what is *new*, that is to say, to create.

IX

MY PATH WITH AND WITHOUT BERGSON

Milestones

Conche shares with Bergson that "the door needs to remain open for numerously different conceptions of man." He does not, however, share Bergson's readiness to use positive science as a model of metaphysics, which leads Bergson to consider the philosopher's life and personality as unimportant. For Conche, they are important and he notes his path has followed a trajectory opposite to Bergson's: the latter began with naturalism and he ended up believing in Christianity, while Conche started with Christianity and ended up believing in Naturalism.

Conche means to find the reason for Bergson's trajectory in the near-absence of the idea of infinity in his thoughts. This absence left vast areas of indeterminacy where there was place for God.

Conche notes, however, that it could have been otherwise. Indeed, he shows that Bergson's "unique thought," the concept of real duration, is incompatible with the idea of God, more precisely with the monotheist affirmation of a God who rules with the Providence he has created. On the contrary: Naturalism, not Theism, is the result of the concept of real duration, according to Conche.

In the end, despite all that they share, Bergson and Conche part mainly due to the different place they give to infinity in their philosophies.

Science and Metaphysics

In *Orientation Philosophique*, the book I wrote about my hesitations, I stated that there is no nature of man. That's to say that one cannot define a person *truly*, a person who would be the ideal man—the model who would prevail at all times and in all places. There exist numerous ways to be "human" and numerous human ideals, each and every one having its time and place of value. Today, one can live in different ways of being human . . . that is to say, choose different human lifestyles, insofar as those ways of life are acceptable within the limits of respect for the morality of human rights, which represent absolute morality, excluding all that is nothing more than a morality of opinion.

Bergson shares the same point of view; he writes, "I believe that the door needs to remain open for numerous different conceptions of man; that many of these conceptions need to be practised here and there; and there is no such thing—in equal affairs—as a unique ideal that is definable in advance once for all man." He adds, "If I dare to present general considerations—they would only refer to the necessity to perceive the moral point of view as essential."[1] This was written in 1935—when morality that desires the respect of the people and individual rights was denied in the name of the alleged "right" of some to rule over all. This point of view is rather old-fashioned and destined for disaster because it is not harmonious with the spirit of the modern world—the reigning spirit since the French Revolution.

Consequently, if mankind is so different, how can they have the same philosophy? Therefore, the philosophical choice is open and no proof or demonstration can turn it into a necessity. Regarding science however, this is different; through the virtue of proof, it imposes itself on all tendencies. One needs to point out Bergson's error in using positive science as a model of metaphysics, even before the beginning of "collaboration,"[2] being susceptible to "Gradual Perfection,"[3] to "indefinite progress"[4] before becoming a true "Positive Science."[5] What an illusion!

This is still the Kantian dream of a "metaphysical future that may present itself as a science." However, if the metaphysical is no science, Kant wonders, "Where does the continuous pride come from?"

Unimportance of the Philosopher's Life?

Given that metaphysics has no right to claim itself as a science; the moment has arrived when it must be accepted that it is something completely different from a science, from *the* science. Due to the role argumentation plays in its method, we can be certain of one thing: art it is not. However, it *is* unceasingly the work of a *creator*—a statement that inevitably leads to the rejection of the logical consequence, of the assimilation of metaphysics and science: the unimportance, regarding Bergson, of the philosopher's personality.[6] Nietzsche's philosophy is not intended to be impersonal. The philosophies that strive to be scientific, strive to be impersonal; but no philosophy that expresses a certain intense thought, an intense life experience or something alive—is impersonal. The life of Spinoza is in *Ethics*, his major work.

Bergson does not wish one to talk about oneself. However, following Montaigne's example, I can't find any reason to be mysterious about myself, as if there were something so precious or so disgraceful that it needs to be hidden! To illuminate how I found my path to philosophy, I would like to compare my own personal story with Bergson's. The first thing that occupied my thoughts was the question of God. I could only find the answer after having solved the other questions first: the question of liberty, the question of the relation between the body and the spirit, the question of life, which, time and time again, proved to bear no relation to the question regarding God. I received a Christian education, and religion has always been a riddle for me. At the age of twenty-five, although he came from a Jewish family background, Bergson was not attached to any particular religious faith. Beginning with Christianity, I personally ended up believing in naturalism; beginning with Spencerian naturalism, Bergson ended up believing in Christianity. Well, the outcome is that I am still at the same level of metaphysics while he is not—if one assumes that "metaphysics" is the discourse on the Whole.

Absence of the Idea of Infinity: Open Door to God?

Christianity teaches us that God, the world, and mankind are all there is. When I had rejected the notion of God, following a rationale similar to that of Ivan Karamazov, my thoughts were still oriented toward the totality of all things. Well, the totality of all things in infinite. Thus, the idea of infinity started to germinate at the heart of all my thoughts. Nevertheless, the idea of infinity is nearly absent in Bergson's thoughts—at least as the most significant thought that preoccupies the philosopher's mind; he writes to N. Söderblom in 1909: "It is the religious problem (with its moral and social implications) that arises to me now."[7] That is more the problem of religion than the problem of "the existence and nature of God," which he states in a letter to J. Chevalier in 1928, having "barely addressed" it at all.[8] Is *The Two Sources of Morality and Religion* a work about metaphysics? In a letter to P. Masson-Oursel in 1932, he writes: "I consider my last work as (to be) a book of sociology."[9] Bergson wanted to "introduce the experience in metaphysics."[10] What experience? His own, or another's? I recognize the necessity of an "experimental" base for metaphysics opposed to the traditional constructions.[11] I founded my rejection of monotheism on my experience regarding unjustifiable harm. However, Bergson seeks the mystical experience, as its writings and narratives express. What can one conclude from this? The mystics have a divine experience—of God as being "transcendent from earth."[12] Either way, if I cannot create an equal experience—furthermore—if I have had a contradicting experience—where does this lead me?

Bergson has not continuously pondered the idea of infinity; with a dissociated reality as background to his thinking, he has attempted, in his own words, "to cut the problems according to natural lines and to study each problem as a single occurrence."[13] For these reasons, his vision of reality holds several vast areas of indeterminacy where there is place for God.

The "Élan Vital" does not allow one to ascend to God, at least not to the "complete" God of monotheism, but it allows one to pronounce the name: "I ascend to an 'Élan Vital.' Without any doubt, this élan erupts from somewhere, but from where? I do not speak about this because—with the resources I possess as the author of 'L'Évolution créatrice'—I do not know anything about this. I have given this cause a name and from the moment I did this, I could do nothing else but give it the name of God. However, if I hold on to the Evolution of Creation, this God is only known as cause x of a finite and imperfect world. Nothing allows us to give it the traditional attributes: in particular, nothing reveals it as being providence."[14]

In my opinion—on the other hand—having erased the idea of a transcendent God, and obliterating it constantly from the first experience renewed every day—I can only ponder on the infinite ensemble of finite objects. For every ensemble, in dispersion, I tried the word *Appearance*, then, considering all ensembles as one, I pronounced the word *Nature*. The "Élan Vital" is derived from somewhere, states Bergson, from a cause and "from the moment I named it, he adds, I could do nothing else but give it the name God." Why not call it "Nature"? Man either comes from beyond him or from below him, or from spiritualism, or naturalism. Bergson discovered the first solution from the moment he considered the liberty of man the "reason for being of our life on earth." It is therefore no huge leap to assume that that kind of liberty is derived from another liberty, and that "creation is at the origin of every world as there is creation in every world created once."[15] This is an aspect of Bergson I would rather ignore, not only from a different and exterior perspective, but starting from another aspect of Bergson, which I accept.

Real Duration: Incompatible with God?

Following Schopenhauer's *einziger Gedanke*, there is one "unique thought" that unites all aspects of a great philosopher's philosophy. If this is true, the "unique thought" of Bergson is obviously the "real duration." In my view, this thought appears to be correct, apart from the fact that I prefer to talk about a universal, real, and unique time that Einstein's theory of relativity does not rule out, and that is—moreover—*given*, that is, accessible to all, in any place and at any time.

So, what is the meaning of "real duration," if not "the continuous creation of unforeseeable novelty which seems to be going on in the universe"?[16] Bergson writes further, "As far as I am concerned, I feel I am experiencing it constantly. No matter how I try to imagine in detail what is going to happen to me, still how inadequate, how abstract and stilted is the thing I have imagined in comparison to what actually happens! The realization brings along with it an unforeseeable nothing which changes everything."[17] This never-ending novelty—brought to us by every passing minute of our lives—is also what I am experiencing—with the possibility—at every moment—to change the course of events by decision. I could say, as does Bergson, that "perfection is neither a state nor a thing, but a continuous creation"[18]—only I would replace "perfection" with "reality."

So then, where do we go from here? Obviously, the future is unpredictable; nobody, not even a God, can anticipate it. Epicurus was already ruminating on these thoughts. Bergson recognizes that "God," the cause of the "Élan Vital," is nothing but "the cause of a finite and imperfect world" and that nothing suggests that we should "allow him traditional attributes." However, he adds, albeit wrongly, "The ideas raised in 'L'Evolution Créatrice' have nothing incompatible with the affirmation of a God that I allow myself to name 'complete,' that God to whom people pray."[19] The concept of "real duration" is, on the contrary, incompatible with the monotheist affirmation of a God who rules with the Providence he has created. That same God does not hold the "knowledge of vision" (*scientia visionis*). Saint Thomas Aquinas wrote: "God, in his eternity, knows all that is or could be in whatever time. Therefore if we think something exists at a certain given moment, it is necessary to add that God has known this eternally."[20] In this way, one accepts the ineffectiveness of Ontological Time, which is exactly the opposite of Bergson's idea. Thanking Louis Lavelle—who has sent him his book *De l'Acte*, in which God is depicted as an absolute Self and timeless Act, Bergson nevertheless subtly contradicts him: "[I wonder] if Time has no superior reality than what you assume."[21]

Certainly! Because Time is the essence of reality, what we call "temporalism": "If I insist on the perception of "real duration," Bergson writes to O. Lovejoy, "it is because of the condition sine qua non regarding the acceptance of 'temporalism' that I find in it." This has "already tried to form itself if only with Heraclitus," he adds.[22]

Where Bergson Parts with Heraclitus

What difference is there then with the author of *panta rhei* (everything passes)? Bergson accepts Heraclitism but assumes it to be incomplete: "It does not suffice to consider the change and the flow; one needs to truly see them,"[23] that is to say, reality must be seen as a continuous creation. Is he correct in reproaching Heraclitus for not having sought to "truly" see the change? "One does not descend twice in the same flow"—those that are tomorrow's flows, one cannot know them now. The future cannot be foreseen. There is, in the universe, for Heraclitus, a "continuous creation of unpredictable new things." Moreover, it is exclusive and of the "eternal return." However, this has not been stated very clearly. What differentiates Heraclitus from Bergson is that he trembles at the idea of infinity. For the "Élan Vital," there is the need for "a cause x." Why is this? Based on the *anankè stènai* of Aristotle perhaps? It is more philosophical, that is to say less theological and more rational, to admit that indefinite continuous creation exists *a parte ante* and *a parte post*. This forms the origin of the "Élan Vital." It is not a cause, but already an undefined creativity. What is this creator, "God," who cannot see in advance what he will create, as a painter cannot see his painting, nor a poet sing, read, or perform his poem? Because we have assumed that Time was the creator and was not there for nothing. This "God"—infinitely fertile, but also blind—cannot be anything other than Nature. Naturalism, not Theism, is the result of the "unique thought" of Bergson.

What We Share and What Divides Us

Regarding what precedes, Bergson and I have completely diverse thoughts. Like him, I am convinced, though what remains, that the philosopher does not need to have "any other worry than that one of the truth"[24]; that there need not to be, in his eyes, "any other source of truth than experience and reasoning"[25]; that "the spirit of simplicity is the trademark of a true philosopher"[26]; that the time of systems is gone[27]; and in general, that the philosopher does not need to "construct," but needs to "see"; that it is not about searching, in metaphysics, for the kind of certainty that can be demanded of the "rigorous science"[28]; that the metaphysical discourse can use metaphors as well as concepts, to suggest as well as to express.[29] On the contrary, I am not more convinced than Bergson of the "*unity* of nature,"[30] although we do not only divide it into "two different regions,"[31] but rather into an infinity of regions.

This idea of infinity revives our differences. Certainly, one needs "to search for the *immediately given*."[32] However; this is not "immediately" given, because one has to "search" for it, so, one needs to return to the "crude, immediate experience free of settings in which the actions oblige us to let it enter."[33] Therefore, one needs to emerge from the natural attitude that implies a limited attention, merely an application of the mind to what has sense regarding the acting subject, and therefore a rejection of the infinity that would erase the effect. It is true that, in *Matière et Mémoire*, Bergson confronts himself with the ensemble of all images: "[T]his ensemble," he says, "I name the universe."[34] However; he was careful to say "infinity," and in this regard he retains something of the natural attitude. Nevertheless, it is always at the center of the omnipresent infinity, albeit in the background, that the clarity of our limited interests is revealed.

X

WITH PASCAL AND WITHOUT HIM

Milestones

Contrary to other chapters, "without him" in this chapter's title does not imply criticism against Pascal but Conche's self-admission that he would be inept at doing so. In this chapter, he successively comments on Pascal's three orders of infinity.

First, infinity in the order of the "bodies" (stars, the earth, kingdoms, cities, living creatures . . .), in Nature, enables man to estimate things and himself according to their true proportion. In this infinity, the law of the greater force over the lesser prevails. Force and power are the pillars of the greatness of flesh, of "those great in carnal sense," who are nearer to animals than to "people of mind."

Second, infinity in the order of the mind means infinity in the domain of knowledge, which, thanks to the senses and reason, without respect for authority, progresses indefinitely. Indeed, infinity in Nature reduces us to points in space, moments in time, yet we are equal to it through thought which is like an opening onto infinity. Nature, although it likes to hide, also allows itself to be known, thereby posing an infinite task to human reason and giving it complete freedom to extend itself indefinitely—as are the ideas of knowledge and freedom inextricably linked. This leads to a double infinity: on one hand, free and impersonal, "scientific" reason helps us to know Nature with its laws and its habits, as well as to master its functions with formulae, though we never reach complete intellectual satisfaction. The task is infinite and the progress of knowledge limitless. On the other hand, the same Nature, unique, not to say one, explodes through philosophies or the lives of each living creature, into a multiplicity of innumerable and infinite worlds. As such, all human beings are self-creators by right, having within themselves the means to forge their own interpretation of the world and having a vocation to become philosophers.

Third, infinity in the order of "charity," which Conche calls love, also unravels a double infinity: love is itself infinite, and it reveals the infinite to us. It is itself infinite by bringing an infinite freedom with regard to all the worries of social or material life. Love is deliverance from the world and the joy of deliverance. Then, there is the joy of loving itself and the need "to know everything" about the one whom we love which reveals to us infinity in two ways. First, because when questioned indefinitely, the one we love will always have more to say as we not only want the details, but the details of the details. And second, being alive, the one we love is in motion, always changing. This accomplished infinity makes for the perfection of love. But is such infinity ever really accomplished? Conche remarks that every love is singular and that the joy of loving encompasses the hope of happiness, though it is not happiness itself. Happiness appears when one joy responds to another. But since there is no method to love or to be loved, happiness just happens. And since happiness is the meaning of life, the meaning of life happens to life. The appearance of love between singular people, who are unique and irreplaceable, is therefore neither in the "plan" of Nature nor in any plan: rather, it is a sublime creation of Nature, the immanent poet, continuously improvising. Nature is hereby not contradicted, but transcended.

Finally, Conche remarks that time may lead passionate love to evolve into passionate affection but both remain infinite. While the infinity of passionate love is without exterior, in the sense of enclosing the lovers, the infinity of passionate affection is also without exterior but in the sense that it extends to the exterior, to every gesture, every word, and every activity. There is nothing that, when touched by the loving heart, does not have a sort of inherent joy.

The Three Orders of Infinity

Let it be understood that in writing "and without him," I do not intend to imply my advantage, rather my ineptitude. Being one who has read him so much, I can only write: "It is I myself I portray"—and "*myself only.*" I certainly don't mean to direct any criticism against one whom I have admired, or I should say, venerated. During my adolescent years, when, with a copy of *Les Pensées* in hand, I would walk the Corrèze woods of the Limousin in solitude, hoping to retain only the truest and deepest of the most moving or sublime thoughts.

There is one segment in *Les Pensées* that holds the key to unlocking what it is I wish to explain. This refers to the "three orders"[1] of infinity:

- Infinity in the order of "bodies"—Nature;
- Infinity in the order of the "mind"—Freedom;
- Infinity in the order of what Pascal calls "Charity" and I call "Love."

Yet these are "three orders differing in kind": "All bodies, the firmament, the stars, the earth, and its kingdoms are not worth the lowest of minds. For it knows all of them, and itself, and bodies know nothing. All bodies together, and all minds together, and all their products are not worth the least impulse of charity. That is of an infinitely higher order."

1. Infinity in the Order of "Bodies": Enabling Man to Estimate Things According to Their True Proportion

The infinity of the first order is depicted for us in the famous passage "on the two infinities."[3] Moreover, it will be sufficient for me to consider the magnitude of infinity, where the truest sense of what Nature actually is reveals itself. It is useful to compare the first draft of this passage with the final edition.

Pascal's mind is at first focused on man and the earth, and then with enthusiasm it moves on to immensity. The first heading of the fragment, "Man's *incapacity*," was intended to curb human pride; it is subsequently amended to "Man's *disproportion*." In addition, the word *disproportion* appeals directly to the geometrician's mind, as it encompasses the idea of "measure"—"disproportion of measure," as Montaigne wrote,[4] it is now Nature itself that puts man in his miniscule place. First, the "little cell in which he finds himself wedged" is the earth, from where he observes a "universe that appears to be of such astonishing immensity, whereas it is merely an imperceptible atom in the grand scheme of things." But then, it is the universe itself that becomes the little cell. Pascal writes:

> Let man . . . regard himself as lost in this remote corner of Nature; and from the little cell in which he finds himself lodged, I mean the universe, let him estimate at their true value the earth, the kingdoms, the cities and himself.

On two occasions he emphasises the word *infinite*; compare how the sentence below changes: "We may enlarge our conceptions; we only produce atoms in comparison with the reality of this infinite sphere. It is an amazing sphere the centre of which is everywhere, the circumference nowhere." And: "We may enlarge our conceptions beyond all imaginable space; we only produce atoms in comparison with the reality of things. It is an infinite sphere, the centre of which is everywhere, the circumference nowhere."[5]

For the geometrician, the expression "infinite sphere," with its inherent contradiction, poses a challenge to understanding and is infinitely more striking than the expression "infinite vastness," which merely stokes the imagination.

Finally, Pascal asks us: "What is man in Nature?" but corrects himself with: "What is man in the Infinite?"—Because Nature is the infinite in flesh and bone, infinity in action.

Pascal makes explicit, but doesn't add anything to, what can already be found in Montaigne, although implicit. Rather, he abstracts. Let us reread the following passage, already quoted in chapter VI:

> But whoever considers as in a painting the great picture of our mother Nature in her full majesty; whoever reads such universal and constant variety in her face; whoever finds himself there, and not merely himself, but a whole kingdom, as a dot made with a very fine brush; that man alone estimates things according to their true proportions. This great world, which some multiply further as being only a species under one genus, is the mirror in which we must look at ourselves to recognize ourselves from the proper angle.[6]

With regard to the idea, Pascal dilutes this passage, because the infinity he holds on to is only infinite in scale, not infinite in diversity and variety. He develops the same visionary image implicit in Montaigne. He positions himself in the sun, which he describes as the "vast circle" and from there, sees the earth as a point—this is in the first draft. However, he corrects this first wording to take the contrasting step of going from the earth to the sun and accommodating the progression: the earth, the sun's orbit, the stellar orbit, the vastness of space, thus stimulating the imagination and suggesting the opening out to infinity.

From this infinity, thought, while pondering the universe, sees it as a "cell." We find the idea in Montaigne: "You see only the order and government of this little cave you dwell in, at least if you do see it. His divinity has infinite jurisdiction beyond; this part is nothing in comparison with the whole: 'The sky, the land, the sea, and all are nothing to the universal all' said Lucretius.[7] It is a municipal law that you allege; you do not know what the universal law is."[8]

This "great world," in the scheme of things, infinity in the vastness of Nature, is only a "cave"; Pascal calls it a "cell." He also read the verses of Lucretius that Montaigne is citing; both of them envision the innumerable worlds of Epicurus, which Pascal calls "universe," and his universe is only one of those worlds—something akin to today's "Big Bang's Universe." In the wider universe there would be infinity of such universes. Furthermore, there is no difference between the word *universe* that Pascal prefers and the word *world* that Montaigne chooses, other than the fact that Pascal uses the expression "infinity of universes."[9] He happens to have written "world" in an earlier draft.[10]

The Epicureans recognize in Nature an infinite diversity and variety, whether it concerns species, individuals, or aspects of the world. "There is no calf," said Lucretius, "that is not recognised by its mother, no grains of wheat or shellfish that are indiscernible." This theme can also be found among the Stoics and Montaigne. Pascal disregards it here, but elsewhere he takes up the idea again and gives as an example two grapes which can never be the same:

> Diversity is so great that all the tones of voice, ways of walking, coughing, blowing one's nose, sneezing [are different]. We distinguish vines by their fruit, and call them from Condrieu, or from Desargues, and from such and such a stock.[11] Is that all? Has a vine ever produced two identical bunches, and have two bunches of grapes ever been alike?[12] It is not possible for two individuals to be the same. Each individual, by the fact of being different from all others, encompasses infinity. Nature, which is an infinite collection of individuals wherein each one encompasses infinity, is outside the range of this Concept. It is the unique and absolute Individual which can only offer itself to us through empirical intuition.

Infinity in Nature is infinity in the order of "bodies," where Pascal allocates their position in opposition to "minds." It is therefore necessary to think not only of material bodies, but also living ones, and even of those men that Pascal calls "those great in a carnal sense." What sort of man is he referring to? "Kings," "rich men," and "captains" top his list, but we might ask him, what is it that makes them great? In Nature the law of the greater force over the lesser prevails, of the strongest over the weakest. Force and power are the pillars of the greatness of flesh. "Those great in a carnal sense" know only force.

Napoleon knew them well; in 1806 he wrote to his brother Joseph commenting that "[m]en are low, grovelling before force alone." Pascal adds to this by writing: "All bodies . . . are not equal to the simplest mind," and "those great in a carnal sense" are at the bottom of the value scale. Certainly, men are equal under law, but how unequal in value. Let us recall the words of Montaigne: "Plutarch says somewhere that he does not find so much difference between one animal and another as he does between one man and another. He is taking about the capacity of the soul and the inward qualities. In truth, I find Epaminondas, as I imagine him, so remote from some men I know—I mean, men capable of common sense—that I would willingly outdo Plutarch and say that there is more distance from a given man to a given man than from a given man to a given animal."[13]

In Pascal's view, the "great in a carnal sense" are nearer to animals than to "people of mind." The law of force reigns among the "great in a carnal sense." Force is what they admire, what they respect, and what they covet. That is their Nature. In this they are of Nature, and the history of men, insofar as they make it, is a natural one. So, is it not necessary then to place them below animals? For, "what in animals is nature, we call in man wretchedness; by which we recognise that, his nature being now like that of animals, he has fallen from a better nature which once was his."[14]

Pascal wants an ideal man, someone who is "upstanding," thus making it possible to build hope for one who in his current form, is "properly *omne animal*."[15]

We only have "factual" men, and what makes them lesser than animals is that they employ a perverse and malicious form of force we know as violence. The animal uses force by its natural means, it is never violent but man acting "great in a carnal sense," makes an ignoble and violent use of force.

2. Infinity in the Order of the Mind: Enabling Man to Be His World's Self-Creator

Let us now address the second order of infinity where the "people of mind" achieve their "greatness," these people who, if measured by their force, are astonishingly weak.

Man, as a mind or a thinking being, "is but a reed, the feeblest thing in Nature, but he is a thinking reed. The entire universe need not arm itself to crush him. A vapour, a drop of water will suffice. But, if the universe were to crush him, man would still be nobler than that which killed him, because he knows that he dies"[16]

Let us reread a sentence from fragment 339,[17] quoted above: "All bodies, the firmament, the stars, the earth and its kingdoms are not worth the lowest of minds; for mind knows all these and itself; and bodies know nothing." Infinity in the order of the mind will therefore be infinity in the domain of knowledge. Knowledge, thanks to the senses and to reason, without respect for authority, progresses indefinitely.

Nature is infinite. This infinity reduces me to a point in space, a moment in time. Yet I am equal to it through thought, not in this sense that I have an "idea" of the infinite, as Descartes said we have of God, but in the sense that thought is like an opening onto infinity—which is no other than Nature offering itself to the consciousness and reason of man. Pascal says "By space the universe encompasses and swallows me up like an atom; by thought I comprehend it."[18] Yet as soon as I think or "understand" the universe or Nature, I think of them as *to be known*.

Pascal writes "Nature always begins the same things again."[19] However, this very law of constantly restarting is characterized in the infinite according to phenomena and beings. Let us consider: "A town, a village, is from afar a town and a village. But, as we draw near, there are houses, trees, tiles, leaves, grass, ants, limbs of ants, ad infinitum. All this is contained under the name of a 'country-place.' "[20]

Yet from one day to the next, as the hours and minutes elapse, there is nothing that does not move, and at first, the play of light and shadow on the trees and on the roofs of the houses; all things are in variation. Light and shadow depend on the sun and it in turn depends on the stars. Reason gives birth to laws, habits of Nature, a universal order, and conceives Nature as "always beginning the same things again" from itself and its immanent ability for self-organization.

Not only does Nature deploy itself in its infinity for thought, but it offers itself to be known, it does not make a mystery of itself for those who choose the right method, which is simply rational. Since natural subjects of study "fall under meaning or under reason," "only reason alone has the ability to know them."[21]

Such subjects, all those that concern Nature, are "placed in proportion within the mind's range," that is to say, to its capacity to resolve problems.

Also, "it finds complete freedom to expand itself; its inexhaustible fertility produces continually, and its inventions can all be together without end and without interruption."[22] Nature, as Heraclitus said, "likes to hide itself"[23] but also allows itself to be known; it poses an infinite task to human reason. That reason carries infinity within itself; Pascal recognized this and said as much before Kant or Husserl entered the scene. He places man's reasoning and the instinct of animals in parallel, and marks the difference, which is from the finite to the infinite, because "the effects of reasoning increase unceasingly, while Instinct remains always in the same state."[24] Nature keeps animals "in an order of perfection that is limited": "It is not the same for man, who is produced only for infinity."[25] Man as a reasoning being, not a being of instinct, accomplishes his vocation under the Idea of knowledge.

"Man," as he is understood, is the universal man, who fulfills his vocation through the collaboration of all the "people of mind." The early knowledge that we owe to the ancient philosophers served as "stages" to those that followed, and thanks to the memory of knowledge, progress is continuous: "Not only does each man advance from day to day in the sciences, but all men together find a continual progress in them as the universe ages, because the same thing happens in the succession of men as in the different ages of an individual, in such a way that the continuation of men, during the course of so many centuries, must be considered as a single man who still exists and learns continually."[26]

There is violent history, forever enacted by men whom Pascal considers to be "those great in a carnal sense," and which consists of wars, conquests, revenge, pillaging, destruction, treachery, etc., contemporaneous with the reign of false values and unhealthy hierarchies. Then there are, through another more intelligent history, the likes of Copernicus who takes up and continues the work of Ptolemy, and Pascal that of Archimedes. The "people of mind" must ignore those of the violent order, just as Archimedes ignored the soldier who killed him.

There was a time when the Idea of knowledge could have been called "Idea of philosophy," as philosophy, which had knowledge of the totality of things in view, encompassed all the sciences. That time has finished. Philosophy has dissociated itself from the sciences and Knowledge has been replaced by interpretation—even though the quest remains unfinished. Montaigne said: "Who does not see that I have taken a road along which I shall go without stopping and without effort, as long as there is ink and paper in the world?"[27]

Montaigne said and wrote what seemed, for him, to be *true*. As long as the truth of knowledge retains the character of necessity, the truth of interpretation holds the character of contingency. Philosophies are only interpretations of reality. The physical system of Descartes is false; he does not enable us to know Nature: it is only "fictional work," said Pascal.[28]

Nevertheless, Descartes believed it was true. In any event, Leibniz believed the truth to be something else; and Hegel, something else again: a contingency of truths. Their mistake was not to say what seemed true to them, because it was their right, but to present their truth as a truth of certainty. They misunderstood the Nature of knowledge, which is not to accept its limit, because we will never know everything.

Violent history is criss-crossed with intelligent history, the work of "people of mind" dedicated to knowledge. Philosophers, by putting aside the part of them that also makes them learned, will also resort to interpretation. Do the interpretations of reality which are philosophies constitute history? For there to be "history," there needs to be a link between facts. The conversion of the king of Navarre to Catholicism assured his place on the throne of France. Aristotle, as much as Archimedes, made possible Galileo. But such a link of condition to the conditioned only exists between certain philosophies—such as those emanating from Descartes or Kant—but not between all. There are therefore various histories of philosophy, always partial and not just one. Henri of Navarre was likely to have been privy to the prevalent mind-set in Paris and accordingly took it into account, and Galileo must have studied Archimedes and Aristotle. But has Bergson read Hegel? Has he read Nietzsche? Everything is, in his case, different from theirs. It can be said that as there have been violent histories on earth, so too have scientific ages blossomed periodically—Greek science, or Chinese, or Indian, etc. There was nothing incompatible to the unification of these eras; indeed, they tended in that direction but differences in interpretation prevented them from being merged into one.

Reason is unequally free, that is to say liberated of everything that influences judgment to give it a particular slant, such as psychological motivations, educational and social pressures, and preconceived ideas—what we call "prejudices," and which do not allow the mind to awaken to the only truth. The condition of knowledge and its progress resides in its perfect freedom to perceive well and judge ably. Thus, the "Idea of Knowledge" only exists by means of the "Idea of Freedom," one and the other progressing to infinity. In order for there to be evolution in knowledge, what is established must not be by means of chains but by stages, so that the fields of knowledge and freedom are one and the same. In the subjects that "are proportioned within reach of the mind" as far as what happens in Nature is concerned, Pascal says the mind "finds complete freedom to extend itself" (text quoted above). Descartes opposes "will" and "understanding," recognizing infinity by extension only to will or freedom, as ability to apply itself to all possible subjects. But if knowledge is always strongly limited, it covers by right all that can be known. It is a totality that cannot be calculated because it is infinite, like Nature. Thus, the Idea of knowledge and the Idea of freedom are inextricably linked.

Reason is free in Galileo and in Newton as scientists, and grants us access to knowledge; it is free also in the case of Descartes the geometrician or Pascal the physicist. It is, however, preoccupied in the case of Descartes the metaphysician, who, instead of weighing things without bias, dispenses with an idea of God that comes to him from elsewhere, namely, his contingent Christian education; like the idea itself that he falsely wants to present to us as necessary.

Interpretations of what is real are false when presented not as interpretations, but as knowledge; that is what systems are. "Hegelianism is to my eyes completely false," says Bergson.[29] It would be impossible for him to say if this system brought real knowledge, or if it were something that should necessarily be taken into account. The character of falseness disappears by reflection, which resolves the system in interpretation. "I put forward formless and unresolved notions," said Montaigne.[30] True philosophy has no scientific pretentions and declares its subjective element. Reason is no longer pure reason, purely available for truth. It is argued reason, governed by the convictions of philosophy, evident *in fact* perhaps for itself, but *by right* not for itself only. Is it not then unfree, being governed by a psychological causality? But here, it must be said, with Bergson: "Either freedom is just an empty word or it is itself the psychological causality"[31]—a causality that is quite different from physical causality, because it is the creator. Reason is not free on its own, but it is free through the personality that uses it, and being through the self, is in essence freedom itself. Of course, human beings are not, *in fact*, "personalities" in this sense; they are only so *by right*. All human beings are self-creators by right, having within themselves the means to forge their own interpretation of the world, and having a vocation, as a human, to become philosophers and accomplish themselves as such. However, only philosophers per se, who are deserving of the name and title, serve the purpose of man, which is thinking about the world, and, in this way, not leaving the world as it was.

The fact that philosophers exist does not go unnoticed in the world, but rather affects the world down to its very being (if it is true that the world is made only of "appearances," as we saw, with Pyrrho, in chapter II, "Presence of the Infinite: Plato and Science in Opposition to the Infinite").

Thus, on one hand, free and impersonal reason help us to know Nature in its laws and habits, and to master its functions with formulae, though we never reach complete intellectual satisfaction, so that the task facing us is infinite, but so also is the progress of knowledge, because it is limitless. On the other hand, this same Nature, unique, not to say one, explodes into a multiplicity of innumerable and infinite worlds, whether it concerns worlds that are simply lived, or worlds that are thought, and thought rather by concepts or metaphors, or even by pencil sketches or splashes of color.

3. Infinity in the Order of Love: Enabling Man to Open Up to Infinity

Beyond the concept of metaphors, philosophy or poetry and the infinities that are discovered through them, there is infinity of another order: not that of the mind and intelligence, but of the heart because "of all the bodies and spirits, we would not know how to produce a single act of real charity," which is "of another, supernatural order." Infinity is that next to which the finite counts for nothing, is nothing. Yet, charity has this power of invalidation which belongs to infinity: "If I have the gift of prophesy, understanding all the mysteries there are, and knowing everything, and if I have faith in all its fullness, to move mountains, but without love, then I am nothing at all. If I give away all that I possess, piece by piece, and if I even let them take my body to burn it, but I am without love, it will do me no good whatever."[32]

So speaks the Apostle of the pagans. "Charity" (*agape*) which he has in mind is the virtue by which the believer loves God, above all else, for Himself, and his neighbour as himself for the love of God.

Naturally, charity finds itself somehow made *finite*, if it is calculated, such as charity as "alchemy" which Yves de Paris speaks of: "The Christian who is indifferent [to riches] gives with pleasure that which will soon be useless to him and that he will for eternity wish he had been generous with, which is worth treasure to him in heaven and gives him the grace of God. In this, charity is as a marvellous alchemy, which transforms an earth into a sun, something indifferent into a necessary good, a matter of corruption into a subject of piety and glory."[33]

However, charity is the "bond of perfection."[34] Yet this perfection of charity, that is to say the love of God, is compromised if feelings of hope and fear reveal the believer's introspection. If he believes in Heaven and Hell then his love is not pure. That is why the bishop Jean-Pierre Camus, disciple of Francois de Sales, depicts Charity as destroying Paradise and Hell. He imagines it as a woman carrying a jug of water in one hand and a flaming torch in the other: "With this torch, she says, 'I want to set fire to Heaven and reduce it so much to ashes that it will never be spoken of again; and, pouring this water on the flames of Hell, I plan to extinguish them; so that henceforth God will be loved and served for the love of himself and in a way that is so pure and disinterested that it is no longer the fear of Hell that chiefly removes us from sin forever, and that we devote ourselves to good works without making of our last and sovereign aim reward alone.' "[35]

It is difficult, nay impossible, forgetting oneself, to be forgotten in the love of God. The Evangelist himself does not present charity as infinite: "Give alms in secret; and your father who sees in secret, will return them to you"[36]; "If you forgive others their transgressions, your heavenly father will forgive you"[37]; "Judge not and thou shalt not be judged"[38]; etc. By the "if . . . then," charity finds itself made finite.

Let us see if the infiniteness of love is easier to find in the case of human love. It is possible, because you love a being of flesh and blood, who can be seen, who lives, who speaks to us, while the believer has no representation of God—only writings and words. Also the love of the Christian is focused on Jesus Christ, or, for simple people, on the Virgin Mary, of whom images are made. The spirit of calculation prevents charity (*agapè*) from being perfect. It also prevents human love (*erôs*) to reach perfection. Only the elite of believers are capable of pure love.

According to troubadours, the singers of courtly love, true love is only possible between such elite personalities. The absolute gratuitousness of love presupposes inner nobility, which is the prerogative of the best.

Ardent love wraps a double infinity: it is itself infinite, and it reveals the infinite to us. It is in itself infinite because all that mattered for us up until then—material interests, careers, the opinions of others, social success, "worldly" pleasures or others, laws and rules, political preoccupations or commitments, scientific or philosophical quests for the truth, etc.—losing all importance, to the point where success or failure leaves us indifferent. In that, love brings an infinite freedom with regard to all the worries of social or material life. One is released from what was causing worry, vague fear, or anguish. Love is deliverance from the world and the joy of deliverance. It seems that we are reborn in a rejuvenated world where false values have been swept away. The troubadours sang of joy, the "joy of love." Of course, at first it is a complex joy: to no longer live in the day-to-day world of financial difficulties, constraints, problems, worries, modest hopes, little pleasures, and little joys requires major adjustments.

It is joy that is given by this new freedom that I have just spoken about. Then, there is the joy of loving itself, as if a wondrous new horizon suddenly presented itself to us. We feel, even when we had a vague feeling of sadness in us, full of vitality, exuding new confidence and markedly more generous, as if we had become better people. Certainly, there is suffering, if love, by the "cruelty" of the woman, remains unsatisfied, yet this rapturous joy and intense suffering, hand in hand, make up the passionate life of love. The joy of loving is the joy of feeling utterly alive. Finally, another element of joy is the bliss due to the delight of gazing at our loved one: her smile, her simplicity, her grace, her beauty; because we cannot love without being led to say, "How beautiful you are!" (Naturally, I have chosen the feminine from my masculine standpoint; I could have supposed the opposite.)

Yet, we also feel the need "to know everything" about the one we love, and here, during this profound wanting, what reveals itself to us is indeed infinity. Moreover, everything we will learn from this, we are already inclined to find admirable. Because without doubt, our discoveries, while perhaps quite banal, appear as the opposite of banality owing to the cross-valuation brought about by love. Against a backdrop of general monotony, something bright always shines where she is concerned.

Ordinarily, we do not take an interest in the private lives or backgrounds of others we meet and with whom we form relationships. I have friends I see occasionally, but couldn't say if they are married, have children, etc. In my village, this would be the case with "the" baker, "the" butcher, or "the" neighbor, etc. They have proper names, but whose significance remains abstract, grouping only some characteristics: "likeable," "of a certain age," etc. When it comes to the person one loves, everything changes. All our attention is focused on her; it knows only her. By herself, she erases the rest of the world: love is therefore infinity. Once she was only one individual among a multitude of others in the world, now she is truly quite a world in herself, because she seems inexhaustible to us. We ask her: "Please, tell me about *you*." She begins with her childhood, her first steps, the first words she heard and the first smiles—all those things she can hardly remember, to our regret. Then, she talks about books, school, games, holidays, studies, encounters, and suddenly the horizon begins to expand. She speaks and we are riveted; we hope she never stops. We want to hear about her most subtle and most fleeting impressions, her most vivid and pure emotions, and her reactions to things and events. We are faced with a double infinity. First, because when questioned indefinitely, she—the one we love—will always have more to say because we want not only the details, but details of the details. Then, because, being alive, she is in motion, unceasingly adding to what she is; but as a painter or a poet will add, that is to say in a way that would be predictable even for them, because life is like a poem. The one who is loved, and who loves the questioner, can say—or force herself to say—what she is, what she feels, what she has been, what she has felt, but she cannot say what she will be, or even, from one moment to the next, what she is going to be. Perhaps this is something she will discover at the same time we do. This is why love is not without some anguish, relative to the way the loved one might change unpredictably.

The accomplished infinity makes for the perfection of love. But is such infinity ever really accomplished? The book of Tristan and Iseult can give an idea of such accomplishment, but what about beyond that legend? Love does not hold to the qualities of the lovers—to the courage of Tristan and the beauty of Iseult—but to Tristan and Iseult as singular.

It is well established that love does not depend on the qualities of the loved one, even if these qualities have been able to create passion. It overrides qualities and faults and reveals a singularity which, by virtue of the fact that it reduces the role of qualities and faults to nothing, is infinity.

In the case of Tristan and Iseult, this infinity also nullifies all that is material attachment and rational will, but also what is promise, duty, religion, apprehension about Heaven, Hell, and eternal salvation. Love that is not true love can never reach this point. I have been able to love—and why might I not yet love again? But this love, while truly passionate, was never unlimited. To the one I love, I could bequeath all my worldly goods: my house, my books—and, in my "possessions" I include my very life, which is something that I have, not what I am. However, I could never renounce the philosophical quest for truth, because that is the depth of my very being, and there is some contradiction in saying that I could renounce *myself*. The one who is a self-appointed philosopher is also the one who is in love with Patricia, Priscilla, or anyone who comes his way. That is my affirmative singular essence. Undoubtedly, in the incessant questioning on the subject of the loved one, there is a search for truth concerning what she is, or of the truth that she is, just as when the truth concerned is that of all the reality of Nature. So to say that my love finds its limitations in my own being, is to say that it finds its limitation in what is the very principle and radical source of this love.

Even if my love is nowhere near platonic, I am a philosopher in my manner of loving.

Thus everyone has, without doubt, his or her singular manner of loving. The joy of loving encompasses the hope of happiness, but it is not happiness. Happiness appears when one joy responds to another. There are the little joys of the present life and the happiness of the retired person in love with his garden, but the simple sweetness of living is not Happiness with a capital "H." There is philosophical happiness, but which is only serenity, "absence of troubles" (*ataraxia*), without the intensity that makes for great Happiness. The condition of happiness, of what really deserves this name (I always mentally add a capital letter), is love. The only happiness for man is that of the loved woman. But where does the fact of loving or being loved come from? It depends on chance or fate. There is no method to loving or being loved. Happiness cannot be projected, wanted, sought after, or decided; it happens. Yet, happiness is the meaning of life, for every life.

Thus the meaning of life happens to life.

In the absence of this meaning occurring, one can certainly seek to give meaning to one's life by searching for that in whatever way it can be achieved. Such is the case for the philosopher in his or her quest for truth. If one has to, one can philosophize alone, but we cannot be happy by ourselves.

I speak about the "loved woman." I do not deny that love, and not only friendly love, but even passionate love can exist between people of the same sex. But such a love is not in the Nature of things and its significance stops at the human level. In the love of a man or a woman, it is Nature itself which accomplishes its gesture of self-affirmation and self-creation. What shocks, however, is that love does not content itself with generality. The creative embrace unites this man with that woman. So only, beyond pleasure, the joy of the mind is the joy of the body, as it enters the body and kindles a fire. Sexuality only requires generality, as Lucretius wished, but is sublimated in love. What does Nature intend by this sublimation, which, without doubt, is not required for the perpetuation of the species? Nature does not "want" anything. The appearance of passionate love between singular people who are unique and irreplaceable, was neither in the "plan" of Nature nor in any plan. It is something that nobody, neither

God nor man, could predict. It is a sublime creation of the immanent poet. Nature is not contradicted but transcended.

On his death bed, Paul Valéry sighs "nothing," "nothing," and "nothing." He knows well however, that infinity of reality surrounds him: and that in the immensity there's a multitude of material things, a multitude of living things, and billions of human beings. How can all of that be "nothing," if it is not the case, as Pascal says, that "all bodies together and all minds together" are nothing with regard to what is of an "infinitely higher order," which he calls "charity" and I call "love"? If Valéry had his Iseult at his bedside, different from every other thing (apart from everything else), he would not have said "nothing," having in real presence this infinity, the nostalgia of which made him say "nothing." I understand the joy of the Christian who has faith in the real presence of Christ and his Eucharist. The Breton Iseult was blonde like the one Tristan had left (behind) in Cornwall. What makes it possible to see between them the difference between nothing and infinity? No difference is visible to human eyes without illumination: the other Iseult may be prettier than the real Iseult, be better-natured, etc. Only faith can discern the unique unspeakable under the appearance that is perhaps banal. Does not everyone have his Iseult to search for in the dark? What is life without that, without this need that nothing finite can satisfy, and this hope of meeting the other human being, or the human god, through whom supreme happiness and supreme peace will come?

I don't mean to say that each individual in the world has some particular human destined solely for them. Nothing of the sort: nobody is destined for "that" special somebody. Everything is merely improvisation. There is chance, encounter, looks, words exchanged, and an emotion different from all the others. This emotion is not love; it is only the spark yet to become the inferno. For the fire to "ignite" there needs to be, on both sides of the relationship, a "stark soul"—"the wisest and the best," according to Heraclitus, and who recognize each other, he says, with the "radiance of the look."[39] Stark, the soul is light, not weighed down by calculation or desire. When the fire has "ignited," we have not two fires, but only the one, because it is off each other that they feed. Such is passionate love, a spontaneous creation of Nature, by which it is no longer Nature but "super Nature" and freedom.

Tristan and Iseult are young, very young. Passionate love whose paradigm they provide us with belongs to youth. Is that to say that the later ages must make do with the envy of youth? Poets—who are not necessarily profound—may say this and believe it, as did Mimnermus:

> But what life would there be, what joy, without golden Aphrodite? May I die when I be no more concerned with secret love and assuasive gifts and the bed, such things as are the very flowers of youth, pleasant alike to man and woman. And when dolorous Age cometh, that maketh a man both foul without and evil within, ill cares do wear and wear his heart, he hath no more the joy of looking on the sunlight, to children he is hateful, to women contemptible, so grievous hath God made Age.[40]

That the "flowers of youth" be desirable we will agree, that old age always or even generally, makes man "evil and ugly," we will not. Neither will we agree that the aged man's heart is wasted away with worry, nor that the sun no longer gives him pleasure, or that women have nothing for him but disdain. These seventh century observations do nothing but show us that old age back then was rather more different than it is today.

During later years, passionate love takes on a different form: it becomes passionate affection. We have, for a sister, a brother, a parent, or a friend a calm affection, not a passionate affection because that implies a love of the sort that nourishes passionate love. The embrace is now unreal. It is only there implicitly, as if chance and circumstances wished us to have met while young, to have been able to exist, to have had to exist. The subconscious image of the creative embrace as an unrealizable possibility (in the Stoical sense of "possible" yet unrealizable in this world) casts a golden light on the relationship. In contrast with affection that is calm, simply pleasant, the joy of love is there with the feeling of fullness because time itself stands still when affectionate lovers are together, when they see and reflect each other. The pleasure of sharing love is undoubtedly less intense than in passionate love, but it is deeper because it is lived in reflection, and as if of secondary importance. The infinity of love, too, is something else. It is no longer exclusive to what is not the absoluteness of love, forcing choices and renunciations that one may later regret. It is a pervasively penetrating infinity, which does not leave anything outside itself. It is universal warmth, which is involved in every activity. Certainly, the thought of the affectionate lover does not leave us, but neither do we obsess on it. We are not less devoted in our tasks, open to others and to "city life," just as we are free to meditate or study. The infinity of passionate love is without exterior, in the sense that it encloses the lovers. The infinity of passionate affection is without exterior in the sense that it extends to the exterior, that is to say, to every gesture, every word, and every activity. There is nothing that, when touched by the loving heart, does not have a sort of inherent cheerfulness.

With love, happiness survives, but the happiness given by affectionate love is not a pinnacle of happiness. It is, rather, a tone of life, which comes not from some received impression, but from within itself—as if one could exclaim: "This *is* living!"

Montaigne knows how to savor the simple fact of living, to "live" it in its purest form. Thus, "when I walk alone in a beautiful orchard, if my thoughts have been dwelling on extraneous incidents for some part of the time, for some other part I bring them back to the walk, to the orchard, to the sweetness of this solitude, and to me."[41] There is an art to enjoying life: "I enjoy it twice as much as others, for the measure of enjoyment depends on what the greater or lesser attention that we lend it is."[42]

Yes, but this concentration of life in itself, this self-reflection of life, is the one that must be lived with the one we love with passionate affection in the union of love; because it is part of the essence of life that we cannot have a full life if we are alone. Without the one who is loved with passionate affection, we are alone.

XI

WITH THE "OLD SAGE" AND WITHOUT HIM

Milestones

This last chapter, with and without Lao Tzu, constitutes for Conche an opportunity to synthesize somewhat his key ideas on Nature. It is an open infinity because it is nothing but continuous creation, tirelessly breaking up into innumerable worlds that are not at all eternal, but are born and perish.

According to Conche, Lao Tzu's Tao, which is "perpetual mutability," is close to Heraclitus's panta rhei ("everything moves") combined with Anaximander's Phusis, the source and principle of birth and growth of individual beings, which deploys a generative force. Now, Nature constantly creates forms that themselves do not or barely evolve. Among them, man is incomplete and knows it. So, to be in accordance with the natural innermost depths of his being, with his Tao, man has to reduce the level of obligations in life as much as possible and to escape, if possible, from the contingent duties arising from fixed forms as well as from making any commitment that can be avoided.

This implies that to live according to the Tao we do not have to "fulfill ourselves," to be socially "recognized," to become "real," "fixed." The Tao Te Ching allows the artist and the philosopher to live according to Nature, to place their confidence in the flow of things, to be led by inspiration, unlike the man of action who attempts to master Nature and the course of things through calculation. The "man of Nature" simplifies his life and can live with the feeling of how tiny we are in the immense and infinite, and of the urgency of living without doing anything other than that: living and nothing more.

The man of Nature is no ordinary man—the one, who, by reflection, can return to natural simplicity—is the philosopher whose infinite activity (which differs from action because he does not build anything) frees him from entice-

ments and fixed forms. The philosopher's activity is a particular application of the method of "non-action" (wu wei). It consists of being open to realities and to allow them to reveal themselves, to meditate.

Such activity requires, first, to be free from anxiety (ataraxia). This serenity is a wisdom which is not the aim of philosophy but its condition. Second, the preoccupation with the self must be absent.

The philosopher's quest for truth gives meaning to his life, while passionate affection (distinct from passionate love) opens him to infinity and gives the life of the one he loves and his own a shared lightness and an overtone of happiness.

Post-Bergsonian Nature: The Pre-Socratic Infinite?

On the day after the death of Bergson in 1941, Jean Wahl wrote: "Right from the outset, this 20th century philosopher modestly but unquestionably involved himself in the dialogue that had taken place twenty-five centuries earlier between Zeno of Elea and Heraclitus. By his critique of the idea of nothingness, it could be said that he is continuing the ideas of Parmenides. By his theory of movement, he is a Heraclitean. Maybe one day we will see that the prestigiousness of Plato, the consummate art of Aristotle to write down and delve deeper into common sense ideas, the severe Cartesian meditation, the Kantian idealism, and the Hegelian dialectic, have all been so many ways to separate the mind from the real. . . . Bergson very often draws us to himself. It would be a lovely dream, and is not an impossible one, that the post-Bergsonians concur with the Pre-Socratics."[1]

Concurring with the Ante-Socratics[2] and therefore recognize, through the "real," the *Phusis* or "Nature," is exactly what happened to me.

Anaximander already understood the essential fact about Nature: that it is *The Incomplete*. It is "the infinite" (*to apeiron*): an infinity which is, in a sense, closed in on itself and without an exterior, because there is only itself, yet this infinity is open, because it is nothing but continuous creation. It is the generator of innumerable worlds, which are as much coexisting—because they are "in infinite number, in infinity, whichever way you turn"[3]—as they are successive to and succeeding each other in infinite time, some created, others destroyed; and which can have no ending, said Aristotle (explaining the position of Anaximander), "because the generations and the destruction of worlds necessarily presuppose movement," which will "always exist."[4]

Nature is that which has always been there. This is also the thinking of Heraclitus. In his eyes, it has always been made up of the world (*cosmos*) as what "was, is and will be."[5] This is to make Nature finite, to diminish its power. Nature did not create itself, that is to say permanently structure itself into the world, but unceasingly and tirelessly builds itself and becomes finite by forming itself into a multiplicity of worlds. This means that it breaks up into innumerable worlds that are not at all eternal, but are born and perish. It is like a perpetual laboratory of endless and multiple trials because it is not only one order (*cosmos*) that is born of Nature, but all systems of the order are born of it at one time or another.

Lao Tzu's Perpetual Mutability: Heraclitus's *panta rhei* Combined with Anaximander's *Phusis*

By his cosmology, Heraclitus is the ancestor of Plato's followers. However, by his *panta rhei*, "everything moves," he is the prime example of all the philosophies of movement, from Montaigne to Bergson, before and after. Furthermore what is the Tao, according to Lao Tzu, but "perpetual mutability itself,"[6] that is to say Heraclitus's river? Yet it must be added: with certain characteristics of Anaximander's *Phusis*, because the "Path" (Tao), which is infinite in that it is unqualified, undetermined, and conceptually incomprehensible, is also the source and principle of birth and growth for individual beings: differentiating themselves and becoming finite, it thus deploys a generative force, *Te*—a word that is generally translated as "Virtue." Nothing prevents this "Virtue" from showing itself in innumerable worlds.

The Tao: Liberating the Incomplete Man from Fixed Forms

Yet, "What is man in Nature?" asked Pascal. Then he removed the word *Nature*, and replaced it with the word *Infinite*. The infinite: the Incomplete. The *Phusis* being all-enveloping, man is not, any more than the other beings, outside Nature. He is even more in accord with the essence of Nature than those species that are fixed. Bees are the same as they were at the time of Virgil, but man is something else. "The very depths of Nature [*der Kern*] are at the heart of man," said Goethe; just like Nature and life itself—whose evolution cannot stop at fixed forms—man is incomplete. He is the being whose essence, I say, is that which is most in accord with the essence of Nature and life, the most natural and living being. However, man *knows* that he is incomplete and possesses the ability to always break with what is stagnant. It reasonably follows that man is spirit.

Life is incomplete, but it constantly contradicts this essential incompleteness, not by the creation of forms, but by the fact that these forms last for millennia without any variation and are like impasses. Man knows himself to be incomplete. However, society is the place of fixed forms, and, by means of the State and its institutions, demands from the individual, under threat, subjugation to these forms so that the individual is unceasingly dispossessed of himself, of his creative essence. Fixed forms do not evolve, or barely evolve.

Hence, at various times throughout history, there are processes of substitution of old fixed forms with new forms such as wars, coup d'états, and revolutions. The individual, who owed respect to a code, institutions, laws, and important people, now owes respect to a different code, to new institutions, to other laws, to other important people. He is told he must go to war. He goes and he dies without having had the time to experience a reality of his own. Existence is necessarily a compromise between society and the self. One cannot completely escape from the pressure of fixed forms (which Plato, with his theory of Ideas, wanted to make absolute to establish his authoritarianism), and live a purely natural life, but one must strive to be in tune with oneself, with one's Tao. It is necessary to reduce as much as possible, the level of obligations in life and to escape, if possible, from the contingent duties coming from fixed forms and from making any commitment that can be avoided.

Living in harmony with the course of things, the flow that unceasingly institutes and causes them, that is to say being in agreement with the natural innermost depths of our being; that is the advice of the "Old Sage," where he concurs with the Greeks and Montaigne. However, the latter wrote of the difficulty of coming back to Nature, through the barbed wire of artificial forms: "Nature is a gentle guide, but no more gentle than wise and just. I seek her footprints everywhere. We have confused them with artificial tracks and for that reason the sovereign of the Academics and the Peripatetics, which is 'to live according to nature,' becomes hard to limit and express; also that of the Stoics, a neighbour to the other, which is 'to consent to Nature.'"[7] The reference to the Academics and Peripatetics is somewhat misleading here, because for them, "nature" means the very nature of man, of reason. For the Stoics, the same applies, if only because reason, before being human, is the immanent *logos* of all things, and unlike human reason, not susceptible to error. The Epicureans do not see in Nature anything like *logos*, which signifies destiny, finality, providence: the nature of things comes from an original chance happening. Yet, it is to this Nature, which is now created, that it is necessary to conform, because what it asks, through the needs that express it, is essentially *finished*, while the desires society gives rise to are insatiable.

The Tao: Renouncing to Fulfill Ourselves to Be in Accord with Nature

Lao Tzu does not theorize on the system of Nature. Like Montaigne, he sticks to the evidence of the conflict between two kinds of living—depending on whether we like to find fulfilment or not in relation to values or ideas linked to fixed forms. Or rather, let us say that in one of these ways of living, we have to *fulfill* ourselves, become real, in the Hegelian sense, meaning by "real" that which is fixed. This can be done if and in so much as we obtain social recognition, qualifying by means of a fixed form. This realization makes it possible to exist in the collective memory and representation, not to say in history. In the other way of living, we consider that we don't have to "fulfill ourselves," if that means becoming settled, because nothing is fixed, and that we have, throughout days and hours, all the true reality of what constitutes life.

Certainly, there is no society without fixed forms, and there is no individual outside society. By means of education, society prepares the child to maintain or even perpetuate forms. Becoming an adult and a man of his time, he fulfils himself in forms defined by the spirit of the era. As he lives not in the immense time of Nature, but in a shrunken time, where ephemeral realities establish themselves like beings, he believes himself to be real, forgets the disappearance of things and nothingness. He has the satisfaction of being "recognized"—a satisfaction that could be considered unsatisfactory because it is obtained at the price of alienation of the self, but he is not aware of such alienation, and in truth there is not much alienation any more, the individual having exhausted himself with regard to what is different, unspeakable, and unique. This is why the satisfactions given by achievement and social promotion repress the obscure fear of missing out on life.

Returning to natural simplicity, following the "Tao," presupposes a minimum commitment to fixed forms. The word *Tao* is composed of a root which means to walk step by step, one step at a time. *Te*, "virtue," is composed of elements of "perfect honesty" and "heart."[8] Living according to the Tao is to be in accord with things, advancing in conformity with things. Everyone has his or her Tao, which can already, by privilege of birth, be attuned to the Tao. Hölderlin writes: "There are two ideals of our existence: a state of extreme ingenuousness, in which our needs themselves are in concord, both with our abilities and with everything related to us, solely through the organisation of Nature, without our interference; and a state of highest culture where the same would take place through the organisation which we are able to give to ourselves."[9]

The Artists' Way of Non-Action

The *Tao Te Ching* allows us, thanks to the power of thought, to establish a state of organization of our being in its relations with itself and the world, similar to that which Nature herself produces spontaneously in the case of certain privileged individuals. These privileged natures are the artists, while the first are philosophers.

"Follow your inspiration," said Bergson to Raïssa Maritain. Such is, in any case, the advice that the artist gives to himself. Because he is about to create, he finds himself on the margins of society and fixed forms. If he consents to a paid profession, it is only to earn what is necessary for life and work. Literally, the artist "works without acting" (*wei wu wei*: Chinese for "non-action"), because, contrary to the entrepreneur who sets an objective for himself and then uses means to obtain it, the artist cannot know in advance what the work will be. He advances step by step, innovating where necessary, incapable of rationalizing his steps. What else does Nature herself do? We can say that she actualizes eternal essences, that, for example, she causes bees to be born by regulating the eternal Idea of the bee? What does the word *bee* signify? This would be impossible to know before Nature created them.

Just as Rimbaud's *The Drunken Boat* could not exist anywhere, not even in the head of the poet, before the poet had written down the words. What is at work in the artist is nothing other than Nature herself, indefinitely incomplete, infinite creator, and pushing blindly the future forward. The man of action is the opposite of the artist, because he wants to know in advance all things concerning his actions, in order to move forward in complete safety. He wants, as much as possible, to avoid risk, which is precisely what the artist cannot avoid. To master Nature and the course of things by calculation is the dream of the man of action; nothing pleases him more than the progress of science and technology. The artist places his confidence in the flow of things, allowing himself to be led by inspiration.

The Philosophers' Way of Non-Action

What is left for he who refuses action and achievement in the world, and who, however, is not artistic in any way due to lack of natural talent? It only remains for him to live poetically, following the example of the "Old Sage." This presupposes that one passes from a state of dependence on fixed forms to a state of simplicity. The individual depends through his roles and functions on a society that encloses him in set obligations, which have been defined without him, and also by what is title, dignity, grade, mark of honor, etc., all things that hold him captive like so many enticements. Who says "enticement" says "lure," who says "lure" says "desire." We must rid ourselves of the desires that enslave us. "Have few desires," Lao Tzu advises us. Epicurus explains: limit yourself to desires without which we cannot live as human beings—and which are, in fact, needs because we have to eat, dress ourselves, find shelter, and have friends. Just as we cut off the useless branches of a tree, we should cut the strings that keep us attached to social forms and fashions, that throw us into the future and that prevent us from living fully in the present because they make us inattentive to others.

The Cynics had already noted that we clutter our lives with innumerable things that we do not need. Having pruned what is of no use to happiness is to be like uncut wood, not like wood that has been cut and worked. This is the origin of Lao-tseu's advice: "Return to the state of uncarved wood."[10] Then what about the individual who has thus simplified his life?

He is as man has always been—the man of Nature, I mean. Regardless of place, era, family and social structures, institutions, that is, regardless of fixed forms, he has to deal with night and day, the sun and the stars, the phenomena of the atmosphere and the necessity to eat and protect his body, in short, the human phenomenon par excellence: meeting the other. This man would be said to be an abstraction; in fact, he cannot abstract himself from his social group. So be it! Yet in societies like ours, where the individual has several degrees of freedom, it is possible to create a situation where the structured social ties are so stretched that there is meaning to speaking about a return to a natural way of living—the man "of nature" being then a product of civilization because we can be relatively indifferent to social reality, to what fills the pages of newspapers or even to notable upheavals, in as much as it concerns the ephemeral, is only passing, and will soon be forgotten. Thus, we can live less with a historic conscience than with a feeling of how tiny we are in the immense and infinite, and so, of the urgency of living without doing anything other than that: living and *nothing more*.

The objection could be made that this condition, where man is stripped of all the things that make up the action of life, would leave him in a void and in boredom. We could quote Pascal about "diversion." Let us listen to the sublime author: "Nothing is so intolerable for man as to be completely at rest, without passions, without business, without diversion, without study. He then feels his nothingness, his forlornness, his insufficiency, his dependence, his weakness, his emptiness. Immediately, from the depth of his heart, will come boredom, gloom, sadness, grief, vexation, despair."[11]

This objection is based on a misunderstanding. It is true that if the ordinary man finds himself "without passions, without business, without diversion, without study," he will be bored and in a void, but we don't have concern for the ordinary man. Until the end of time, men will desire power, riches, honors, and consideration and will need to rival, criticize, dominate, defy one another, and quarrel, etc. They will continue to go to war, to destroy, and to kill. If the *Tao Te Ching* has some effect on the ordinary man, it is the sign that he was not an ordinary man.

The one who, by reflection, can return to natural simplicity, is the philosopher, insofar as he is capable of achieving the state of what Hölderin describes as "that of the highest culture." Not to be haunted by any desire for honors, power, consideration, or glory, to guard against any form of rivalry or confrontation with others, condemn the use of arms, armed revolts, insurrections, or war, not to participate in any violent undertaking at the risk of bringing upon oneself public blame and legal sanctions, which in time of war strike pacifists, to know that we can, "without going beyond the doorstep, know the world,"[12] to have no interest in ourselves, nor "private ends,"[13] to live in a hidden and anonymous way with those who make up obscure history, but yet to reject the life of the hermit, to be welcoming to all, however limited their capacity to listen may be, to live in communion and agreement with all beings—plants, animals, stars—to always be of the same mind as all children of the Earth, and from there, to know internal peace and "serenity"[14]—this is what the philosopher can do. It is not that this serenity is the aim. It is correlative to the activity of the philosopher, which, by itself, frees him from all that has just been said. If the ordinary man is powerless to free himself from enticements and fixed forms, it is because he is not capable of this passion for reason, which is what the philosopher is made of. Pascal reflects upon the man who, without passion, without business, without activity, only finds emptiness and boredom. Yet to philosophize is an activity, and is singularly absorbing because the task of the philosopher is an infinite task.

When I say "activity," I do not say "action." The authors of systems have assimilated the philosopher to a man of action. They conceive the search for truth as an enterprise whereby, through analyses and demonstrations, we arrive at a result. Descartes wanted to rebuild philosophy, like a building that would be the work of a single architect. Philosophy, however, is nothing like a building. "Beware of prejudices," said Descartes. Undoubtedly he is right, but it is also necessary, said Bergson, to be wary of "habits formed in action, [which,] when they find their way up to the sphere of speculation, create fictitious problems there."[15]

What sort of activity is that of the philosopher who follows the Tao? We can say it consists of a particular application of the method of "non-action" (*wu wei*). This method is universal and makes it possible, in all areas, to be efficient without conflict or violence. The way the philosopher applies it to the domain of knowledge consists of this: to be open to realities and to allow them to reveal themselves. Most likely not knowing the Tao, Bergson is close to the idea of "non-acting" by his intuitive method of coincidence with the "actual flow of the real."[16] Let us leave the word *intuition* to Bergson. Let us content ourselves with the word by which we ordinarily design the activity of the philosopher: the word *meditation*. To meditate is to be waiting, like lying in wait, for thoughts that are going to surprise us, bringing sudden clarity. "We will never succeed in having thoughts, they come to us," said Heidegger, with great accuracy.[17] We anticipate, with variable probability, the result of an action, and it is for this reason that we act. Yet we don't anticipate thoughts. The philosopher is, in this regard, similar to the artist. Thought is "work of a poet," said Heidegger.[18]

The Requirements: Ataraxia and Absence from Self-Preoccupation

What is required so that thoughts come to us? First, the soul must reach "freedom from anxiety" (*ataraxia*), serenity, a sort of negative happiness that we can call "wisdom"—a wisdom that is not the aim of philosophy, but its condition. Then and correspondingly, preoccupation with oneself must be absent. "The self is detestable," said Pascal. However, we shouldn't attach so much importance to ourselves that we hate ourselves. We will avoid the trap of *Cogito*, which, by enclosing thought in self-reflection, separates it from things, depriving it of all immediate relations. Above all, it is necessary to empty oneself and put aside all cultural acquisitions—be they beliefs or preconceived ideas—so that there are only things themselves, their elusiveness, their infinity and their immensity under the horizon of eternal Time.

All of this is understood under the inspiration of the "Old Sage." I have therefore called this chapter: "With the 'Old Sage' *and without him*," because Lao Tzu, like Socrates before him, is unique. He reaches the plenitude of wisdom and lacks nothing, like a god. Tuned like an instrument to the flow of things,[19] he is in sympathy and communion with all beings; he shines for them like a benevolent jewel and is a blessing to them by his very existence. Yet, even if the philosopher can perceive something from this height of wisdom, he is himself down in a valley. For, if he has been able to break away from or treat as nothing his social attachments—I do not say "family"—if he has delivered himself from any dependence on fixed forms like trends and fashions, there still remains what he was not able to reduce to nothing within himself, and which comes from the fact of not simply being a human being, but a *masculine or feminine* human being, and—in our hypothesis—a "man" (*vir*, or in Greek, *anèr*).

The Philosopher and His Loved One: A Shared Tone of Happiness

Yet, in this respect, the philosopher is astonishingly similar to the ordinary man we mentioned earlier. He has within himself an ordinary side, by which he simply needs to love a woman and to be loved by one. The kiss that Lou Salomé gave to Nietzsche at Monte Sacro without thinking or at least without attaching any importance to it, was for Nietzsche the opposite of an insignificant event, because whatever brings joy or sadness—according to whether or not it happens only once—and can put more sparkle into living, is not insignificant.

For the philosopher as such, the quest for truth gives meaning to his life, but for the human being, love is the meaning of life. But the philosopher is also a human being. Hölderlin's oak tree, Titan stripped of his chains of social dependence, is the image of the sage, but the poet adds: "If my heart did not attach me to communal life—this heart which cannot give up love—how I would like to be an oak tree!"[20]

Is this in good faith? Who would want the barrenness of a life without love? Neither the soul of a poet nor the soul of a philosopher—if at least the philosopher must really *live* and be more than a thinking sleepwalker.

Real love implies the infinite, because everything else pales in comparison. Are we not then falling into the "Either-or" (the *Enten-Eller* of Kierkegaard)? There is on the one hand, *joy*, the joy of marvelous moments, and on the other hand, the responsibility of the philosopher and the duty of a choice. But we have distinguished the closed infinity of passionate or emotional love, that of Tristan and Iseult, and the open infinity of passionate affection. If "crazy" love excludes all other interests, passionate affection, far from excluding other interests, enfolds them in its infinity. The mutual belonging of affectionate lovers does not prevent each one from having his own activities; and one can devote himself to philosophy, with the other not even having access to it.

Yet love gives each of the two lives a shared lightness, a shared tone of happiness. What about the loving embrace? The lovers live the tension of the inapproachable proximity that is both painful and marvelous. As for the philosopher, he reflects on these words of Hölderlin:

> The deepest thought loves the liveliest life;
> it is after taking a glance at the world that we understand the
>   high virtue;
> and the sages, very often
> finish by clinging to beauty.[21]

All of this, we understand very well, must remain somewhat mysterious. Any conclusion would be contrived. Life ends at death, which is not a conclusion.

APPENDIX

CORRESPONDENCE BETWEEN MARCEL CONCHE AND GILBERT KIRSCHER

1. Marcel Conche to Gilbert Kirscher

Treffort, 30 June 1999

Dear Gilbert,

I am replying to your letter quite quickly as I have something to ask you.

First of all, I'd like to thank you for your thoughts on *Ma vie antérieure* (My earlier life). To tell you the truth, only the first section was written spontaneously. The others were dragged out of me by the friendly editor of a journal published in Corrèze. (He would like the follow-up, which I won't give him as I think my path after the "aggregation" [a prestigious professional qualification for teachers in France] is not remarkable enough.) However, I have no regrets about writing these sections.

So here is what I wanted to ask you. As a philosopher, I must speak with a certain "attitude" and within a certain "category" (to use the words of Éric Weil). But which ones? I don't know if you can reply to this question from the following comments.

1. The aim of philosophy is to think the real as a whole. Hence, these questions arise. What should we understand by "real"? What merits being called *truly* "real"?

2. The real is what remains opposed to what is only passing—but perhaps the Whole of reality is "only passing."

3. We should philosophize not out of belief but from the evidence of what is shown and offered to everyone: the world based on Nature.
4. The Whole of reality is Nature. There may be several worlds (and even infinity) but there's only one Nature: *Totum sive natura.*
5. Nature presents itself as infinite and so incomprehensible. To think Nature is not therefore to understand it. Thinking is therefore not understanding—nor knowing; one cannot know the Whole of reality.
6. Thinking, in the philosophical sense, is completely separate from doing; there is no action which can be applied to the Whole of reality.
7. Thinking is to bring clarity, it is to enlighten.
8. As we philosophize based on *enargeia*, evidence (which is not the Cartesian *evidentia*), the "units of meaning" which imply Revelation do not come under philosophy. The God of revealed religions is not a philosophical notion (*Deus sive natura* is, of course, different). Religious beliefs are cultural facts that come from causal explanation.
9. Thinking Nature in search of the truth does not imply that one is worried about the way the world is going. Philosophy must think of itself as indifferent to history. The philosopher must be detached from contingent interest to what is happening in order to think.
10. The aim of philosophy is truth, not happiness. The intervention of the idea of *eudaimonia* in the future of Greek thought meant decadence.
11. Between philosophers and believers—as such—dialogue has no meaning. Between philosophers in the strict sense—those who philosophize from evidence—dialogue has a meaning.

That said I seem to be talking with one of those "implacable attitudes." But which one?

Please let me know what you think.

Yours sincerely,
Marcel

2. Gilbert Kirscher to Marcel Conche

Lille, 22 July 1999

Dear Marcel,

On my return from a short break in Brittany, where my grandchildren (4 and 7 years old) made me feel like a child again, I read your letter and the questions it raises. You are asking me what might be the categorical area of your own discourse in *Logique de la philosophie* (The logic of philosophy) by Éric Weil. I'm not sure how to reply without writing a book! However, I don't wish to be evasive. After several unsuccessful attempts writing this longhand, I decided to turn to the computer, which allows me to correct more easily what I write. So, please excuse the impersonal appearance of a letter that is, in fact, addressed to you alone.

Allow me to begin with an interlocutory consideration. If the *LP* of É. Weil contains a table of fundamental discourse categories (and corresponding attitudes) this table does not distinguish between the essences but rather between the types of ideas, heuristic fictions which may be used to analyze effective discourses between men (individuals or groups: cultures and civilizations) but not to set them in a would-be definition, like the taxonomy of Gaston Berger. The categories are not *separate* essences, but are more forms of coherence, nodes of meaning, all present and all acting to various degrees in any discourse. For Weil, to understand a singular discourse means detecting which categories are being worked and played out in it in a *privileged manner*.

So a Weilian interpretation of Kant would make way for the significance of categories of *consciousness* (transcendental and practical subjects), of *condition* (phenomenal objectivity), of *God* (postulates of practical reason) and of the formal category of *sense*, though expressed in inadequate ontological language. Effective discourse is not confined to just one category and, even in the case of one category prevailing to the point of erasing the others, it will still retain categories that logically precede it and from which it follows in some way: the category absorbs or supplements the preceding one, or it rejects it, forgets it etc.

Thus the category of *condition*, that is to say, the abandoned nature of God, nature that is just the object of modern determinist science, the category, if we may say so, of atheism and of mathematical physics, seems haunted by the category of God. Kojève had indeed said this, recalling that it is the religion of transcendence, and finally, Christianity-Judaism which allowed (in spite of themselves) the advent of modern science. The nature of modern physics is what remains of the Greek *phusis* when the gods retired and the gods only retired insofar as the transcendent God replaced them.

In this respect, your own discourse is continuously preoccupied with God, but in a negative way. It is much more critical than the discourse based on the category of God. In order to go beyond the attitude of faith you must go further than the affirmative part of your discourses (Nature *Totum sive natura*).Your assertion relies on your repeated negation of God and on the critique of the attitude and discourse of the believer to oppose what you consider the evidence of the world, in other words what can be seen. From Weil's viewpoint, I would say that the category of *God* is very much to the fore in your discourse but that it is seen from the viewpoint of another category, from which the loss of faith is conceptualized, formulated and celebrated, but also at times, it seems to me, regretted.

What could this other category be? There seem to be two options: it could logically be *a posteriori* (as in the *LP*) or indeed logically *a priori*. In fact, on reflection, both solutions seem to apply.

1. On the one hand, it is indeed from the *a posteriori* category of the *condition* (but not only) that you speak of the attitude of the believer when you state that "religious beliefs are cultural facts that come from causal explanation." Scientific assertion? Or scientistic? Positivist? In any case, your overall discourse is not scientistic—in fact, it's far from it! Your reflection on the suffering of children as absolute evil would be totally incomprehensible from the viewpoint of man of the *condition*, of man who is *only* of science, of the scientistic man, who hopes to reduce any illusion of sense to leave room only for causal explanations. So, the negative link to the category of *God* comes from further away, beyond the condition but through the language of the *condition*.

From where? Doubtlessly, from *consciousness* (see what you say about essential equality, of the "duty of substitution" in *Le fondement de la morale* [The foundation of morality], for example) but not just that. However, it seems to me you do not go as far as admitting the autonomy of consciousness, in the way Kant speaks about the noumenal autonomy of the will.

From *intelligence*? You seem to see this attitude as a possibility, as a temptation, but you always point out its unreality. We are not alone. We are in contact with each other. We cannot consider things leaving aside the effective presence of others. We cannot remain at a distance without losing lucidity. We have entered the world with others. We are not purely transcendental subjects without empirical roots.

From *personality*? Certainly, as in your closest argumentation where you establish a universally valid need, you sometimes claim the right to be excluded, often with humor, sometimes maliciously and sometimes solemnly. Yes to reason and yes also to the individual that I am!

In short, these three categories of subjectivity (*consciousness, intelligence and personality*) seem to be linked together in your discourse, with none taking precedence over the other; rather they limit each other. The rational absoluteness of the Kantian moral *consciousness* is limited by the irrational individualism of the *personality* (see Heidegger's critique of the use of the French impersonal pronoun "On") and by the detachment, to the point of forgetting, of the self of *intelligence*, theorizing and interpreting works and human worlds.

2. Before considering the subsequent categories, I would like to go back to the other choice referred to above. You also oppose the category of *God* from the point of view of logically *a priori* categories. Thus the first two points in your letter presented the fundamental distinction of your argument, namely one which is "truly real" at the heart of the real and then a second real which comes from appearance, if we can say that. This distinction is made in *Logique de la philosophie* (The logic of philosophy) in the Archaic categories (this is not a value judgment but a reference to the *archè*): they correspond historically to the pre-Socratics, especially Heraclitus.

The *True-and-false* (linked with the hyphens!) confirms the inextricable link and the impossibility of separating one from the other, the true and the false constituting the Real (night/day, war/peace, etc.). *Certainty* separates the true and the false, distinguishes between essential and unessential and opposes the discourse in truth to that of the "many" who digress. (On this point may I refer you to the two relevant chapters in my book published by PUF, *La philosophie d'Éric Weil*? I'm still pleased with those two chapters!).

The poet-thinker of *True-and-false* calls it the enigmatic unit of the Real; the thinker of *Certainty* repeats the same unit while introducing an opposition that makes him choose one of the elements as the truly real, without for all that eliminating the other element; hence the two "ways" or the two parts of the poem of Parmenides. The categories that are still *a priori*, *Truth* and *Non-Sense*, had only confirmed the Real in its absolute unity, *a priori* to any difference, still unspecified and so evanescent. Your *Pyrrho* would correspond quite well to the discourse of *Non-Sense*, for which *All is appearance*, for which *appearance is all.*

The four Archaic categories are extremely important in your own discourse, and in particular the two categories of *True-and-false* and *Certainty*, which are in keeping with your having devoted a sizeable part of your work to reading, interpreting and reflecting on the most representative Archaic thinkers in these categories, not just for their own sakes as thinkers of *Totum sive natura*, but also as positive counterparts of the category always rejecting *God*.

Of course you have not restricted yourself to these categories; you have integrated them into your discourse and they work insofar as you draw upon them (like Weil's concept of *drawing upon*) from the viewpoint of ulterior categories. In the same way, you take up the category of God to reject it from the *condition* viewpoint.

3. I'll now return to where I was before beginning my point (2). It is certainly not only from the viewpoint of the three categories of subjectivity (*consciousness*, *intelligence and personality*) that you take up the categories of *True-and-false* and of *Certainty*, as it is not only with the viewpoint of *condition* that you reject the category of *God*. So, this needs to be taken further.

The *absolute*? Yes, like all philosophy, with the absolute, which is in Hegel's work, you both define philosophy as reducing belief to thought and as thought of Everything (and oneself), but the dialectic reason and its understanding and the reconciliation of the concept do not satisfy you. You oppose the sense of tragic as well as the need for causal rational explanation (this corresponds, schematically, to Nietzsche's position). You oppose the discourse of the *absolute* (Hegel) a "thought" that is not "understanding," and this thought is associated (paradoxically?) with the scientific rationality of understanding (*Verstand*) rather than the dialectic rationality of reason (*Vernunft*). The thought of the absolute, yes (*Deus sive natura*, *Totum sive natura*) but not in the manner of the category of the *absolute*, where the absolute is spirit (for Hegel, the spirit is born of the death of nature. Spirit *is* resurrected or better resurrecting).

What of the *Work*, then? Yes, insofar as you wish to create individual work, or you recognize yourself as an individual (as already a *personality*). However, you wish to create in the element of language and thought, an element in which the violence of the work is sublimated so that it becomes sensitive. You create your work to clarify but not to transform, let alone to destroy. In this respect it is the *finite* category (which is also Heidegger's) which seems to me to provide the point from which you see and think, and, in particular, that you rethink the Archaic categories, greatly distancing yourself, like Heidegger, from the purely "Greek" categories (according to Weil's terminology) of *discussion* (Socrates), of the *object* (Plato) and the *self* (Epicurus and the Stoics). In the latter category there appears, according to Weil, what for you constitutes decadence: the quest for happiness greater than the quest for truth.

You stop at the *finite* since you reject action. Weil leans toward *action*, history and political and historical reality. This is our world, the world in which and on which philosophy exerts an influence, the world it aims to understand and to transform from the perspective of understanding and with a view to possible understanding for everyone. The political dimension is crucial for Weil: philosophy is political in its essence, even if political philosophy is not the last word in philosophy. Therein, in my opinion and as you point out yourself, lies the main difference between you and Weil, even though you agree that the need for truth is fundamental. *Truth* is the first category of *Logique de la philosophie*. However, Truth eventually leads to action and, inversely, reflection of the action on itself leads to philosophy, to reflection of philosophy on and of itself, to the logic of philosophy.

Thus, Weil recognizes the choice of philosophy as a fundamental choice of truth, without for all that considering that the question of happiness means that this choice leads to decadence, because the choice is that of a finite being, of an individual who is not just a thinker. The fundamental theoreticism of philosophy does not lead to indifference to action. Action, the thought of action and action in accordance with thought, philosophical action and the philosophy of action have their place in philosophy as a whole which thinks the Real and its thoughts about the Real. This is why, according to Weil, action is not the final category: it is the concrete category, the final attitude, but which is only understood when rising above itself. When thought thinks and is thought, it does not act: you and Weil agree on this point (as do Hegel, Spinoza, Plato, Aristotle, etc.) Nevertheless, for thinking to be possible, man must be educated to think: the philosophical organization of the human community is the condition and also the aim (historically speaking) of philosophy and the action of philosophy. If thinking is fundamentally *theoria*, this does not divert from the understanding of history and action, of its own historicity and politicization.

There remains the formal category of *Wisdom*. It seems to me that once again you and Weil—and also Heidegger—agree on the idea of wisdom, but probably, unlike Weil, you would not accept that for every attitude and every category there is a corresponding figure of wisdom.

As you see, I have just given a rough illustration of Weil's thesis, in which all categories are present in all discourse, confirmed or rejected in various ways. If we examine what you reject—mainly the categories of *God* and of *action*, the attitude of the believer and that of the man of action (politician, citizen, reason and the will of the State), we could wonder what, in your opinion, profoundly links these two figures. Would it be the guiding idea of happiness? Is this idea incompatible with that of enlightenment of truth? Why would the idea of happiness bring about the decline of philosophy? Or do you think that these two opposing poles (*God and action*) are independent of one another and without any link to the third, the idea of happiness?

Rereading what I have written, I note how this type of schematic analysis can be unsatisfactory and does not manage to retain the essence of the singular path and the reflection in hand, which is continually questioning and lively. In any case, this perspective which I have done my best to provide is not intended as a demurral or a refutation, but perhaps it will help to define what is in question for one from the point of view of the other and what could be the basis for discussion.

Best wishes,
Gilbert

Acknowledgment by Marcel Conche

I would like to express my gratitude to Gilbert Kirscher for this benevolent reply and truly admirable analysis, which clearly involved much work, effort, and reflection. Thank you for this wonderful lesson in philosophy and friendship.

As I said in the Foreword, the example given here of the power of analysis contained in *Logique de la philosophie* by Weil, may encourage and help novice readers to understand, or have a better understanding of, this philosophy.

In this respect, I suggest reading—or rather, studying—Kirscher's major work *La philosophie d'Éric Weil. Systématicité et ouverture* (PUF, 1989), coll. "Philosophie d'aujourd'hui" (Today's philosophy) (and to supplement this, for example, his book *Éric Weil ou la raison de la Philosophie* [P.U. du Septentrion, 1999], coll. "Problématiques philosophiques").

The latest publications of unpublished works by Weil, *Essai sur la nature, l'histoire et la politique* (P.U. du Septentrion, 1999), coll. *Philosophie et réalité II* (Beauchesne publications, 2003), are of very great interest.

3. Gilbert Kirscher to Marcel Conche

Lille, 20 February 2001

Dear Marcel,

Thank you for sending me your most recent collection of essays *Presence of Nature*. I enjoyed reading it, as one would enjoy meeting a friend true to himself, familiar yet unpredictable, in his thought always starting from the enigmatic evidence of Nature. Faithful to yourself and to this evidence, you give priority to the Greek poet-thinkers and modern poets, putting in its place, as Heidegger did, modern science that "does not think." At the same time, you object to any recourse to the supernatural, while knowing that many would not wish to, or would not dare, share the evidence that you affirm, and that they would prefer to reflect on nature from their belief in something beyond nature. Tolerant and even indifferent, you let them think what they will, perhaps, I may add, because you consider that they are not, or rather are no longer dangerous. As they no longer have the means of imposing their belief, they can go on speaking and believing.

I don't believe in the supernatural either. However, I have to admit that the attitude of the believer has its own coherence. If he interprets anthropomorphism and theomorphism in a strange way, the presence of what there is *(il y a)*, it is that he also hears "the call of the real" (p. 16) to the point of hearing the call coming from someone and addressed specifically to him. If we leave aside the difference between a personal presence and an impersonal presence, the fact remains that in either case, it is based on the presence and on the presence thought as infinite creative origin. Between belief that divine love is the source and the end of creation and the discourse on nature thought as *phusis*, I see a lot of connection, although, of course, I also understand the difference. Nevertheless, the difference of expressions of the absolute presence does not abolish the identity of this absolute of the presence. It seems to me that you avoid this term "absolute" when speaking about nature even though it would suit to use it in its strict meaning; without relation to anything other than itself, and so at the same time one and infinite, All.

You explain the different meanings of "nature" with your usual clarity, the thinker with the Greeks, with the modern philosophers too, such as Nietzsche and Heidegger. You explain the meaning of "nature" by developing the distinction between "what there is" and "what is offered us," between *phusis*, nature in its totality on the one hand, and *cosmos* and *universe*, on the other. Here I have two questions:

1. One is about the distinction between "world" and "universe." Is the "world" the "face" of nature as it appears somehow *before* modern science (in a representation dominated by myth, poetic narrative and art)? Is the "universe" the face of nature as it appears from the methodical investigation of modern science (Galileo, Newton, and Einstein)?

2. The other question is about the distinction between "nature" and "world" and in particular between nature as thought by the Greeks and the world known by modern science. This distinction leads, in my opinion, to a discrediting of the second term (by "accommodation of nature to our understanding," p.8). This is also the case with Heidegger.

However, I am tempted to play the devil's advocate and ask (that is of modern science, which is no less atheist, no less rebellious to the supernatural than the thinker of nature in the Greek sense), about the idea that all in nature, even life, emerges as a mechanism (see contemporary biology), and that deep down there is nothing other than mechanism—infinite mechanism without an engineer; does this idea have less evidence than that of "there is"? Is it incompatible with the Greek idea of nature? Doesn't it mean that nature takes shape by chance, without obeying an external finality, but according to the need inherent in auto-deployment, in time and space, of matter and bodies? What would I lose of your thought of nature by supporting the idea that there is only mechanism, that every becoming, every expression in the form of reality, that every becoming, birth and death, is based on an infinite mechanism? Isn't the distinction between the Greek *phusis* and nature in the sense of modern science only made from the point of view of the finiteness of our knowledge? Must we choose between the learned person and the poet? Wasn't Heidegger himself led to think that the Technique veils and unveils the Being neither more nor less than any other manifestation?

Your book leads me on to another consideration that is not an objection, since it stems from agreement with your discourse, but rather an awareness of my congenital and unrepentant Hegelianism.

The evidence of presence is in the principle of your discourse: presence *of* nature and presence *to* the individual who speaks. For the individual who speaks, the mark of presence, of reality, is the external to the speaking individual; nature is outside, facing.

However, I must add; this externalism is for me, it is said in my discourse; it appears *in* the language and *through* the language. The affirmation of the presence of nature is immanent to the language (not to the individual who speaks, but to the language through which the individual can say "I" and "we" at the same time as reality appears to him). I think Heidegger says something like this when he writes that language is the house of the Being. Likewise Weil, p. 420 of *Logique de la philosophie*: "Every 'there is' for man comes from the language." Hegel used to say it when speaking of reality as "mind"; it is the mind which speaks and thinks what nature is, and it can because it is nothing other than nature, nature having become nature reflected and reflecting on itself. Or it is not the individual, it is "we" who speak nature (which is expressed in your own style by the numerous citations; you think with, you think from the community of thinkers).

However, at this point when nature understands itself in the mind, in the language and the thought of the human community, nature loses its externalism. It has become natural externalism found *in* the poetic, philosophic or scientific language. Of course, I would not agree with Hegel to the very end, because the end for him means externalism would be completely destroyed, which would also be the sign that the individual has completely surrendered (reduced or elevated, lifted up again, *aufgehoben*) to the mind. Weil liked to recall that according to Hegel absolute access to the absolute mind always means death of the individual. You yourself say this clearly at the beginning of your book: "The evidence of Nature and the evidence of death are one and the same evidence." Death overcome would be nature becoming *entirely* spirit. Mortals deal with nature that is present as externalism and at the same time this externalism is already internal, "spiritual" as it is said. We never have to deal with nature itself in its silent presence, but with nature said and thought, even when we are silent and believe we forget ourselves.

The evidence of nature is evidence for the *mind*, and this is why this evidence is not a multiple exception as long as there are figures of the mind or fundamental attitudes. The multiplicity and diversity of figures of the mind are for me evidence equal to the presence of nature even if the latter is so to speak immediate and the former is only discovered progressively though the history of human thought. Yet again when I speak of mind, I speak of nothing other than *nature*, which is reflected in the being who speaks, in the speaking body, because speaking, knows itself to be mortal and can speak the evidence of nature.

It seems to me that in your book, you take an interest especially, if not solely, in nature as externalism. Also don't you turn toward the immanent thrust of nature toward language, toward the speaking of the self, toward poetic and philosophic language, toward what Hegel calls spirit? Yet you chose to interpret one of the greatest poets, about whom it has been said that he had been *the poet*, to show that he understands nature as the Greeks understood it and as you understand it. Isn't this implicitly admitting that the most elevated product of the mind is also the most elevated product of nature, through which nature itself speaks (the "I")—what the poet perceives when saying, "I am Other"? In this respect, Kant, by his theory of genius, deserves a place among the greatest thinkers about nature in the *phusis* sense, even if he expresses himself in unsuitable language, more creationist than Greek.

To speak and think nature would therefore, I think, also be to speak and think that nature is spirit, that is to say that nature is language in power and in action. What really makes it enigmatic is that it can be spoken and is spoken effectively, that it has produced speaking bodies, that it has managed to say "I" and "We" through them, to produce poems and philosophical discourse, even if each time this is in an ephemeral way.

You can tell how much I enjoy reading your letters—and writing to you—by the excessive length of my letter.

Best regards,
Gilbert

4. Marcel Conche to Gilbert Kirscher

Treffort, 23 February 2001

My Dear Gilbert,

I don't want to postpone the pleasure of replying to your letter.

Believers, you say, also hear the "call of the real," coming from someone and specially addressed to them. Yes. That is their business. I am an unbeliever but I am not a-theist, if being atheist is to deny (which would suppose that I give a meaning to the word "God": by which right without Revelation?). On the side of believers, you say, there's a personal presence; for me there's the impersonal presence of Nature. So be it! Nature is present for them but their God is not present for me. Nature has always been there; gods presuppose religions which are human phenomena. "The attitude of the believer has its coherence." I do not wish to dispute that, although the believers quarrel with one another about the solution to the "problem" of evil. Yet, it seems to me that this coherence is not purely philosophical because the "discourse" of believers mixes describable and indescribable elements. Still, I instinctively prefer churches to mosques and synagogues.

Now I'll turn to your questions, starting with the distinction between "world" and "universe." In my view, world (cosmos) is a structured totality, which is organized (*holon*) whereas universe is an additive totality (*pan*)—a set of distinct units. The universe of astrophysicists ("*Big Bang's universe*") is a world. When I speak of the world as a "face" of Nature, I mean the world I see on opening my window (which opens out on the countryside). So, I consider that I am on this side of what is myth, poetic narrative, art or other human creation.

Another question is the distinction "between nature and world, and especially, between nature thought by the Greeks and world known by modern science." A world is structured by definition; Nature is only structurable. But science cannot know Nature without making it a world. What relation is there between this world of modern science and Nature as absolute totality, as a set of all things? Science cannot tell us.[1] Philosophy speculates on the totality of Nature, as you put it, that "all becoming . . . depends on an infinite mechanism"—that according to modern science—Democritus (who would totally agree with all your development) applied it to the totality of Nature, which modern science cannot do. It remains that a philosophical conception of Nature *cannot be falsified*."

Then you apply your "Hegelianism." I find it hard to follow you—you, Hegel, Weil, etc. In my view, language does not reduce externalism of Nature, *because it observes it*. If it "reduced it," it would have been wrong to observe it. "All *there is* for man is born in language," says Weil. Yes, but I say "there is" because there is, and it is not because I say "there is" that *there is*. "It is the mind that says and thinks what Nature is." Yes, but thinking is not "reducing" it, *on the contrary*; it's allowing it to be itself. And what mind? The mind of man. Man says there is, there always has been and there always will be Nature. This was true before he was there to say it and will be true when he is no longer there. Man is but an accident of Nature: the accident cannot "reduce" the substance.

Nevertheless, when you write: "the most elevated product of the mind is also the most elevated product of Nature, through which nature itself speaks" I find myself in complete agreement with you. It is even, in my commentary of the poet, what I wished to say. Also, when you write: "when I speak of mind, I speak of it as nothing other than *nature*, which has been reflected in the being who speaks, in the speaking body . . . ," I see nothing there with which I would disagree but are you sure Hegel would say that?

Thank you most sincerely for your letter, to which I have replied too quickly.

Very best wishes,
Marcel

GLOSSARIUM

Aetius: First or second-century doxographer, eclectic philosopher, and teacher of Eunomius. None of Aetius's works survive today, but he does solve a mystery about two major compilations of philosophical quotes. There are two extant books named *Placita Philosophorum* ("Opinions of the Philosophers") and *Eclogae Physicae* ("Physical and Moral Extracts").

Alexander of Aphrodisias: (fl.AD 200) a Peripatetic philosopher and the most celebrated of the Ancient Greek commentators on the writings of Aristotle. A native of Aphrodisias in Caria, he lived and taught in Athens at the beginning of the third century, where he held a position as scholarch of the Peripatetic school. He wrote many commentaries on the works of Aristotle, and still extant are those on the Prior Analytics, Topics, Meteorology, Sense and Sensibilia, and Metaphysics. Several original treatises also survive, and include a work On Fate, in which he argues against the Stoic doctrine of necessity; and one On the Soul. His commentaries on Aristotle were considered so useful that he was styled, by way of preeminence, "the commentator."

Aquinas, Saint Thomas (1224–1274): the greatest of the medieval philosopher-theologians.

Amor fati: a Latin phrase coined by Nietzsche loosely translating to "love of fate" or "love of one's fate." It is used to describe an attitude in which one sees everything that happens in one's life, including suffering and loss, as good. Moreover, it is characterized by an acceptance of the events or situations that occur in one's life.

Anaxagoras (c.500–428 BC): a pre-Socratic Greek philosopher. Born in Clazomenae in Asia Minor, Anaxagoras was the first philosopher to bring philosophy from Ionia to Athens. He attempted to give a scientific account of eclipses, meteors, rainbows, and the sun, which he described as a fiery mass larger than the Peloponnese.

Anaximander (c.610–c.546 BC): a pre-Socratic Greek philosopher who lived in Miletus, a city of Ionia; Milet in modern Turkey. He belonged to the Milesian school and learned the teachings of his master Thales. He succeeded Thales and became the second master of that school where he counted Anaximenes and, arguably, Pythagoras among his pupils. Anaximander claimed that an "indefinite" (*apeiron*) principle gives rise to all natural phenomena. Carl Sagan claims that he conducted the earliest recorded scientific experiment.

Augustine of Hippo (354–430): Bishop of Hippo Regius (present-day Annaba, Algeria). He was a Latin-speaking philosopher and theologian who lived in the Roman Africa Province. According to his contemporary, Jerome, Augustine "established anew the ancient Faith." In his early years he was heavily influenced by Manichaeism and afterward by the Neoplatonism of Plotinus. After his conversion to Christianity and baptism (387), Augustine developed his own approach to philosophy and theology, accommodating a variety of methods and different perspectives. He believed that the grace of Christ was indispensable to human freedom, and he framed the concepts of original sin and just war.

Baillet, Adrien (1649–1706): a French scholar, biographer of René Descartes, and critic.

Beaufret, Jean (1907–1982): a French philosopher and Germanist tremendously influential in the reception of Martin Heidegger's work in France.

Bernard, Claude (1813–1878): the first man to define the term *milieu intérieur*. Among many other accomplishments, he was one of the first to suggest the use of blind experiments to ensure the objectivity of scientific observations.

Benrubi, Isaak (1876–1943): a philosopher of Greek-Jewish extraction; he opposed the conventional character of the act of knowing in "subject" and "object" to the reality that is interested in both subject and object: "I can't exist without the universe; neither can the universe exist without me."

Bonne, Herman (b.1952): CEO of a family business (geographical information systems). After a classical education (Greek-Latin), trained as LLM (Law Dept. Ghent University 1977), philosophy being his chosen field of interest.

Bréhier, Émile (1876–1952): a French philosopher and successor to Bergson at the Sorbonne. His interest was in classical philosophy and the history of philosophy. He wrote a *Histoire de la Philosophie*, translated into English in seven volumes.

Callicott, J. Baird (1941): an American philosopher whose work has been at the forefront of the new field of environmental philosophy and ethics. He is a University Distinguished Research Professor and a member of the Department of Philosophy and Religion Studies and the Institute of Applied Sciences at the University of North Texas. Callicott is widely considered to be the leading contemporary exponent of Aldo Leopold's land ethic. He has written, among others: *In Defense of the Land Ethic* (1989), *Beyond the Land Ethic* (1999), and *Earth's Insights* (1994).

Camus de Pontcarré, Jean-Pierre (1584–1652): a French bishop, preacher, and author of works of fiction and spirituality.

Chrysippus of Soli (c.279–c.206 BC) a Greek Stoic philosopher. He was a native of Soli, Cilicia, but moved to Athens as a young man, where he became a pupil of Cleanthes in the Stoic school. When Cleanthes died, around 230 BC, Chrysippus became the third scholarch of the school. A prolific writer, Chrysippus expanded the fundamental doctrines of Zeno of Citium, the founder of the school, which earned him the title of "Second Founder of Stoicism."

Cicero, Marcus Tullius (106–43 BC): a Roman philosopher, statesman, lawyer, political theorist, and constitutionalist. He came from a wealthy municipal family of the equestrian order, and is widely considered one of Rome's greatest orators and prose stylists.

Cleanthes (c.330–c.230 BC): of Assos, a Greek Stoic philosopher and the successor to Zeno as the second scholarch of the Stoic school in Athens. Originally a boxer, he came to Athens where he took up philosophy, listening to Zeno's lectures. He supported himself by working as water-carrier at night. After the death of Zeno (c.262 BC), he became the scholarch of the school, a post he held for the next thirty-two years.

Collobert, Catherine: French philosopher and associate professor at the University of Ottawa (philosophy, classics).

Comte, Auguste (1798 1857) a French philosopher, a founder of the discipline of sociology and of the doctrine of positivism. He may be regarded as the first philosopher of science in the modern sense of the term.

Comte-Sponville, André (b.1952): a French philosopher born in Paris, France. He studied in the *École Normale Supérieure*, and is aggregated in philosophy. He is a proponent of atheism and materialism, but in a particular form, because of his spiritualistic aim.

Confucius (551–479 BC): a Chinese thinker and social philosopher of the Spring and Autumn Period. The philosophy of Confucius emphasized personal and governmental morality, correctness of social relationships, justice, and sincerity. These values gained prominence in China over other doctrines, such as Legalism or Taoism during the Han Dynasty (206 BC–AD 220). Confucius's thoughts have been developed into a system of philosophy known as Confucianism.

Dastur, Françoise (b.1942): a French philosopher and historian of philosophy. Emeritus professor of the University of Nice Sophia-Antipolis, her work focuses on French and German phenomenology.

Democritus (c.460–370 BC): an Ancient Greek philosopher born in Abdera, Thrace, Greece. He was an influential pre-Socratic philosopher and pupil of Leucippus, who formulated an atomic theory for the cosmos.

Descartes, René (1596–1650): a French philosopher and writer who spent most of his adult life in the Dutch Republic. He has been dubbed the "Father of Modern Philosophy," and much subsequent Western philosophy is a response to his writings, which are studied closely to this day. In particular, his *Meditations on First Philosophy* continue to be a standard text at most university philosophy departments. Descartes's influence in mathematics is equally apparent; the Cartesian coordinate system—allowing geometric shapes to be expressed in algebraic equations—was named after him. He is credited as the father of analytical geometry. Descartes was also one of the key figures in the Scientific Revolution.

Dion (408–354 BC): tyrant of Syracuse in Sicily, the son of Hipparinus, and brother-in-law of Dionysius I of Syracuse.

Dionysos: born from the thigh of Zeus, the great Olympian god of wine, vegetation, pleasure, and festivity.

Dixsaut, Monique: a professor of philosophy at the Sorbonne, Paris, who writes on the dialogues of Plato.

Donahue, James (b.1967) an American college teacher. He has published *Between Two Worlds* (2013), a multicultural coming-of-age anthology. He has helped Ledoux and Bonne translate this book.

Dostoyevsky, Fyodor Mikhaylovich (1821–1881): a Russian writer of realist fiction and essays. He is best known for his novels *Crime and Punishment*, *The Idiot*, and *The Brothers Karamazov*.

Epicurus (341–270 BC): a Greek philosopher and founder of the school of philosophy called Epicureanism. Only a few fragments and letters remain of Epicurus's three hundred written works. Much of what is known about Epicurean philosophy derives from later followers and commentators. For Epicurus, the purpose of philosophy was to attain the happy, tranquil life, characterized by *ataraxia*, peace and freedom from fear, and *aponia*, the absence of pain, and by living a self-sufficient life surrounded by friends. He taught that pleasure and pain are the measures of what is good and evil; that death is the end of the body and the soul and should therefore not be feared; that the gods do not reward or punish humans; that the universe is infinite and eternal; and that events in the world are ultimately based on the motions and interactions of atoms moving in empty space.

Gast, Peter (1854–1918), real name Johann Heinrich Köselitz: a German author and composer. He is known for his longtime friendship with Friedrich Nietzsche, who gave him the pseudonym Peter Gast.

Gierczynski, Zbigniew: a contemporary philosopher, specialist on Montaigne and Rabelais. Wrote the *Que sais-je* volume on Montaigne, *Rabelais et la religion : le problème du libertinage au XVIe siècle* (*Rabelais and religion*), and *Rabelais ou l'Humanisme des Lumières* (*Rabelais and the Humanism of Enlightenment*).

Godin, Christian (b.1949): a French philosopher, teaching at the Université Blaise-Pascal of Clermont-Ferrand (France).

Granarolo, Philippe (b.1947): a French philosopher.

Halévy, Daniel (1872–1962): a French historian and essayist, famous for his biography of Nietzsche.

Hán Yù (768–824): born in Nanyang, Henan, China, a precursor of neo-Confucianism as well as an essayist and poet, during the Tang dynasty.

Hegelianism: a collective term for schools of thought following or referring to G. W. F. Hegel's philosophy, which can be summed up by the dictum that "the rational alone is real," which means that all reality is capable of being expressed in rational categories. His goal was to reduce reality to a more synthetic unity within the system of transcendental idealism.

Heidegger, Martin (1889–1976): an influential German philosopher known for his existential and phenomenological explorations of the "question of Being."

Heisenberg, Werner (1901–1976): a German theoretical physicist who made foundational contributions to quantum mechanics and is best known for asserting the uncertainty principle of quantum theory.

Heraclitus (c.535–475 BC): a pre-Socratic Greek philosopher, a native of the Greek city Ephesus, Ionia, on the coast of Asia Minor. Little is known about his early life and education, but he regarded himself as self-taught and a pioneer of wisdom. From the lonely life he led, and still more from the riddling nature of his philosophy and his contempt for humankind in general, he was called "The Obscure" and the "Weeping Philosopher."

Herodotus (c.484–425 BC): an ancient Greek historian who was born in Halicarnassus, Caria (modern day Bodrum, Turkey). He has been called the "Father of History" since he was the first historian known to collect his materials systematically, test their accuracy to a certain extent and arrange them in a well-constructed and vivid narrative.

Hofmannsthall, Hugo von (1874–1929): an Austrian novelist, librettist, poet, dramatist, narrator, and essayist.

Hölderlin, Johann Christian Friedrich (1770–1843): a major German lyric poet, commonly associated with the artistic movement known as Romanticism. Hölderlin was also an important thinker in the development of German Idealism, particularly his early association with and philosophical influence on his seminary roommates and fellow Swabians Georg Wilhelm Friedrich Hegel and Friedrich Wilhelm Joseph Schelling.

Jerome, Saint (c.347–420): an Illyrian Catholic priest and apologist. He was the son of Eusebius, of the city of Stridon, which was on the border of Dalmatia and Pannonia. He is best known for his translation of the Bible into Latin (the Vulgate), and his list of writings is extensive. He is recognized by the Catholic Church as a saint and Doctor of the Church and the Vulgate is still an important text in Catholicism. He is also recognized as a saint by the Eastern Orthodox Church, where he is known as St. Jerome of Stridonium or Blessed Jerome.

Khayyám, Omar (1048–1131): a Persian mathematician, astronomer, philosopher, and poet. He also wrote treatises on mechanics, geography, and music.

Kirscher, Gilbert: Emeritus philosophy professor at the University of Lille, France, and a specialist on Éric Weil.

Kierkegaard, Søren Aabye (1813–1855): a profound and prolific writer in the Danish "golden age" of intellectual and artistic activity.

Kojève, Alexandre (Moskou 1902–Brussels 1968): a French philosopher of Russian origin, known for the reintroduction of Hegel to the French philosophical scene.

Koyré, Alexandre (1892–1964): a French philosopher of Russian origin who wrote on the history and philosophy of science.

Lao Tzu: (fl.6th century BC): a mystic philosopher of ancient China, and best known as the author of the *Tao Te Ching*. His association with the *Tao Te Ching* has led him to be traditionally considered the founder of Taoism (also spelled "Daoism"). He is also revered as a deity in most religious forms of the Taoist religion, which often refers to Laozi as Taishang Laojun, or "One of the Three Pure Ones." Laozi translated literally from Chinese means "old master" or "old one," and is generally considered honorific.

Ledoux, Laurent (b.1966): a Belgian manager, currently President of the Belgian Ministry of Mobility & Transports. He is also the director of Philosophie & Management (www.philoma.org), an association organizing philosophy seminars for managers.

Leibniz, Gottfried Wilhelm (1646–1716): a German philosopher and mathematician. Leibniz occupies a prominent place in the history of mathematics and the history of philosophy. He developed the infinitesimal calculus independently of Isaac Newton, and Leibniz's mathematical notation has been widely used ever since it was published.

Leibowitz, Yeshayahu (1903–1994): an Israeli philosopher and scientist known for his outspoken, often controversial opinions on Judaism, ethics, religion, and politics.

Leyssenne, Jean (1921–2009): a French aquarellist, a lifelong friend to Marcel Conche.

Littré, Émile (1801–1881): a French lexicographer and philosopher, best known for his *Dictionnaire de la langue française*, commonly referred to as "The Littré."

Lucretius (c.99–55 BC): a Roman poet and philosopher. His only known work is an epic philosophical poem laying out the beliefs of Epicureanism, *De rerum natura*, translated into English as *On the Nature of Things* or *On the Nature of the Universe*. Virtually no details have come down concerning the life of Lucretius; Saint Jerome tells how he was driven mad by a love potion, and wrote his poetry in between fits of insanity, eventually committing suicide in middle age.

Malebranche, Nicolas (1638–1715): a French Oratorian and rationalist philosopher. In his works, he sought to synthesize the thought of St. Augustine and Descartes, in order to demonstrate the active role of God in every aspect of the world. Malebranche is best known for his doctrines of Vision in God and Occasionalism.

Malinowski-Charles, Syliane: professor of philosophy at the *Université du Québec à Trois-Rivières*, Canada.

Marcus Aurelius (121–180): Roman emperor from 161 to 180. He ruled with Lucius Verus as co-emperor from 161 until Verus's death in 169. He was the last of the "Five Good Emperors" and is also considered one of the most important Stoic philosophers.

Maritain, Raïssa Oumansoff (1883–1960): a Russian-Ukrainian poet and philosopher, married to Jacques Maritain, French philosopher.

Mimnermus (fl. c.630–600 BC): a Greek elegiac poet from either Colophon or Smyrna in Ionia. He was strongly influenced by the example of Homer yet he wrote short poems suitable for performance at drinking parties and was remembered by ancient authorities chiefly as a love poet. Mimnermus exerted a strong influence on Callimachus and Roman poets such as Propertius.

Melissos (fl.5th century BC): the third and last member of the ancient school of Eleatic philosophy, whose other members included Zeno and Parmenides. Little is known about his life except that he was the commander of the Samian fleet shortly before the Peloponnesian War. Melissus's contribution to philosophy was a treatise of systematic arguments supporting Eleatic philosophy. Like Parmenides, he argued that reality is ungenerated, indestructible, indivisible, changeless, and motionless. In addition, he sought to show that reality is wholly unlimited, and infinitely extended in all directions; and since existence is unlimited, it must also be one.

Montaigne, Michel Eyquem de (1533–1592): one of the most influential writers of the French Renaissance, known for popularizing the essay as a literary genre, and is popularly thought of as the father of Modern Skepticism. He became famous for his effortless ability to merge serious intellectual speculation with casual anecdotes and autobiography—and his massive volume *Essais* (translated literally as

"Attempts") contains, to this day, some of the most widely influential essays ever written. Montaigne had a direct influence on writers the world over, including René Descartes, Blaise Pascal, Jean-Jacques Rousseau, Ralph Waldo Emerson, Friedrich Nietzsche, Stefan Zweig, Eric Hoffer, Isaac Asimov, and perhaps William Shakespeare.

Nemesius (c.AD 390): a Christian philosopher, and the author of a treatise *De Natura Hominis* (*On Human Nature*). According to the title of his book, he was the Bishop of Emesa (in Syria). His book is an attempt to compile a system of anthropology from the standpoint of Christian philosophy.

Nicias (c.470–413 BC): an Athenian politician and general during the Peloponnesian War.

Omnès, Roland: author of several books that aim to close the gap between our commonsense experience of the classical world and the complex, formal mathematics that is now required to accurately describe reality at its most fundamental level.

Ontological: the philosophical theory that there might be no objects at all, i.e., that there is a possible world in which there are no objects at all; or at least that there might be no concrete objects at all, so that even if every possible world contains some objects, there is at least one that contains only abstract objects.

Overman: the *Übermensch* (German for "Overman, Overhuman, Above-Human, Superman") is a concept in the philosophy of Friedrich Nietzsche. Nietzsche posited the *Übermensch* as a goal for humanity to set for itself in his 1883 book *Thus Spoke Zarathustra*. There is no overall consensus regarding the precise meaning of the *Übermensch*, nor on the importance of the concept in Nietzsche's thought. The German prefix *über* can have connotations of superiority, transcendence, excessiveness, or intensity, depending on the words to which it is prepended. Mensch refers to a member of the human species, rather than to a man specifically. The adjective *übermenschlich* means superhuman, in the sense of beyond human strength or out of proportion to humanity.

Panta rhei: Πάντα ῥεῖ, ("everything flows") either was not spoken by Heraclitus or did not survive as a quotation of his. This famous aphorism used to characterize Heraclitus's thought comes from Simplicius, a Neoplatonist, and from Plato's *Cratylus*. The word *rhei*, adopted by rhe-o-logy, is the Greek word for "to stream, and to the etymology of

Rhea according to Plato's *Cratylus*." Compare with the Latin adages *Omnia mutantur* and *Tempora mutantur* and the Japanese tale *Hōjōki*, which contains the same image of the changing river.

Parmenides of Elea (fl. early 5th century BC): an ancient Greek philosopher born in Elea, a Greek city on the southern coast of Italy (now Velia). He was the founder of the Eleatic school of philosophy. The single known work of Parmenides is a poem, *On Nature*, which has survived only in fragmentary form. In this poem, Parmenides describes two views of reality. In "the way of truth" (a part of the poem), he explains how reality (coined as "what-is") is one, change is impossible, and existence is timeless, uniform, necessary, and unchanging. In "the way of opinion," he explains the world of appearances, in which one's sensory faculties lead to conceptions that are false and deceitful. These ideas strongly influenced the whole of Western philosophy, perhaps most notably through their effect on Plato.

Pascal, Blaise (1623–1662): a French mathematician, physicist, inventor, writer, and Catholic philosopher. He was a child prodigy who was educated by his father, a tax collector in Rouen. Pascal's earliest work was in the natural and applied sciences where he made important contributions to the study of fluids and clarified the concepts of pressure and vacuum by generalizing the work of Evangelista Torricelli. Pascal also wrote in defense of the scientific method.

Pasteur, Louis (1822–1895): a French chemist and microbiologist who was one of the most important founders of medical microbiology. He is remembered for his remarkable breakthroughs in the causes and preventions of diseases.

Plutarch (c.AD 46–120): a Greek historian, biographer, essayist, and Middle Platonist known primarily for his *Parallel Lives* and *Moralia*.

Phusis or *Physis*: in the pre-Socratic philosophy it developed a complex of other meanings. The word *physis* occurs very early in Greek philosophy, and in several senses; generally, these senses match rather well the current senses in which the English word *nature* is used. The etymology of the word *physical* shows its use as a synonym for *natural* in about the mid-fifteenth century. Since Aristotle, the physical (the subject matter of physics, properly "Natural things") has often been contrasted with metaphysical (the subject of metaphysics). In *The Odyssey*, Homer uses the word once (its earliest known occurrence), referring to the intrinsic way of growth of a particular species of plant.

Philo (c.20 BC–AD 50): Philo Judaeus or Philo of Alexandria was the foremost Jewish philosopher of the Hellenistic age, a leader of Alexandria Jewry, who defended his co-religionists in an embassy to Caligula and in sophisticated apologetics. Philo's thoughtful, cosmopolitan, often allegorical Greek commentaries on the Septuagint Bible synthesize Platonic, Stoic, and Jewish values and ideas, laying a foundation for Christian, and later Muslim and Jewish rational theologians.

Posidonius "of Apameia" or "of Rhodes" (c.135–51 BC): a Greek Stoic philosopher, politician, astronomer, geographer, historian, and teacher native to Apamea, Syria. He was acclaimed as the greatest polymath of his age. None of his vast body of work can be read in its entirety today, as it exists only in fragments.

Positivism: refers to a set of epistemological perspectives and philosophies of science that hold that the scientific method is the best approach to uncovering the processes by which both physical and human events occur.

Pyrrho (c.360–270 BC): a Greek philosopher of classical antiquity, is credited as being the first Skeptic philosopher, and the inspiration for the school known as Pyrrhonism, founded by Aenesidemus in the first century BC.

Pyrrhonism, or Pyrrhonian Skepticism: a school of skepticism founded by Aenesidemus in the first century BC and recorded by Sextus Empiricus in the late second century or early third century AD. It was named after Pyrrho, a philosopher who lived from c.360 to c.270 BC, although the relationship between the philosophy of the school and of the historical figure is murky. A renaissance of the term is to be noted for the seventeenth century when the modern scientific worldview was born.

Reid, Thomas (1710–1796): a Scottish philosopher, contemporary of David Hume, the founder of the Scottish School of Common Sense, and played an integral role in the Scottish Enlightenment. The early part of his life was spent in Aberdeen, Scotland, where he created the "Wise Club" (a literary-philosophical association) and graduated from the University of Aberdeen.

Sartre, Jean-Paul (1905–1980): a French existentialist philosopher, playwright, novelist, screenwriter, political activist, biographer, and literary critic. He was one of the leading figures in twentieth-century

French philosophy, particularly Marxism, and was one of the key figures in literary and philosophical existentialism.

Schmitt, Gérard: professor of philosophy at the University of Nancy (France), and redactor in chief of the *L'Enseignement philosophique*.

Spencer, Herbert (1820–1903): an English philosopher, biologist, sociologist, and prominent classical liberal political theorist of the Victorian era. Spencer developed an all-embracing conception of evolution as the progressive development of the physical world, biological organisms, the human mind, and human culture and societies. He was "an enthusiastic exponent of evolution," and even "wrote about evolution before Darwin did."

Spinoza, Baruch de (1632–1677): a Dutch Jewish philosopher, famous for his *Ethica*.

Swan, Ian (b.1965): an Irish writer and communications consultant based in Paris. He helped Ledoux and Bonne translate this book.

Tchouang-Tse or Zhuangzi (fl.4th century BC): an influential Chinese philosopher who lived during the Warring States Period, a period corresponding to the philosophical summit of Chinese thought—the Hundred Schools of Thought, and is credited with writing—in part or in whole—a work known by his name, the *Zhuangzi*.

Temporalism: the philosophical doctrine that emphasizes the ultimate reality of time instead of the reduction of time to a manifestation of the eternal.

Theophrastus (c.371–287 BC): a Greek native of Eresos in Lesbos and the successor of Aristotle in the Peripatetic school. He came to Athens at a young age, and initially studied in Plato's school. After Plato's death he attached himself to Aristotle. Aristotle bequeathed to Theophrastus his writings, and designated him as his successor at the Lyceum. Theophrastus presided over the Peripatetic school for thirty-six years, during which time the school flourished greatly. His successor as head of the school was Strato of Lampsacus.

Tristan and Iseult: the legend of Tristan and Iseult is an influential romance and tragedy, retold in numerous sources with as many variations. The tragic story is of the adulterous love between the Cornish knight Tristan (Tristram) and the Irish princess Iseult (Isolde, Yseult, etc.). The narrative predates and most likely influenced the Arthurian romance of Lancelot and Guinevere, and has had a substantial impact on Western art, the idea of romantic love, and literature since it first appeared in the twelfth century. While the details of the story differ from one author to another, the overall plot structure remains much the same.

Tudor, Dan (b.1967): an American entrepreneur, CEO of Tudor Collegiate Strategies, who works with colleges around the United States, teaching their coaches to recruit more effectively. He helped Ledoux and Bonne translate this book.

Valéry, Paul (1871–1945): a French poet, essayist, and philosopher. His interests were sufficiently broad that he can be classified as a polymath. In addition to his poetry and fiction (drama and dialogues) and aphorisms on art, history, letters, music, and current events, he also wrote many misanthropic diatribes on human nature.

Vallentin, Antonina (1893–1957): a German intellectual and writer best known for her biographical works.

Wahl, Jean (1888–1974): a French philosopher. He was professor at the Sorbonne from 1936 to 1967, broken by World War II. He was in the U.S. from 1942 to 1945, having been interned as a Jew at the Drancy internment camp (northeast of Paris) and then escaped. He began his career as a follower of Henri Bergson and the American pluralist philosophers William James and George Santayana. He is known as one of those introducing Hegelian thought in France in the 1930s, ahead of Alexandre Kojève's more celebrated lectures. He was also a champion in French thought of the Danish proto-existentialist Kierkegaard. These enthusiasms, which became the significant books *Le malheur de la conscience dans la philosophie de Hegel* (1929) and *Études kierkegaardiennes* (1938), were controversial, in the prevailing climate of thought. However, he influenced a number of key thinkers including Emmanuel Levinas and Jean-Paul Sartre. In the second issue of *Acéphale*, Georges Bataille's review, Jean Wahl wrote an article titled "Nietzsche and the Death of God," concerning Karl Jaspers's interpretation of this work. He became known as an antisystematic philosopher, in favor of philosophical innovation and the concrete.

Weil, Eric (1904–1977): a French philosopher, Jewish survivor of the Holocaust, emigrant from the Rhine. His philosophy contribution is his research *The Logic of Philosophy*, called *A Fresh Look at Philosophy*. His publications include *Hegel and the State*, *Philosophy and Reality: Recent Trial and Conferences*, *Texts on The Nature*, *History and Politics*. Not related to Simone Weil.

Weil, Simone: (1909–1943): a French philosopher, Christian mystic, and social activist.

Whitehead, Alfred North (1861–1947): a British mathematician, logician, and philosopher.

Yves de Paris (1588–1678): a Capuchin theologian, humanist, and spiritual writer. Born as Charles de la Rue, ordained to the priesthood 1630, he studied law at the University of Orléans and was admitted into the bar of the Parliament of Paris in 1608. In Italy he discovered the Neoplatonism of Marsilio Ficino (1433–1499), the chief scholar of the Platonic Academy founded by Cosimo de' Medici. In addition to Ficino, he appeared to have absorbed the writings of Ramón Llull (c.1232–1316), the Stoics, and the French Humanists.

BIBLIOGRAPHY OF MARCEL CONCHE

1. History of Philosophy

Montaigne ou la conscience heureuse, Ed. Seghers 1964, 1966, 1970; reedited Ed. Mégare, 1992; PUF 2002, 2007, 2011.

Lucrèce et l'expérience, Ed. Seghers 1967; reedited Ed. Mégare 1981, 1990, 1996; ed. Fides, coll. "Noésis," 2003; PUF 2011.

Pyrrhon ou l'apparence, Ed. de Mégare 1973; reworked and augmented ed. PUF 1994.

Epicure: Lettres et Maximes, Ed. de Mégare 1977; reedited PUF 1987, 1990, 1992, 1995, 1999, 2003, 2009.

Sur le "De Fato," unpublished work of Octave Hamelin, published and annotated by M. Conche, Ed. de Mégare, 1978.

Héraclite: fragments, PUF 1986, 1987, 1991, 1998, 2003, 2011.

Montaigne et la philosophie, Ed. de Mégare 1987, 1992; reedited PUF 1996, 1999, 2003, 2007, 2011.

Anaximandre: fragments et témoignages, PUF 1991, 2004, 2009.

Parménide. Le Poème: fragments, PUF 1996, 1999, 2004, 2009.

Montaigne. Les Essais. Foreword and Supplement (pp. 1335–65), PUF, coll. "Quadrige" 2004.

2. Oriental Thought

Nietzsche et le bouddhisme, Cahiers du Collège international de philosophie, no. 4, November 1987; reed. Encre Marine 1997, 2007, 2009. Translated into Italian.

Lao-Tseu, Tao-Te-king, PUF 2003, 2004, 2005, 2006, 2008, 2011.

3. Metaphysics

Orientation philosophique, Ed. de Mégare 1974; 2nd reworked and augmented edition, with foreword by André Comte-Sponville, PUF 1990, 1996; 3rd reviewed and augmented edition, Les Belles Lettres, coll. "Encre Marine" 2011. Translated into Russian and Portuguese.

La mort et la pensée, ed. de Mégare 1974, 1975; reedited Ed. Cécile Defaut 2007.

Temps et destin, Ed. de Mégare 1980; 2nd augmented edition, PUF 1992, 1999.

L'aléatoire, Ed. de Mégare 1989, 1990; 2nd reedited PUF 1999; 3rd augmented ed. *Les Belles Lettres*, coll. "Encre Marine" 2012.

Le sens de la philosophie, Encre Marine 1999; augmented and reedited 2003.

Présence de la nature, PUF 2001; augmented and reedited PUF, coll. "Quadrige" 2011.

Quelle philosophie pour demain? PUF, 2003.

Philosopher à l'infini, PUF 2005, 2006. Translated into Polish.

La liberté, Les Belles Lettres, coll. "Encre Marine" 2011.

Métaphysique, PUF 2012.

4. Ethics and moral philosophy

Le fondement de la morale, Ed. de Mégare 1982, 1990; reedited PUF 1993, 1999, 2003. Translated into Portuguese.

Vivre et philosopher, réponses aux questions de Lucile Laveggi, PUF 1992, 1993, 1998; reedited Livre de Poche 2011.

Analyse de l'amour et autres sujets, PUF 1997, 1998, 1999; reedited Livre de Poche 2011. Translated into Portuguese.

Interview with Sébastien Charles, in S. Charles, *La philosophie française en question*, Livre de poche, 1999.

Confession d'un philosophe, réponses à André Comte-Sponville, Albin Michel 2003; reedited Livre de Poche, 2003. Translated into Spanish.

La voie certaine vers "Dieu," Les cahiers de l'Égaré 2008.

5. Literature

Ma vie antérieure, Encre Marine 1997, and *Le destin de la solitude*, Encre Marine 1999; reedited as *Ma vie antérieure & Le destin de la solitude*, Encre Marine 2003.

Essais sur Homère, PUF 1999; reed. coll. "Quadrige" 2003.

De l'amour, pensées trouvées dans un vieux cahier de dessin, Les cahiers de l'Égaré, 2003; reedited Cécile Defaut 2008.

Heidegger par gros temps, Preface by Philippe Granarolo, *Les Cahiers de l'Égaré*, 2004. Translated into Spanish.

Avec des "si." Journal étrange I. PUF 2006, 2008, 2011.

Oisivetés. Journal étrange II, PUF 2007.

Noms. Journal étrange III, PUF 2008.

Diversités. Journal étrange IV, Les Belles Lettres, coll. "Encre Marine" 2009.

Corsica. Journal étrange V, PUF 2010, 2011.

Le silence d'Émilie, Les Cahiers de l'Égaré 2010. Prix des Charmettes—Jean Jacques Rousseau.

Interview with Gilbert Moreau in *Les moments littéraires*, no. 26, 2011. Foreword by Syliane Malinowski-Charles.

Ma vie (1922–1947), un amour sous l'Occupation, HDiffusion 2012.

And numerous articles in philosophical journals, such as *Raison Présente*, *Enseignement Philosophique*, *Revue philosophique*, *Le Nouvel Observateur hors série*, *Magazine littéraire*, etc.

Pilar Sánchez Orozco, *Actualité d'une sagesse tragique—La pensée de Marcel Conche*, Les Cahiers de l'Égaré 2005.

NOTES

I. Flashback

1. Henri Bergson, *Philosophical Intuition*, in *Henri Bergson, Key Writings*, trans. Melissa McMahon, ed. Keith Ansell Pearson and John Mullarkey (New York: Continuum, 2002), 233. Also: *The Creative Mind, An Introduction to Metaphysics*, trans. Mabelle L. Andison (New York: Dover, 2007) (reprint of 1948), 87.

2. Ibid., 235; also: ibid., 90.

3. Montaigne, *Essays*, in *The Complete Works*, trans. Donald Frame (New York: Everyman's Library, 2003), 476.

4. Philo, *De Josepho*, Online Text Philo of Alexandria, ed. Charles Duke Yonge, 1854; http://www.earlyjewishwritings.com/philo.html.

5. Parmenides, in Diels-Kranz, *Die Fragmente der Vorsokratiker*, 6th ed. (Zürich: Weidmann, 2004), *Fragment* 8, 9. Also: Parmenides, trans. Harold North Fowler, Loeb Classical Library (Cambridge: Harvard University Press and London: William Heinemann, 1926).

6. Ibid., 8, 5.

7. νῦν in Ancient Greek.

8. Aristotle, *Metaphysica*, in *The Complete Works, the Revised Oxford Translation*, ed. Jonathan Barnes (Princeton: Princeton University Press, 1984), A, 2, 983 a 13.

9. *Vis*, in Lucretius, *De rerum natura*, trans. Alice Stallings (London: Penguin Classics, 2008), I, 13.

10. Φύσις κρύπτεσθαι φιλεῖ, in Heraclitus, in Diels-Kranz, *Die Fragmente der Vorsokratiker*, 6th ed. (Zürich: Weidmann, 2004), *Fragment* 123. Also: Heracleitus, in Hippocrates, vol. IV, *Nature of Man*, trans. W. H. S. Jones, Loeb Classical Library (Cambridge: Harvard University Press and London: William Heinemann, 1931).

11. Φιλέω.

12. Herodotus writes for example αὔρη φιλέει πνέειν (the North wind is wont to blow). *Histories* (London: Penguin Classics, 2008), II, 27.

13. Heraclitus, in Diels-Kranz, *Die Fragmente der Vorsokratiker*, 6th ed. (Zürich: Weidmann, 2004), *Fragment* 54. Also: Heracleitus, in Hippocrates, vol. IV, *Nature of Man*, op. cit.

II. Presence of the Infinite.

1. Quoted by Jean Hamburger, *Monsieur Littré* (Paris: Flammarion, 1988), 231.

2. Quoted by Pasteur Vallery-Radot, *Les plus belles pages de Pasteur* (Paris: Flammarion, 1943), 320–21 (from the speech by L. Pasteur in reception to the French Academy, 1882).

3. Henri Bergson, *On Aristotle's Conception of Place*, trans. D. Hauptmann and P. Healy (Delft School of Design Publication Series, forthcoming).

4. Paul Janet, quoted by Bergson, in Henri Bergson, *Mélanges* (Paris : PUF, 1972), 377 (from a critique Bergson wrote on *Principes de métaphysique et de psychologie* of Paul Janet, published in *Revue philosophique* of November 1897).

5. Henri Bergson, *On the Pragmatism of William James, Truth and Reality*, in *Henri Bergson, Key Writings*, trans. Melissa McMahon, ed. Keith Ansell Pearson and John Mullarkey (New York: Continuum, 2002), 273. Also, *The Creative Mind, An Introduction to Metaphysics*, trans. Mabelle L. Andison (New York: Dover, 2007), 186.

6. Letter to Jacques Chevalier, 2 mars 1926, in Henri Bergson, *Correspondance* (Paris : PUF, 2002), 1187.

7. Adrien Baillet, *Vie de Monsieur Descartes* (Paris : La Table Ronde, 1946), 291.

8. Gustave Thibon, *Ils sculptent en nous le silence* (Paris: F. X. de Guibert, 2003), 200.

9. *Hegel's Preface to the Phenomenology of Spirit*, trans. and running commentary Yirmiyahu Yovel (Princeton: Princeton University Press, 2005), 102, also Introduction, 31–34.

10. Henri Bergson, *The Creative Evolution*, trans. Arthur Mitchell (London: Macmillan, 1922), 201. See Toronto University: http://openlibrary.org/books/OL7240000M/Creative_evolution).

11. Isaac Benrubi, *Souvenir sur Henri Bergson* (Memories of Henri Bergson) (Neuchâtel: Delachaux & Niestlé, 1942), 77.

12. Plato, *Theaetetus* (London: Penguin Classics, 1987), 173 c.

13. Ibid., 174 a.

14. Plato, *Laches* (Oxford: Oxford University Press, 2009), 198 c.

15. Ibid., 192 d.

16. Yeshayahu Leibowitz, *Judaïsme, peuple juif et Etat d'Israël* (Judaism, Jewish people and the State of Israel), trans. G. Roth, ed. Jean-Claude Lattès (Paris: 1985), 200, taken from an article on bravery, published (in Hebrew) in 1967.

17. The Greek words are αἰτίας λογιςμῷ in Plato, *Meno* (Oxford: Oxford University Press, 2009), 98 a.

18. The Greek word for Science is here ἐπιστήμη and for the enchainment of ideas is δεσμός.

19. In Greek: εἴδη.

20. Plato, *The Republic* (London: Penguin Classics, 2008), VII, 521 d.

21. Plato, *Phaedo* (Oxford: Oxford University Press, 2009), 97 c. The Greek word used for "intelligence" is νοῦς.

22. Ibid., 97 c.

23. Plato, *Parmenides*, trans. Harold North Fowler, Loeb Classical Library (Cambridge: Harvard University Press and London: William Heinemann, 1926), 130 b-c.

24. Plato, *The Republic*, X, 596 a.

25. The Greek words used are: γένεσις εἰς οὐσιαν, in Plato, *Philebus*, trans. Harold North Fowler, Loeb Classical Library (Cambridge: Harvard University Press and London: William Heinemann, 1925), 26 d.

26. Greek words for "principles for beings": ἀρχὰς τῶν ὄντων.

27. Aristotle, *Metaphysica*, in *The Complete Works, the Revised Oxford Translation*, ed. Jonathan Barnes (Princeton: Princeton University Press, 1984), A 6, 987 b.

28. Ibid., 987 b 29–30.

29. Ibid., 987 b 18.

30. Ibid., 987 b 21. The Greek word for principles is ἀρχαί.

31. Ibid., 987 b 23. The Greek word for substance is οὐσία.

32. As we learn from Plato, *The Republic*, Book VI.

33. Aristotle, *Metaphysica*, 987 b 22–23.

34. Theophrastus, *Metaphysica*, trans. W. D. Ross (Whitefish, Montana: Kessinger Legacy Reprints, 2010), 6 b 8–14.

35. The Greek word for Undefined Dyad is ἀόριστος δυάς.

36. Aristotle, *Metaphysica*, N 5, 1092 b 8.

37. Ibid., N 6, 1093 a 13–16.

38. Friedrich Nietzsche, *Philosophy in the Tragic Age of the Greeks*, trans. Marianne Cowan (Washington, DC: Regnery, 1996). Conche, in the edition he uses (Nietzsche, *La naissance de la philosophie à l'époque de la tragédie grecque*, trans. G. Bianquis [Paris: Gallimard, 1938]) refers to a fragment from Nietzsche's *Nachlass*, not translated in the English edition.

39. The Greek word for "conversions" is τροπαί.

40. Marcel Conche, *Héraclite* (Paris: PUF, 2005), fragment 82 = Diels-Kranz, *Die Fragmente der Vorsokratiker*, 6th ed. (Zürich: Weidmann, 2004), fragment 31.

41. The Greek word is περαςς.

42. Nietzsche, op. cit., 177 (in the French edition of *Philosophy in the Tragic Age of the Greeks*, not translated in the edition of Marianne Cowan; see note 38 supra).

43. Ibid., 175 (in the French edition of *Philosophy in the Tragic Age of the Greeks*, not as in the edition of Marianne Cowan, see note 38 supra).

44. Émile Bréhier, *The Hellenic Age* (Chicago: University of Chicago Press, 1964), 129.

45. Plato, *Sophist*, in *Complete Works*, trans. John M. Cooper (Cambridge, MA: Hackett, 1997), 253, b.

46. Ibid., 259 e.

47. Ibid., 248 e. The Greek words for the totality of being is παντελῶς ὄν.

48. This notion of "totality of the being" was used by Plato before he wrote *Timaeus*.

49. Plato, *Timaeus*, trans. Desmond Lee (London: Penguin Classics, 2008), 31 a.

50. André Lalande, *Vocabulaire technique et critique de la philosophie* (Paris : PUF, Quadrige, 2002).

51. Alexandre Koyré, from a conference given at the American Society for the advancement of Science, Boston, 1954, cf. *The Scientific Monthly*, 1955. Published (abridged) as "Influence of Philosophical Trends on the Formulation of Scientific Theories," in *The Validation of Scientific Theories*, ed. Philipp Frank (Boston: Beacon Press, 1956), 194. Original French text in *Études d'histoire de la pensée philosophique* (Paris: Gallimard, 1971), 259.

52. Ibid., 267 in the French text, not in the English publication (see note 51 supra).

53. Plato, *Timaeus*, 31 a.

54. *Bulletin de la Société française de philosophie* (Bulletin of the French Society of Philosophy), séance du 23 janvier 1999 (Paris : Vrin, 1999), 29.

55. Ibid., 41–42.

56. Alain Blanchard, *L'Univers (The Universe)* (Paris: Flammarion, 1995), 110.

57. Werner Heisenberg, *Physics and Beyond*, trans. Arnold Pomerans (New York: Harper and Row, 1971), xvii.

58. *The Born-Einstein letters, Correspondence 1916–1955*, trans. I. Newton-John and Irene Born, introduction Werner Heisenberg (London: Macmillan, 1971), x.

59. Werner Heisenberg, *The Physicist's Conception of Nature*, trans. Arnold Pomerans (Westport, CT: Greenwood Press, 1970), 15.

60. The Greek words are λόγους ποιεῖσται πρός τινα.

61. Antonina Vallentin, *The Drama of Albert Einstein* (New York: Doubleday, 1954).

62. Werner Heisenberg, *Reality and Its Order*, trans. M. B. Rumscheidt, N. Lukens, and I. Heisenberg; http://werner-heisenberg.unh.edu/t-OdW-english.htm.

63. Roland Omnès, *Philosophie de la science contemporaine* (Paris: Gallimard, 1994), 358. See *Quantum Philosophy, Understanding and Interpreting Contemporary Science*, trans. Arturo Sangalli (Princeton: Princeton University Press, 1999) (not a complete translation).

III. With and Without Aristotle

1. Aristotle, *Physica*, in *The Complete Works, the Revised Oxford Translation*, ed. Jonathan Barnes (Princeton: Princeton University Press, 1984), II 1, 193 a.

2. Aristotle, *Metaphysica*, in *The Complete Works, the Revised Oxford Translation*, ed. Jonathan Barnes (Princeton: Princeton University Press, 1984), Δ 14, 1020 a 34.

3. In Greek: φυσις.

4. Aristotle, *Physica*, II 1, 192 b 9–12.

5. Aristotle, *De partibus animalium*, in *The Complete Works, the Revised Oxford Translation*, ed. Jonathan Barnes (Princeton: Princeton University Press, 1984), I, 640 b 28–29.

6. In Greek: εἶδος.

7. In Greek: σύνολον.

8. Aristotle, *Metaphysica*, Z 8, 1033 b 32.

9. In Greek: ὡς ἔτυχε, in Aristotle, *De caelo* in *The Complete Works, the Revised Oxford Translation*, ed. Jonathan Barnes (Princeton: Princeton University Press, 1984), II 8, 290 a 31.

10. In Greek: ἀλόγως.

11. Aristotle, *De caelo*, II 11, 291 b 13.

12. In Greek: μάτην in Aristotle, *De generatione animalium*, in *The Complete Works, the Revised Oxford Translation*, ed. Jonathan Barnes (Princeton: Princeton University Press, 1984), II 5, 741 b 5.

13. In Greek: περίεργον in ibid., II 4, 739 b 19.

14. In Greek: ἕνεκα τοῦ in Aristotle, *De partibus animalium*, I 1, 641 b 12.

15. Not yet polluted at the time of Aristotle.

16. In Greek: ἄνθρωπος φρόνιμως in Aristotle, *De partibus animalium*, IV 10, 687 a 12.

17. In Greek: δυίουργική in ibid., I 5, 645 a 9 and *De generatione animalium*, I 23, 731 a 24.

18. Claude Bernard, *Introduction à la médecine expérimentale* (*Introduction to Experimental Medicine*), II, 2 § 1, 6e ed. (Paris: Delagrave, 1934), 147–48. *An Introduction to the Study of Experimental Medicine*, trans. H. C. Greene (New York: Dover, 1927).

19. Ibid., 140.

20. André Bremond, *Le Dilemme aristotélicien* (*The Aristotelian Dilemma*), Archives de Philosophie, vol. X, cahier 2 (Paris: Beauchesne, 1933), 111.

21. In Greek: τὸ βέλτιστον in Aristotle, *De caelo*, II 5, 288 a 3.

22. Marcel Conche, *Anaximandre* (Paris : PUF, 1991), 226. Also : Charles H. Kahn, *Anaximander and the Origins of Greek Cosmology* (Indianapolis/Cambridge: Hackett, 1960/1994).

23. Lucretius, *rerum natura creatrix*, in *The Nature of Things* (London: Penguin Classics, 2008), I, 629; II, 1116; V, 1362.

24. Latin: *natura gubernans*, in Lucretius, op. cit., V, 77.

25. Aristotle, *Physica*, III 8, 208 a 13.

26. In Greek: πῶς.

27. In Greek: δυναμει.

28. In Greek: ἐπὶ τῆς νοήσεως in Aristotle, *Physica*, III 8, 208 a 16.

29. In Greek: ἐνεργείᾳ.

30. Aristotle, *Physica*, III 6, 206 b 33–207 a 2.

31. André Lalande, *Vocabulaire technique et critique de la philosophie* (Paris : PUF, collection Quadrige, 2002), see "infini actuel" ("current infinite").

32. In Greek: τόδε τι.
33. In Greek: ὡς οὐσία τις.
34. In Greek: ἀεὶ ἐν γενέσει ἢ φθορᾷ.
35. Aristotle, *Physica*, III 6, 206 a 29–33.
36. Lucretius, op. cit., IV, 375–76.
37. Aristotle, *Physica*, III 6, 207 a 8–10.
38. Ibid., III 6, 207 a 12.
39. In Greek: τέλειον.
40. In Greek: ἀεί γε ἕτερον καὶ ἕτερον in Aristotle, *Physica*, III 6, 206 a 33.
41. André Lalande, op. cit., see "acte," meaning "E."
42. That is "in actualization," "in action" (ἐν ἐνέργειᾳ) not "currently" (ἐν ἐντελεχείᾳ).
43. Elsewhere, I distinguish action from activity (or spontaneity, the Taoist *ziran*). Here the word *action* is equally valid for these two forms of actualization.
44. In Greek: κατὰ πλάτος, in *Arius Didymus*, 26, in Hermann Diels, *Doxographi Graeci* (Berlin: W. de Gruyter, 1965), 461, 32.
45. Plutarch, *Moralia*, *Against the Stoics on common conceptions*, 42, 1082 b in *Plutarch*, vol. XIII, trans. Harold Cherniss, Loeb Classical Library (Cambridge: Harvard University Press and London: William Heinemann, 1976), 841.
46. In Greek: ἀτελής in Aristotle, *Metaphysica*, Θ 6, 1048 b 29.
47. Aristotle, *Physica*, III 1, 201 a 10.
48. In Greek: ἐνέργεια.
49. In Greek: ὑπαρχειν.
50. In Greek: δυνάμει.
51. Aristotle, *Metaphysica*, Θ 6, 1048 a 30–32.
52. Marcel Conche, *Temps et destin* (*Time and destiny*) (Paris: PUF, 1992), Appendix: "*La question du réel et la question de l'événement.*" See also *L'aléatoire* (*The Aleatory*) (Paris: Les Belles Lettres, coll. "Encre Marine," 2012), 151–160.
53. Friedrich Nietzsche, *Œuvres* (Paris: Gallimard, 1982), 342. *The Gay Science*, "*Unedited fragments*," fragment not available in English editions such as Cambridge University Press, Stanford University Press, or Walter Kaufmann.
54. Marcus Aurelius, *Meditations*, trans. A. S. L. Farquharson (Oxford: Oxford University Press, 1998), II, 14.

IV. With and Without Chrysippus

1. Émile Bréhier, *Chrysippe* (Paris: Alcan, 1910), 73.
2. In Greek: ἄδηλον.
3. In Greek: οὐσία.
4. Diogenes Laertius, *Lives of Eminent Philosophers*, trans. R. D. Hicks, Loeb Classical Library (Cambridge: Harvard University Press and London: William Heinemann, 1989), vol. 2, VII, 148.

5. In Greek: διὰ τοῦ ζῆν.

6. Diogenes Laertius, *Lives of Eminent Philosophers*, VII, 147.

7. Émile Bréhier, *La théorie des incorporels dans l'ancien stoïcisme* (*Theory of the un-corporeals in ancient Stoicism*) (Paris: Vrin, 1928), 21.

8. Carlo Diano, *Forme et événement. Principes pour une interprétation du monde grec* (*Form and Event. Principles for an Interpretation of the Greek World*) (Combas: Ed. de l'Eclat, 1994), 14.

9. In Greek: εἶδος. Cf. Simplicius, in Hans von Arnim, *Stoicorum Veterum Fragmenta (SVF)*, (Stuttgart: Teubner, 1958), vol. II, n° 395.

10. In Greek: ἰδίως ποιόν.

11. In Greek: ἀνθόως.

12. "infinitely and without end" = εἰς ἄπειρον καὶ ἀτελευτήτως, cf. Nemesius, in *SVF*, op. cit., vol. II, n° 625.

13. Lactantius, in *SVF*, op. cit., vol. II, n° 623.

14. Nemesius, l.c.

15. Diogenes Laertius, VII, 137.

16. After Aristocles, in *SVF* I, n° 98.

17. In *SVF*, II, n° 624.

18. In Greek: συμβεβηκότα.

19. In Greek: ποιόν.

20. In Greek: ὑποκείμενον.

21. In Greek: τι.

22. In Greek: πὼς ἔχον.

23. In Greek: πρὸς τι πὼς ἔχον.

24. Cicero, *Academica*, II, 26, 85, in *Academica*, trans. H. Rackham, Loeb Classical Library (Cambridge: Harvard University Press and London: William Heinemann, 1922), 575.

25. Ibid., 539.

26. In Greek: ἀπαραλλάκτως.

27. Nemesius, in *SVF*, II, n° 625.

28. Plutarch, *Moralia*, *Stoic Self-contradictions*, trans. Harold Cherniss, Loeb Classical Library (Cambridge: Harvard University Press and London: William Heinemann, 1976), 595.

29. *Nisi libenter ac libere*.

30. Cicero, *Paradoxa stoicorum*, trans. H. Rackham, Loeb Classical Library (Cambridge: Harvard University Press and London: William Heinemann, 1968), 284.

31. Ibid., 286.

32. Aristotle, *De generatione et corruption*, in *The Complete Works*, *the Revised Oxford Translation*, ed. Jonathan Barnes (Princeton: Princeton University Press, 1984), II 11, 338 b.

33. Aristotle, *Meteorologica*, in ibid., I 14, 352 a.

34. In Greek: since the ἰδίως ποιά are εἴδη.

V. With and Without Epicurus

1. Lucretius, *De rerum natura*, trans. Alice Stallings (London: Penguin Classics, 2008), VI, 678.

2. Schopenhauer, *The World as Will and Representation*, trans. E. Payne (New York: Dover, 1966), 21.

3. Daniel Schulthess, *Philosophie et sens commun chez Thomas Reid* (*The Philosophy and Common Sense of Thomas Reid*) (Bern: Ed. Peter Lang, 1983), 129.

4. Ibid., 223, n. 169.

5. *Minimae partes*.

6. In Greek: παρέγκλισις.

7. In Greek: εἴδωλα.

8. Regarding all this, cf. my *Lucrèce* (Lucretius), 6th ed. (Paris: PUF, 2011) and my translation with comments of the *Lettre à Hérodote* (Letter to Herodotus), in my *Épicure, Lettres et maxims*, 8th edition (Paris: PUF, 2009).

9. Descartes, *Letter to William Cavendish, Marquess of Newcastle*, October 1645 in *The Philosophical writings of Descartes, vol. 3, The Correspondence* (Cambridge: Cambridge University Press, 1991), 275.

10. Strait line: *deorsum rectum* (see also note 172).

11. Lucretius, *De rerum natura*, II, 217–19.

12. Ibid., 445–46.

13. Auguste Comte, *System of positive polity*, 3rd vol., *Social Dynamics, or the General Theory of Human Progress*, trans. Edward Spencer Beesly (London: Longmans, 1876).

14. André Comte-Sponville, "Matérialisme," in *Dictionnaire philosophique* (*A Dictionary of Philosophy*) (Paris: PUF, 2013). Cf. also *Une éducation philosophique* (*A Philosophical Education*) (Paris: PUF, 1989), 99.

15. Comte-Sponville, "Matérialisme."

16. Marcel Conche, *L'aléatoire* (*The Aleatory*) (Paris: Les Belles Lettres, coll. "Encre Marine," 2012), 179.

VI. With and Without Montaigne

1. Montaigne, *Essays*, in *The Complete Works*, trans. Donald Frame (New York: Everyman's Library, 2003), 553.

2. Ibid., 554. In Plato, the one, coextensive to the being, is often put together with *tauto*, the same. For Aristotle, the one and the being are correlative notions. Cf. also Leibniz: "What is not really *one* being cannot be really one *being*" in a letter to Arnauld, 30 April 1687, in *The Leibniz-Arnauld Correspondence*, ed. H. T. Mason (New York: Garland, 1985).

3. Montaigne, *Essays*, 860.

4. Montaigne, *Journal de Voyage*, in *The Complete Works*, 1243. Marcel Conche uses the French translation of Meunier de Querlon's (1774), ed. Fausta Garavini (Paris: Gallimard, Folio-series, 1983), 331.

5. Montaigne, *Essays*, 286.
6. Ibid., 1041–43.
7. Ibid., 161.
8. Ibid., 162. Donald Frame translates "nature" whereas Villey (of the French edition) gives "God," as found in the A and B version of the *Essais*; the manuscript version, however (the most recent version by Montaigne himself), has "nature."
9. Ibid.
10. Ibid., 993.
11. Ibid., 1042.
12. Ibid., 555.
13. Ibid.
14. Cf. our *Orientation Philosophique* (Paris: Les Belles Lettres, coll. "Encre Marine," 2011), 37–38.
15. Montaigne, *Essays*, 140.
16. Ibid., 460.
17. Pascal, "Man's Disproportion," in *Pensées*, intro. T. S. Eliot (New York: Dutton, 1958); http://www.gutenberg.org/files/18269/18269-h/18269-h.htm.
18. Montaigne, *Essays*, 141. The sentence starting with "This great world" does not exist in the original edition (1580).
19. Ibid., 842.
20. Ibid., 401.
21. Cf. our *Orientation Philosophique* (Paris, PUF, 1990), 208–209.
22. Montaigne, *Essays*, 474.
23. Ibid., 743.
24. Ibid., 404.
25. Ibid., 726.
26. Ibid., 938.
27. Ibid., 977.
28. Ibid., 750.
29. *Eirmos aitiôn*. Cf. Aetius, *Placita Philosophorum*, I, 28, 4, In Hermann Diels, *Doxographi Graeci* (New York: W. de Gruyter, 1965), 324.
30. After Stobaeus, *SVF* II, op. cit., n° 913.
31. Montaigne, *Essays*, 416.
32. Ibid., 487.

VII. A Moment with Omar Khayyam

1. All quotes in this chapter from Omar Khayyam's *Robâiyat* are based on a translation of the original Persian version into French by Franz Toussaint (*Robâïyat de Omar Khayyâm*, foreword by Ali Nô-Rouze [Paris, Ed. H. Piazza, 1925]). I prefer this version in prose to the usual poetic translations, but in no way holding those poetic renderings in low esteem.

Translator's Note: the English translation of Toussaint's version used in this book was prepared by Hans Van Rossum and can be found on his Web site (http://home.kpn.nl/hansvanrossum/rubaiyat2.html). A few minor changes have been brought to Van Rossum's version in order to stick as much as possible to the French version as quoted by Marcel Conche. Parenthetical numbers refer to numbers of the quatrains in Hans Van Rossum's version.

2. King of Iran, of whom the following adage is told: "Be just and generous, and you will be a Freidoun." Cf. Ferdowsi, *The Book of Kings*, (London: Penguin Classics, 2007).

3. Montaigne, *Essays*, 301.

4. Scholars cannot determine with certainty which of the *Robâiyat* attributed to Khayyam are authentic. I doubt this one is authentic since it is not included in the first systematic collection, including 158 quatrains that can be found in the manuscript of the Bodleian Library of Oxford University dated 1460. Madhy Fouladvind keeps this *robâï* but does not classify it among the 155 most "Khayyamian" (Omar Khayyam, *Les Quatrains* [Paris: Éditions du Rocher, 1996]). Gilbert Lazard does not keep it as such but his selection is very severe and only retains 101 quatrains. See his edition of *Omar Khayyam, Cent un quatrains de libre pensée* (*101 Quatrains of Free Thinking*) (Paris: Gallimard, 2002).

5. "That such a book may circulate as freely in a Muslim country is a surprise. We can't find in European literature a book where not only positive religion, but all moral belief is negated with an irony so subtle and bitter" dixit Ernest Renan, in *Journal Asiatique* (Paris: L'Imprimerie Nationale, July-August 1868), 56–57; "This absolute freedom of thought, at a time when the most superstitious credulity reigned in Europe, is astonishing. Only the most daring modern thinkers come close to it" dixit Théophile Gautier, in *Moniteur Universel* (a newspaper founded in 1789), Paris, 8 December 1867.

6. Marcel Conche chooses here Charles Grolleau's translation (quatrain 94, in *Quatrains* [Paris, Mille et une Nuits: 1995]), which I translate literally into English. Here is Hans Van Rossum's version, based on the one by Jean Rullier (in Franz Toussaint's book, see note 1):

> This is the only truth:
> We are pawns in that mysterious chess game, played by Allah.
> He moves us or makes us stay where we are, moves us again, to finally throw us,
> one by one, into the box of nothingness. (103)

Gilbert Lazard keeps this quatrain among the 101 of his corpus (quatrain 50); Madhy Fouladvind classifies it as one of the most authentic "Khayyamian" (quatrain 93).

7. In Bernard Ducourant, *Sentences et proverbes de la sagesse chinoise* (*Sentences and Proverbs of Chinese Wisdom*) (Paris : Albin Michel, 1995), no. 48.

8. *L'Algèbre d'Omar al-Khayyami* (*Omar al-Khayyami's Algebra*) (Paris: Ed. F. Woepcke, 1851).

9. *Histoire légendaire des rois de Perse* (*Legendary History of the Persian Kings*), trans. Frouzandéh Brélian-Djahanshahi (Paris: Ed. Imago, 2001), 275.

VIII. Concerning Nietzsche

1. Philippe Granarolo, *L'individu éternel. L'expérience nietzschéenne de l'éternité* (*The Eternal Individual. The Nietzschean Experience of Eternity*) (Paris: Vrin, 1993), 31.

2. Ibid., 77.

3. Daniel Halévy, *Nietzsche* (Paris: Grasset, 1944), 269. *The Life of Friedrich Nietzsche*, trans. J. M. Hone (London: Fisher Unwin, 1911) is an abridged translation now available from Forgotton Books (Hong Kong, 2012).

4. ἀεὶ ὄντες in Greek.

5. ἀείζωον in Greek.

6. ἄναρχον, ἄπαυστον in Greek.

7. Melissos, in Diels-Kranz, *Die Fragmente der Vorsokratiker*, 6th ed. (Zürich: Weidmann, 2004), *Fragment* B 4.

8. Hesiod, *Theogony and Works and days*, (Oxford: Oxford University Press, 2009), v. 310.

9. Halévy, op. cit.

10. αἰών in Greek.

11. Aristotle, *Nicomachean Ethics*, in *The Complete Works, the Revised Oxford Translation*, ed. Jonathan Barnes (Princeton.: Princeton University Press, 1984), X 3, 1174 b 8.

12. Nietzsche, *Untimely Meditations*, ed. Daniel Breazeale (Cambridge: Cambridge University Press: 1997), Second Meditation, § 2, February 1874.

13. Ibid.

14. Nietzsche, *Œuvres philosophiques complètes* (*Complete Philosophical Works*), vol. II, 1, trans. P. Rusch (Paris: Gallimard, 1990), 410. No translation available in current English publications (from Cambridge University Press, Stanford University Press, Walter Kaufmann).

15. Nietzsche, *La volonté de puissance* (*The Will to Power*), vol. II, trans. G. Bianquis (Paris : Gallimard, 1948), 286. Cf. *Œuvres*, vol. IX, 677. No translation available in current English publications (from Cambridge University Press, Stanford University Press, Walter Kaufmann).

16. Ibid., 284; cf. *Fragments posthumes 1884* in *Œuvres*, vol. X, trans. Jean Launay, 82. No translation available in current English publications (from Cambridge University Press, Stanford University Press, Walter Kaufmann).

17. Ibid., 285; cf. *Œuvres*, vol. X, 277. Cf. Nietzsche, *Kritische Studienausgabe (KSA)*, ed. Colli-Montinari (München, Deutscher Taschenbuch Verlag & Berlin, W. de Gruyter: 1999), vol. 11, 250. No translation available in current English

publications (from Cambridge University Press, Stanford University Press, Walter Kaufmann).

18. Ibid., 288; cf. *Œuvres*, vol. V, trans. Pierre Klossowski, *Le gai savoir*, 383. No translation available in current English publications (from Cambridge University Press, Stanford University Press).

19. *Œuvres*, vol. X, 20; Colli-Montinari, *KSA*, 11, 10. No translation available in current English publications (from Cambridge University Press, Stanford University Press, Walter Kaufmann).

20. Ibid., 20–21 ; Colli-Montinari, *KSA*, 11, 10–11. No translation available in current English publications (from Cambridge University Press, Stanford University Press, Walter Kaufmann).

21. *La volonté de puissance*, 286; cf. *Œuvres*, vol. IX, 678. No translation available in current English publications (from Cambridge University Press, Stanford University Press, Walter Kaufmann).

22. Ibid.

23. Ibid.; cf. *Œuvres*, vol. X, 251; Colli-Montinari, *KSA*, 11, 10. No translation available in current English publications (from Cambridge University Press, Stanford University Press, Walter Kaufmann).

24. *La volonté de puissance* (*The Will to Power*) (H. Albert, 1942), vol. II, § 414. No translation available in current English publications (from Cambridge University Press, Stanford University Press, Walter Kaufmann).

25. Ibid., 288; cf. *Œuvres (Works)*, vol. X, 251; Colli-Montinari, *KSA*, 11, 225. No translation available in current English publications (from Cambridge University Press, Stanford University Press, Walter Kaufmann).

26. Ibid., 229. No translation available in current English publications (from Cambridge University Press, Stanford University Press, Walter Kaufmann).

27. *Œuvres*, vol. V, 452. No translation available in current English publications (from Cambridge University Press, Stanford University Press, Walter Kaufmann).

28. Ibid., vol. II, 277. No translation available in current English publications (from Cambridge University Press, Stanford University Press, Walter Kaufmann).

29. Ibid., 213–14. No translation available in current English publications (from Cambridge University Press, Stanford University Press, Walter Kaufmann).

30. Ibid., 215. No translation available in current English publications (from Cambridge University Press, Stanford University Press, Walter Kaufmann).

31. Marcel Conche, *Orientation philosophique* (Paris: Les Belles Lettres, coll. "Encre Marine," 2011), 224–225.

32. See *supra*, ch. 2, "Presence of the Infinite: Plato and Science in Opposition to the Infinite."

33. *Œuvres*, vol. V, 415. No translation available in current English publications (from Cambridge University Press, Stanford University Press, Walter Kaufmann).

34. Ibid., 342; cf. *La volonté de puissance*, vol. I, 290. No translation available in current English publications (from Cambridge University Press, Stanford University Press, Walter Kaufmann).

35. Ibid., 530. No translation available in current English publications (from Cambridge University Press, Stanford University Press, Walter Kaufmann).

36. *Fragments posthumes*, Autumn 1885-Autumn 1887, in *Œuvres*, vol. XII, trans. J. Hervier, 290; cf. Colli-Montinari, *KSA*, 12, 300 (7 [15]); cf. Nietzsche, *Writings from the Late Notebooks*, trans. Kate Sturge (Cambridge: Cambridge University Press, 2012), 133.

37. *Fragments posthumes*, 306–307; cf. Colli-Montinari, *KSA*, 12, 307 (7 [62]); cf. Nietzsche, *Writings from the Late Notebooks*, 140.

38. *Œuvres*, vol. V, 420. "Chaos sive natura" is repeated on p. 531. No translation available in current English publications (from Cambridge University Press, Stanford University Press, Walter Kaufmann).

39. Pascal, *Pensées*, fragment 64 in the French Brunschvicg edition, or fragment 568 in the Levi edition. See infra (chapter on Pascal).

40. *Œuvres*, vol. V, 321; *La volonté de puissance*, vol. I, 300–301. Analysis by Henri Poincaré on the problems posed by the evolution of laws hypothesis: "Evolution of Laws," in *Dernières pensées* (*Final Thoughts*) (Paris: Flammarion, 1913), 48–67. No translation available in current English publications (from Cambridge University Press, Stanford University Press, Walter Kaufmann).

41. See Marcel Conche, *Lucrèce*, § 12.

42. Nietzsche, *The Gay Science*, § 374.

43. See Marcel Conche, *Orientation Philosophique* (Paris: PUF, 1990), 212.

44. *Œuvres*, vol. II, 1, 210. No translation available in current English publications (from Cambridge University Press, Stanford University Press, Walter Kaufmann).

45. Cahiers de Royaumont, *Nietzsche* (Paris: Ed. Minuit, 1967), 98

46. *Œuvres*, vol. XII, 298; cf. Colli-Montinari, *KSA*, 12, 307 (7 [38]); cf. Nietzsche, *Writings from the Late Notebooks*, 2012), 133.

47. *Œuvres*, vol. X, 326; cf. *La volonté de puissance*, 390. No translation available in current English publications (from Cambridge University Press, Stanford University Press, Walter Kaufmann).

IX. My Path with and Without Bergson

1. Henri Bergson, *Correspondence* (Paris: PUF, 2002), 1499 (in a letter to G. de Reynold, 11 March 1935).

2. Ibid., 514 (in a letter to V. Norström, 28 April 1913), 562 (in a letter to J. Landquist, 16 February 1914).

3. Ibid., 366 (in a letter to A. Chiapelli, 15 July 1910).

4. Ibid., 1405 (in a letter to R. Flewelling, 6 April 1933).

5. Ibid., 91 (in a letter to G. Papini, 21 October 1903).

6. Ibid., 1176 (in a letter to J. Chevalier, 2 March 1926).

7. Ibid., 285 (in a letter to N. Söderblom, 27 July 1909).

8. Ibid., 1255 (in a letter to J. Chevalier, 8 April 1928).

9. Ibid., 1387 (in a letter to P. Masson-Oursel, 8 September 1932).

10. Ibid., 1377 (in a letter to H. Gouhier, 9 June 1932).

11. Ibid., 261 (in a letter to G. Papini, 5 May 1909): Bergson used this very word (experimental) himself.

12. Ibid., 1377 (in a letter to H. Gouhier, 9 June 1932).

13. Ibid., 1491 (in a letter to C. Bouglé, 24 January 1935).

14. Ibid., 1183 (in a letter to Jacques Chevalier, 2 March 1926).

15. Ibid., 992 (in a Draft letter, s.d., to Forti?).

16. Henri Bergson, *The Creative Mind* in *Bergson—Key Writings*, trans. Melissa McMahon, ed. Keith Ansell Pearson and John Mullarkey (New York: Continuum, 2002), 223.

17. Ibid.

18. *Correspondence*, 1626 (in a letter to Ch. Werner, 31 May 1939).

19. Ibid., 1184 (in a letter to Jacques Chevalier, 2 March 1926).

20. Saint Thomas Aquinas, *Summa Theologica*, First Part (God), question 14, article 15. See: http://www.gutenberg.org/cache/epub/17611/pg17611.html.

21. *Correspondence*, 1582 (in a letter to L. Lavelle, 8 (December 1937).

22. Ibid., 421 (in a letter to O. Lovejoy, 4 July 1911).

23. Ibid.

24. Ibid., 464 (in a letter to É. Borel, 24 June 1912).

25. Ibid., 1365 (in a letter to J. Chevalier, 2 March 1932).

26. Ibid., 1649 (in a letter to P. Martin, 6 January 1940).

27. Ibid., 366 (in a letter to A. Chiapelli, 15 July 1910).

28. Ibid., 442 (in a letter to Ch. Dunan, s.d.—1911 ?).

29. Ibid., 273–74 (in a letter to G. Prezollini, 12 July 1909), 461 (in a letter to A. Gibbons-Howe-James, 14 June 1912), 511 (in a letter to Algot Ruhe, 3 April 1913).

30. Ibid., 163 (in a letter to H. van Keyserling, 9 April 1907).

31. Ibid., 164.

32. Ibid., 188 (in a letter to J. Baldwin, 6 February 1908).

33. Ibid., 234 (in a letter to A. Simmel, 8 December 1908).

34. Henri Bergson, *Images and Bodies*, in *Henri Bergson, Key Writings*, op. cit., 87.

X. With Pascal and Without Him

1. Pascal, *Pensées*, ed. Anthony Levi, trans. Honor Levi (Oxford: Oxford University Press, 1995), fragment 339.

[Translator's Note: Levi follows the numbering of the Pascal fragments by Philippe Sellier (Paris: Mercure de France, 1976); also in Philippe Sellier and Gérard Ferreyrolles, *Pascal, Pensées* (Paris: Livre de Poche, 2000).]

2. Pascal wrote "of charity."

3. Pascal, *Pensées*, ed. Levi, fragment 230 "Disproportion of man."

4. Montaigne, *Essays*, 747.

5. "Infinite sphere": as in Pascal Blaise, *Pensées*, ed. Michel Le Guern, collection La Pléiade (Paris: Gallimard, 2000), fragment 185 (= fragment 339 in the Levi edition), as in *Pensées*, Louis Lafuma (Paris, Seuil: 1963), fragment 390 (= fragment 9 in the Levi edition), among others, rightly reinsert the word *infinite*, misread by Brunschvicg—whose edition I quote, as it's the one I have always used (*Pensées et Opuscules*, Paris: Hachette, 1953).

6. Montaigne, *Essays*, 141.

7. Lucretius, op. cit., VI, 679.

8. Montaigne, *Essays*, 473.

9. Pascal, *Pensées*, ed. Levi, fragment 230.

10. Pascal, *Pensées et Opuscules*, ed. Léon Brunschvicg (Paris: Hachette, 1953), fragment 72, 349, note 11.

11. The geometrician Desargues had a vineyard in Condrieu, on the banks of the Rhône.

12. Pascal, *Pensées*, ed. Levi, fragment 465.

13. Montaigne, *Essays*, 229.

14. Pascal, *Pensées*, ed. Levi, fragment 149, "Man's greatness."

15. Pascal, *Pensées et Opuscules*, ed. Brunschvicg, 373, note 2 (fragment 94). For fragment 94 in Brunschvicg, see fragment 523 in Levi.

16. Pascal, *Pensées*, ed. Levi, fragment 231.

17. Ibid., fragment 339.

18. Ibid., fragment 145, "Thinking reed."

19. Pascal, *Pensées et Opuscules*, ed Brunschvicg, fragment 121 (note: this fragment is not translated in the English edition of Anthony Levi [fragment 544]).

20. Pascal, *Pensées*, ed. Levi, fragment 99, "Diversity."

21. Pascal, Fragment of the *Traité du Vide* (*The Treatise on Vacuum*), in Pascal, *Pensées et Opuscules*, ed. Brunschvicg, 76. Not translated in the English edition of Anthony Levi.

22. Ibid.

23. Heraclitus, in Diels-Kranz, *Die Fragmente der Vorsokratiker*, 6th ed. (Zürich, Weidmann, 2004), *Fragment* 123. Also: Heracleitus, in Hippocrates, vol. IV, *Nature of Man*, trans. W. H. S. Jones, Loeb Classical Library (Cambridge: Harvard University Press and London: William Heinemann, 1931).

24. Ibid., 79.

25. Ibid.

26. Ibid., 80.

27. Montaigne, *Essays*, 876.

28. Pascal, *Œuvres Complètes*, ed. Le Guern, collection La Pléiade (Paris : Gallimard, 2000), II, 1087.

29. After Isaac Benrubi, *Souvenir sur Henri Bergson* (*Memories of Henri Bergson*) (Neuchâtel: Delachaux and Niestlé, 1942), 77.

30. Montaigne, *Essays*, 278.

31. In a letter to L. Brunschvicg, 26 February 1903, in Henri Bergson, *Mélanges* (Paris: PUF, 1972), 586.

32. 1 Corinthians 13:2–3.

33. Yves de Paris, *De l'indifférence* (*On Indifference*), ed. R. Bady (Paris, Les belles Lettres: 1966), 54.

34. Colossians 3:14.

35. Yves de Paris, *De l'indifférence* (*On Indifference*), Introduction, XII.

36. Matthew 6:4.

37. Matthew 6:14.

38. Matthew 7:1.

39. Heraclitus, in Diels-Kranz, *Die Fragmente der Vorsokratiker*, 6th ed. (Zürich, Weidmann, 2004), *Fragment* 118. Which is *Fragment* 97 in my edition (Conche, *Héraclite*, [Paris: PUF, 2009]). Also: Heracleitus, in Hippocrates, vol. IV, *Nature of Man*, trans. W. H. S. Jones, Loeb Classical Library (Cambridge: Harvard University Press and London: William Heinemann, 1931).

40. Mimnermus, *Elegies*, trans. M. L. West, in *Greek Lyric Poetry* (Oxford: Oxford University Press: 2008), I.

41. Montaigne, *Essays*, 1036.

42. Ibid., 1040.

XI. With the "Old Sage" and Without Him

1. *Henri Bergson, Essais et témoignages* (*Essays and testimonies*), 2nd ed., collected by A. Béguin and P. Thévenaz (Neuchâtel: À la Baconnière, s.d.), 25–26.

2. Marcel Conche prefers "Ante-Socratics" over "pre-Socratics."

3. Anaximander, in Diels-Kranz, *Die Fragmente der Vorsokratiker*, 6th ed. (Zürich: Weidmann, 2004), Fragment 12 A 17. Also: Charles H. Kahn, *Anaximander and the origins of Greek Cosmology* (Indianapolis/Cambridge: Hackett, 1960/1994), 46.

4. Aristotle, *Physica*, in *The Complete Works, the Revised Oxford Translation*, ed. Jonathan Barnes (Princeton: Princeton University Press, 1984), VIII I, 250 b 20–21.

5. Heraclitus, in Diels-Kranz, *Die Fragmente der Vorsokratiker*, 6th ed. (Zürich: Weidmann, 2004), *Fragment* 30. Also: Heracleitus, in Hippocrates, vol. IV, *Nature of Man*, trans. W. H. S. Jones, Loeb Classical Library (Cambridge: Harvard University Press and London: William Heinemann, 1931).

6. J.-J.-L. Duyvendak, *Tao tö king. Le livre de la Voie et de la Vertu* (Adrien Maisonneuve, 1987), passim.

7. Montaigne, *Essays*, 1042.

8. Lao Tse, *Le Vieux Sage*, trans. Cheng Wing fun and Hervé Collet (Millemont, France: ed. Moundarren, 1993), 3.

9. Foreword of the fragment of the *Thalia*, quoted by E. Tonnelat, *L'oeuvre poétique et la pensée religieuse de Hölderlin* (*Poetry and religious thought of Hölderlin*) (Paris: Didier, 1950), 78.

10. Marcel Conche, *Lao Tseu—Tao Te king* (Paris: PUF, 2003), ch. XXVIII. See also *Lao Tzu Tao Te Ching*, trans. D. C. Lau (London: Penguin Books, 1963), 33.

11. Pascal, *Pensées*, ed. Levi, fragment 515, "Boredom."

12. Conche, *Lao Tseu*, ch. XLVII.

13. Ibid., ch. VII.

14. Ibid., ch. XXXVII.

15. Foreword to *Matter and Memory*, in *Henri Bergson, Key Writings*, trans. Melissa McMahon, ed. Keith Ansell Pearson and John Mullarkey (New York: Continuum, 2002), 85.

16. Henri Bergson, *The Creative Evolution*, trans. Arthur Mitchell (Macmillan, 1922), 201, 362; see Toronto University: http://openlibrary.org/books/OL7240000M/Creative_evolution).

17. Martin Heidegger, *Poetry, Language, Thought*, trans. A. Hofstadter (New York: HarperCollins, 2001), 6.

18. Ibid. 37.

19. "Tuning in with the flow of things, with the music of things, is the only way to fair living (as fair singing)," as Cheng Wing fun and Hervé Collet wrote, op. cit., 3.

20. From "The Oaks" (Die Eichbäume), in Hölderlin, *Poèmes—Gedichte*, trans. G. Bianquis (Paris: Aubier-Montaigne, 1943), 99.

21. From "Sokrates und Alcibiades," ibid., 153; see also *Friedrich Hölderlin, Poems and Fragments*, trans. Michael Hamburger (Cambridge: Cambridge University Press, 1980), 67.

Appendix: Correspondence between Marcel Conche and Gilbert Kirscher

1. Science as such is a principle of illusion. It insists on the structure of the logical-mathematical logos as a unifying power so that the cosmologist deals with a sole universe that seems to be necessarily "the All" to him. But is the universe of the cosmologist the All of what there is? It is here that the philosopher opens up a specifically metaphysical perspective: Why would the "big bang's universe" not be like an Epicurean world where there is infinity? Science, however, considers its object (of all the aspects of Nature that it deals with) a world beyond which there is nothing: that is where the illusion lies. Science, of necessity, only gives us an extremely narrow vision of Reality in its entirety (*Note of 2004*. See Chapter II of this book: "Presence of the Infinite: Plato and Science in Opposition to the Infinite").

INDEX